Internet Law

The Reference Shelf
Volume 92 • Number 4
H.W. Wilson
A Division of EBSCO Information Services, Inc.

Published by
GREY HOUSE PUBLISHING
Amenia, New York
2020

The Reference Shelf

The books in this series contain reprints of articles, excerpts from books, addresses on current issues, and studies of social trends in the United States and other countries. There are six separately bound numbers in each volume, all of which are usually published in the same calendar year. Numbers one through five are each devoted to a single subject, providing background information and discussion from various points of view and concluding with an index and comprehensive bibliography that lists books, pamphlets, and articles on the subject. The final number of each volume is a collection of recent speeches. Books in the series may be purchased individually or on subscription.

Publisher's Cataloging-In-Publication Data
(Prepared by The Donohue Group, Inc.)

Names: Grey House Publishing, Inc., compiler.
Title: Internet law / [compiled by Grey House Publishing].
Other Titles: Reference shelf ; v. 92, no. 4.
Description: Amenia, New York : Grey House Publishing, 2020. | Includes bibliographical references and index.
Identifiers: ISBN 9781642656039 (v. 92, no. 4) | ISBN 9781642655995 (volume set)
Subjects: LCSH: Internet--Law and legislation--United States. | Network neutrality--Law and legislation--United States. | Intellectual property--United States. | Computer security--Law and legislation--United States. | LCGFT: Reference works.
Classification: LCC KF390.5.C6 I58 2020 | DDC 343.7309944--dc23

Printed in Canada

The
Reference Shelf®

Contents

3

Digital Copyright Law and Open-Source Software

4

Privacy and Cybercrime

5

Digital Nationalism and the Splinternet

Preface

The Rise of Internet Regulation

In a recent article on digital nationalism, New York University's Akash Kapur reminds us that "The internet was never just a technology or an engine of globalization. It was, at its core, an idea."[1] Those working in the heady days of the Internet's infancy saw only its limitless potential. Their absolute commitment to the free flow of information created both what is wonderful about the Internet and what is not, and it began a strain of thought that flows through digital regulation debates to this day. There are those who still believe that any attempt to regulate the Internet is anathema to its purpose and well-being.

Given how drastically the Internet has changed our lives, it's hard to believe that it's only been 50 years since it evolved out of the U.S. Department of Defense Advanced Research Project Agency Network (ARPANET). Its early users, before the advent of the personal computer, were mainly government, military, and academic institutions. Despite rhetoric about being its own borderless "space," the Internet has always been tethered to its physical infrastructure and the people who use it, who in turn are subject to regulation. Real-world laws are used to prosecute digital-equivalent crimes, often bringing into play conflicting laws for transactions that cross borders. Laws have also been passed specifically for information technology; Internet law is a part of this. In the United States, these include the Telecommunications Act of 1996, which includes the Communications Decency Act (CDA) and its controversial Section 230 as well as net neutrality classifications; the Digital Millennium Copyright Act (DMCA); the Computer Fraud and Abuse Act (CFAA); and the Electronic Communications Privacy Act (EPCA), among others.

If regulation is unavoidable, who should do the regulating? Governments, which may be slow to understand technological developments and motivated by politics? Corporations, which if powerful enough can become de facto regulators and are primarily driven by profit? Although most agree (or at least pay lip service to the idea) that any regulation should benefit the end user, what is the best way to achieve this? In 1999 Harvard Law School professor Lawrence Lessig's influential "code is law" maxim highlighted how the underlying software and hardware of the Internet effectively control it. He envisioned building a system of protections (such as open source code) into this underlying structure not unlike the checks and balances of America's democratic government.[2]

White Hat, Black Hat, Red Hat, Blue Hat

Hackers were an essential part of how the Internet developed. The word "hacker" has become part of our general lexicon, along with its plethora of "hats," or types. White hats are the "good" guys who protect information and remove threats. Black hats are the "bad" guys who steal money and create havoc. Grey hats fall somewhere in between, infiltrating systems on a smaller scale. Green hats are newbies intent on proving themselves to the hacking community. Red hats attempt to stop black hats by launching counter cyberattacks. Blue hats are motivated by revenge. Script Kiddies don't know code but use existing software to launch attacks. Hacktivists are black hats with political reasons.[3] The Computer Fraud and Abuse Act was put in place to prosecute criminal hackers, but it has also hampered important cybersecurity research and imposed outsized penalties on things like violating websites' terms of service. The intricacies of hacker culture encapsulate many of the problems of trying to regulate something that is not quite "in the world" and yet has a profound effect on it.

The first hackers at the Massachusetts Institute of Technology (MIT) in the 1950s and 1960s were mainly interested in pushing the limits of computers, as recounted by journalist Maureen Webb in *Coding Democracy: How Hackers Are Disrupting Power, Surveillance, and Authoritarianism*. A group of engineering and physics students discovered early "keypunch" machines in a basement room while looking for parts for an elaborate model train set and began to experiment with them, self-deprecatingly referring to themselves as "hackers." Webb incorporates a well-known history of hacking, Steven Levy's *Hackers: Heroes of the Computer Revolution*, which delineates the ethic of these early hackers:

1. Access to computers—and anything that might teach you how the world works—should be unlimited and total. Always yield to the hands-on imperative.
2. All information should be free.
3. Mistrust authority. Promote decentralization.
4. Hackers should be judged by their hacking, not by bogus criteria such as degrees, age, race, or position.
5. You can create art and beauty on a computer.
6. Computers can change your life for the better.

In the 1970s the mission of the next generation was to "bring computers to the people." Groups like the Homebrew Computer Club (Apple's Steve Wozniak was a member) were experimenting with build-your-own computers, and many members ultimately ended up in Silicon Valley, bringing the hacker spirit with them. But a divide occurred during the 1970s and 1980s between the original hacker ethos and a commercial, for-profit one. The latter began developing proprietary code and were hired by corporations. In response, Richard Stallman, who had been part of hacking's "golden age," changed the course of software history (and created legal headaches) with his open source system and "copyleft" licensing.

In an attempt to describe where modern hackers fit in to the digital landscape, Webb writes: "Code, more than law, will soon determine what kind of societies we live in and whether they end up resembling democracies at all. Yet code is incomprehensible to most people. . . . Who controls code?" She describes a common conflicting attitude about hackers: "A struggle is taking place right now as corporations, states, criminal elements, and parts of civil society vie to build the coded environment around us. Hackers are savants in this world. But their identity is protean. Sought after for their talents, almost folkloric in stature, they've been recruited and reviled, celebrated and thrown into prison."[4] Webb sees the hackers of today as continuing in the spirit of the original hacker ethos and as a social force dedicated to disrupting authoritarian tendencies.

Manifesto Mania

Manifestos have been written around the idea that the Internet has no physical boundaries and so there is no real jurisdiction over it. A seminal and still-influential one was written by Electronic Frontier Foundation (EFF) founder John Perry Barlow in 1996. His "Declaration of the Independence of Cyberspace" states:

> Governments of the Industrial World, you weary giants of flesh and steel, I come from Cyberspace, the new home of Mind. On behalf of the future, I ask you of the past to leave us alone. You are not welcome among us. You have no sovereignty where we gather.[5]

Barlow wrote this primarily in response to the 1996 Telecommunications Act, which attempted to place rules on emerging information technology based on those for the telephone and cable industries. But the Internet's physical parts—tubes, wires, data storage facilities—exist in particular places with laws. People—Internet users—live in physical locations. As a recent *Foreign Affairs* article explains,

> Cyberspace is not, as is often thought, simply part of the global commons in the way that the air or the sea is. States assert jurisdiction over, and companies claim ownership of, the physical infrastructure that composes the Internet and the data that traverses it. States and companies built the Internet, and both are responsible for maintaining it. Actions taken in the public sector affect the private sector, and vice versa. In this way, the Internet has always been hybrid in nature.[6]

Columbia University law professor Tim Wu describes how regulations placed on companies that maintain the physical side of the Internet are necessary to prevent corporate monopolies and protect public access to the Internet. Wu, who coined the term "net neutrality" in 2003, believes that the 2017 reversal of these policies under the Trump administration breaks from a long history of regulating how network providers can treat content and what they can charge for their services.[7]

A World of Uncensored Voices

Section 230 of the Communications Decency Act gives Internet service providers (ISPs) immunity for user content in the same way a telephone company is not responsible for its customers' conversations. But this has also been interpreted to mean that tech companies can't be sued when they do remove content. In other words, Section 230 gives them the necessary breathing room to police content in the first place. It's just that many feel they should be doing more in the wake of real-world violence related to online hate speech. But will tinkering with Section 230 help with this problem? Or will it just restrict what's available on line to a much smaller body of professionally generated content deemed safe from litigation?

EFF legal director Corinne McSherry testified in support of a strong Section 230 in a 2019 congressional hearing:

> Section 230 has ushered in a new era of community and connection on the Internet. People can find friends old and new over the Internet, learn, share ideas, organize, and speak out. Those connections can happen organically, often with no involvement on the part of the platforms where they take place. Consider that some of the most vital modern activist movements—#MeToo, #WomensMarch, #BlackLivesMatter—are universally identified by hashtags.[8]

Copyright in the Digital Age

The ability to share unlimited files with unlimited people—music is especially popular—has resulted in a lot of copyright infringement on the Internet. The Digital Millennium Copyright Act's Section 512 is designed to address this with its notice and takedown system, but many artists argue that the system is ineffective in removing unauthorized copies of their work. Others note that the system can be abused by sending false takedown notices to harm business competitors or to suppress political speech. Section 512 also contains safe harbor provisions that limit liability for ISPs when users upload copyrighted material. This is credited with the development of the Internet as we know it in a similar manner to that of the CDA's Section 230, and many warn of an Internet populated with a lot less content if changes are made to Section 512. A more controversial provision is Section 1201, which is meant to preempt getting around copyright protections built into software or devices. This section has narrowed fair use, particularly for educational purposes, and it's also curtailed legitimate research into software vulnerabilities. Because software has become a component in almost everything, Section 1201's reach has also been interpreted to extend to such things as unlocking smartphones and fixing tractors, considered an overreach by many. Recent "right to repair" exceptions have been made to the law, but their permanence and the vehicles they cover are still in play, as are whether or not they will void product warranties.[9]

Balancing Privacy with Safety

The Electronic Communications Privacy Act, passed in 1986, restricts government and law enforcement access to our digital communications. It prohibits intentional interception of electronic communications and prevents such interception from being used as evidence; it protects the content of files stored by ISPs; and it mandates a warrant for using pen register and trap and trap devices, which track numbers and other information about calls.[10] When the ECPA was updated by the USA Patriot

Act after 9/11, these restrictions were eased. Former National Security Agency (NSA) contractor Edward Snowden downloaded approximately 1.5 million documents while exposing the agency's surveillance activities in 2013, which included collection of telephone records of millions of Verizon customers; collection of data from Google and Facebook through the Prism program; collection of email metadata through EvilOlive; an XKeyscore program that allowed searching through databases of emails, browsing history, and online chats; the monitoring of vast amounts of Americans' international emails; and other international spying and cyberattacking activity.[11] The Patriot Act, passed under the rubric of preventing further terrorist attacks, changed Americans' awareness and attitudes toward government surveillance. Companies like Apple have also refused to build backdoors into their devices to allow law enforcement access.

What's in a Name?

The Internet Corporation for Assigned Names and Numbers (ICANN) is a crucial cog in how the Internet functions because Internet protocol (IP) addresses are what allows computers to find one another. A nonprofit organization formed in 1998 and headquartered in California, ICANN was initially set up to help the U.S. government manage Internet infrastructure functions. ICANN manages the domain name system and root servers and is responsible for coordinating IP addresses and for maintaining their central repository.[12] Domain name disputes account for most Internet trademark litigation, when companies that have invested heavily in a name or brand can't use it in a domain name because someone else has purposely purchased it for the sole purpose of selling it back to them for profit, a technique known as "cybersquatting." The Anti-Cybersquatting Act of 1999 (ACPA) holds cybersquatters liable for registering, trafficking in, or using a recognizable trademark name.[13] Sometimes who should own domain names is less clear-cut, as with retail giant Amazon's recent dispute with several South American governments over the domain name .amazon. Applications involving geographical locations require the approval of local governments. According to ICANN Latin America regional vice president Rodrigo de la Parra, "It's not the classic issue of two different parties applying for the same name. . . . The governments didn't apply for .amazon—they only have concerns about its usage by a private company given its cultural and natural heritage for the region."[14]

ICANN was initially overseen by the U.S. Department of Commerce's National Telecommunications and Information Administration (NTIA), but control was handed over to an international coalition under the Obama administration in 2016. Adelphi University Internet law professor Mark Grabowski points out that this transition into international governance has not gone as smoothly as envisioned. Some governments, like the European Union (EU) and Brazil, have begun rejecting ICANN's authority, the organization is facing budgetary issues that could put its objectivity under strain, and they are facing increasing pressure to censor hate speech, among other problems. Grabowski contends that, although the United

States should investigate these issues, they should not, as the Trump administration has proposed, try to take back U.S. control of ICANN.[15]

Tales from the Dark Side

At the opposite end of a philosophy based on the transparent and free flow of information is one dedicated to anonymity and the hidden flow of transactions. A 1992 manifesto by cryptoanarchist Timothy May declares: "Just as the technology of printing altered and reduced the power of medieval guilds and the social power structure, so too will cryptologic methods fundamentally alter the nature of corporations and of government interference in economic transactions."[16] Cryptoanarchists, or cypherphunks, believe that encryption and decentralized computer networks can create a world of personal freedom hidden from government and corporate surveillance, and by extension taxation and other laws. Some famous members include 3-D gun manufacturer Cody Wilson and WikiLeaks founder Julian Assange. Early crypto programs like MIT's 1977 RSA (named after its three developers) got the attention of the NSA, which wanted the program classified as a munition under federal arms trafficking laws. The 1991 release of public-key encryption freeware Pretty Good Privacy (PGP) helped spread the movement internationally, and in 1993 the Clinton administration attempted to develop and make mandatory a processor with a backdoor for law enforcement (research showed that it could be circumvented, and the plan was abandoned). In 1995 cypherphunk Jim Bell devised an elaborate, anonymous assassination scheme with a list of targeted government employees and payment schemes for would-be assassins (the plan was never put into practice). The 1999 case of *Bernstein v. U.S. Department of Justice* established that code was free speech protected under the first amendment after UC Berkeley graduate student Daniel Bernstein sued the State Department after being told that his encryption program would be considered a munition. This level of encryption, whatever its philosophical roots, is linked to terrorist attacks and dark web black markets.[17]

The Splinternet

From a vision of global unity, the steady rise of regulation, surveillance, and cyberwarfare have created the possibility of a final fracturing of the World Wide Web. Some countries heavily censor the Internet (China, Iran, Saudi Arabia, and Thailand, to name a few), other countries may be building their own network (Russia, Brazil, India, and South Africa). Once unheard-of censorship acts like blocking access to social media sites are becoming commonplace in a number of countries. China, whose Great Firewall blocks everything from Winnie-the-Pooh (memes of Pooh were used to mock President Xi Jinping) to searches for the Tiananmen Square student protests to the *New York Times*, is trying to import its version of the Internet to other Southeast Asian countries. As technological tools to censor the Internet become cheaper and more available, more governments are willing to try it, especially in the wake of political uprisings like the Arab Spring. But social media companies and free speech have come under fire in the United States and Europe as well, in response to intensified online hate speech. Often referred to as the "splinternet" or "cyberbalkanization," the idea has been around since the 1990s but the process is accelerating. Seattle-based cyberlaw firm president Venkat Balasubramani notes, "It feels like a chunk of the Internet is gone or different. People feel the Internet is not as we knew it." Ed Black, who runs the Computer and Communications Industry Association in Washington, D.C., believes that more should have been done to preserve online free speech and counter censorship: "It's death by a thousand cuts. We now face a situation where we have Chinese and authoritarian models being aggressively proselytized around the world, and we haven't done enough to counter that."[18]

Works Used

Darlington, Shasta. "Battle for .amazon Domain Pits Retailer Against South American Nations." *The New York Times*. Apr. 18, 2019. https://www.nytimes.com/2019/04/18/world/americas/amazon-domain-name.html.

Dyson, Lauren. "Code Is Law, Law Is Code: Law.gov & the Local Challenge for Legal Transparency." *Code for America*. Feb. 22, 2011. https://www.codeforamerica.org/blog/2011/02/22/code-is-law.

"Electronic Communications Privacy Act." *ScienceDirect*. https://www.sciencedirect.com/topics/computer-science/electronic-communications-privacy-act.

Flournoy, Michèle, and Michael Sulmeyer. "Battlefield Internet: A Plan for Securing Cyberspace." *Foreign Affairs*. September/October 2018. https://www.foreignaffairs.com/articles/world/2018-08-14/battlefield-internet.

Grabowski, Mark. "Should the U.S. Reclaim Control of the Internet? Evaluating ICANN's Administrative Oversight Since the 2016 Handover." *Nebraska Law Review*. Aug. 6, 2018. https://lawreview.unl.edu/Should-the-U.S.-Reclaim-Control-of-the-Internet%3F.

Greenberg, Andy. "It's Been 20 Years Since This Man Declared Cyberspace Independence." *Wired*. Feb. 8, 2016, https://www.wired.com/2016/02/its-been-20-years-since-this-man-declared-cyberspace-independence.

"Hacker Hat Colors: An Inside Look at the Hacking Ecosystem." *Alpine Security*. https://alpinesecurity.com/blog/hacker-hat-colors-an-inside-look-at-the-hacking-ecosystem/.

Harmon, Elliot, and Ernesto Falcon. "EFF Defends Section 230 in Congress." *Electronic Frontier Foundation*. Oct. 16, 2019. https://www.eff.org/deeplinks/2019/10/eff-defends-section-230-congress.

"Internet Regulation." *Encyclopedia.com*. June 12, 2020. https://www.encyclopedia.com/law/encyclopedias-almanacs-transcripts-and-maps/internet-regulation.

Kapur, Akash. "The Rising Threat of Digital Nationalism." *The Wall Street Journal*. Nov. 1, 2019. https://www.wsj.com/articles/the-rising-threat-of-digital-nationalism-11572620577.

May, Timothy C. "The Crypto Anarchist Manifesto." Nov. 22, 1992. https://www.activism.net/cypherpunk/crypto-anarchy.html/

Milner, Greg. "The Wild, Baffling, and Sometimes Terrifying History of

Crypto-Anarchy." *BreakerMag*. Sept. 14, 2018. https://breakermag.com/the-wild-baffling-and-sometimes-terrifying-history-of-crypto-anarchy/.

Roberts, Jeff John. "The Splinternet Is Growing." *Forbes*. May 29, 2019. https://fortune.com/2019/05/29/splinternet-online-censorship/.

Szoldra, Paul. "This Is Everything Edward Snowden Revealed in One Year of Unprecedented Top-Secret Leaks." *Business Insider*. Sept. 16, 2016. https://www.businessinsider.com/snowden-leaks-timeline-2016-9.

Webb, Maureen. *Coding Democracy: How Hackers Are Disrupting Power, Surveillance, and Authoritarianism*. Cambridge, MA: MIT Press, 2020.

"What Is ICANN and Why Does It Matter?" *Data Foundry*. July 11, 2016. https://www.datafoundry.com/blog/what-is-icann.

"Will 'Right to Repair' Be a Thing of the Past for Motorcyclists?" *Ultimate Motorcycling*. Mar. 10, 2020. https://ultimatemotorcycling.com/2020/03/10/will-right-to-repair-be-a-thing-of-the-past-for-motorcyclists/.

Wu, Tim. "How the FCC's Net Neutrality Plan Breaks with 50 Years of History." *Wired*. Dec. 6, 2017. https://www.wired.com/story/how-the-fccs-net-neutrality-plan-breaks-with-50-years-of-history/.

Notes

1. Kapur, "The Rising Threat of Digital Nationalism."
2. Dyson, "Code Is Law, Law is Code: Law.gov & the Local Challenge for Legal Transparency."
3. "Hacker Hat Colors," Alpine Security.
4. Webb. *Coding Democracy: How Hackers Are Disrupting Power, Surveillance, and Authoritarianism*.
5. Greenberg, "It's Been 20 Years Since This Man Declared Cyberspace Independence."
6. Flournoy and Sulmeyer. "Battlefield Internet: A Plan for Securing Cyberspace."
7. Wu, "How the FCC's Net Neutrality Plan Breaks with 50 Years of History."
8. Harmon and Falcon, "EFF Defends Section 230 in Congress."
9. "Will 'Right to Repair' Be a Thing of the Past for Motorcyclists?" *Ultimate Motorcycling*.
10. "Electronic Communications Privacy Act," *ScienceDirect*.
11. Szoldra, "This Is Everything Edward Snowden Revealed in One Year of Unprecedented Top-Secret Leaks."
12. "What Is ICANN and Why Does It Matter?" *Data Foundry*.
13. "Internet Regulation," *Encyclopedia.com*.
14. Darlington, "Battle for .amazon Domain Pits Retailer Against South American Nations."
15. Grabowski, "Should the U.S. Reclaim Control of the Internet? Evaluating ICANN's Administrative Oversight since the 2016 Handover."
16. May, "The Crypto Anarchist Manifesto."
17. Milner, "The Wild, Baffling, and Sometimes Terrifying History of Crypto-Anarchy."
18. Roberts, "The Splinternet Is Growing."

1
The Communications Decency Act and Section 230

In May of 2020, Donald Trump signed an Executive Order on Preventing Online Censorship, aimed at preventing the perceived online suppression of conservative viewpoints. Many consider the order unconstitutional and its effect doubtful at best.

Who Is Responsible for Online Content?

The aspect of Internet law that has generated most recent headlines is the Section 230 provision of the Communications Decency Act (CDA), which is part of the mammoth Telecommunications Act of 1996 that attempted to address legal issues arising from emerging information technologies. Widely known as "the 26 words that created the Internet," Section 230 states that:

> No provider or user of an interactive computer service shall be treated as the publisher or speaker of any information provided by another information content provider.

Before the passage of the CDA, the New York Supreme Court held that online service providers could be held responsible for user content in *Stratton Oakmont, Inc. v. Prodigy Services Co.* (1995) after a user posted comments about Stratton's fraudulent stock offerings. Prodigy marketed itself as a family-friendly provider that moderated pornographic material, and the court ruled that this was exercising editorial control over content and that the company should be treated as a publisher. The message to the industry was alarming: if you moderate any content, you will be considered legally liable for all content. Public outcry over the Stratton case was used to help pass the CDA, but the federal law contained two concessions that have since had unintended consequences. First, only actual creators are liable for harmful content. Second, removing offensive user content does not incur liability on the part of Internet service providers (ISPs) and websites.[1]

The CDA was intended to regulate pornography and indecent material, especially by limiting access to such content for children. As detailed in a 2014 *Verge* article by Matt Stroud, a couple of legal cases that followed shortly after its passage are considered to have shaped how the Internet developed.

In *Reno v. American Civil Liberties Union* (1997), federal judges and then the Supreme Court struck down a provision calling for criminal prosecution of any individual who knowingly sent pornographic content to someone under 18, establishing online free speech protection. As University of California Berkeley Professor Brian W. Carver explained, "The court had to struggle with whether the internet should be regulated like a print medium, a broadcast medium, or as something new altogether. The Court paved the way for our understanding that on the internet, the government cannot reduce the adult population to only what is fit for children and that less-restrictive means of controlling online content, such as parent-controlled filtering software, were preferred."

The next influential legal battle established the precedent of not holding websites responsible for user content. The case dealt with many of the same elements that Facebook and other online platforms are facing today, calling the basis of Section 230 into question. In *Zeran v. America Online, Inc.* (1998), the U.S. Court of

Appeals for the Fourth Circuit ruled against Seattle resident Kenneth M. Zeran when he tried to sue America Online for false content posted on a message board. After the April 1995 Oklahoma City bombings, posts appeared with Zeran's contact information (including his phone number) advertising items for sale printed with "Visit Oklahoma. . . . It's a BLAST!" and "McVeigh for President 1996." Zeran claimed to have no knowledge of the message board or the sale items, but the incident went viral after an Oklahoma City radio disc jockey drew attention to it, and Zeran received hundreds of angry phone calls, eventually needing Federal Bureau of Investigation (FBI) protection. According to Santa Clara University professor Eric Goldman: "It's no exaggeration to say that the Zeran case is responsible for our entire UGC [user-generated content] economy." Former director of Harvard's Citizen Media Law Project Jeffrey Hermes adds: "Think about YouTube. If [Zeran] had gone the other way, Google today would need to hire people with sophisticated legal backgrounds to review every single piece of content on that site. There would not be enough hours in the day. You would need to have literally millions of lawyers whose only responsibility would be reviewing user videos."[2]

Section 230 and Social Media

However, as the stakes have gotten higher and the real-world consequences of online content more deadly, Section 230 immunity has come under increasing fire. Striking a balance between protecting free speech and taking action against content that can incite violence has become more difficult. The global popularity of platforms like Facebook and Twitter add variations in international law to the mix.

Attempting to respond to its role in the ethnic cleansing of the Rohingya in Myanmar, Facebook belatedly banned four militant Myanmar groups by designating them "dangerous organizations," an action that banned not only the groups from the platform but also "all related praise, support and representation" of them. But local human rights groups worry that there is no transparency or oversight to such decisions in a country where Facebook is, for most citizens, equivalent to the Internet. Some consider it an overreaction that will ultimately tip the balance in the government's favor over the many ethnic armed organizations that have been fighting for self-determination for decades, setting a precedent of ignoring human rights violations that are state-sanctioned.[3]

The amount of hate speech on platforms like Facebook continues to spiral out of control despite recent content moderation efforts, and it is becoming hard to keep track of the number of mass shooter "manifestos" posted to social media. The live-streaming of the Christchurch, New Zealand, mosque shootings in New Zealand, which left 51 worshippers dead, is the most infamous misuse of social media to date. But the recent phenomenon of "performance crime"—such as a Facebook video of the apparently random murder of a Cleveland man[4]—is another example of what advocates of Section 230 reform hope to address.

The Rallying Cry of Reform

Section 230 was revised in 2018 by the Senate's Stop Enabling Sex Traffickers Act and the House's Victims to Fight Online Sex Trafficking Act (FOSTA-SESTA). Aimed at stopping online sex trafficking, the law also weakened Section 230 by holding online services responsible if their users facilitated illegal sex acts in any way over their platforms. Many believe it also removed vital health and safety forums for sex workers at the same time it increased online censorship.[5]

In June 2019 Senator Josh Hawley (R-Mo.) introduced a bill to remove Section 230 immunity for big tech companies unless they submitted to an external audit proving that their algorithms and content-removal practices are politically neutral (the legislation would not apply to small- and medium-sized tech companies). According to Hawley, "There's a growing list of evidence that shows big tech companies making editorial decisions to censor viewpoints they disagree with. Even worse, the entire process is shrouded in secrecy because these companies refuse to make their protocols public. This legislation simply states that if the tech giants want to keep their government-granted immunity, they must bring transparency and accountability to their editorial processes and prove that they don't discriminate."[6] Hawley and other Republicans, most notably President Trump, believe that social media companies are censoring conservative viewpoints.

In a highly publicized recent battle with Twitter, Trump issued an executive order to government agencies asking them to penalize companies for removing content if the removal is deemed politically biased. Twitter stamped two fact-checking labels on two of Trump's tweets about mail-in voting, and later labeled the president's tweet about the Minneapolis protests—"when the looting starts, the shooting starts"—as glorifying violence. Several tech organizations have labeled the order unconstitutional, and many believe it lacks authority. Facebook, meanwhile, has publicly declared that it is not up to them to censor political content. The real danger for tech companies is the effect the battle could have on Section 230 legislative reform. As *Politico*'s Steven Overly and Nancy Scola point out, "The fight that Twitter set off by stamping fact-check labels on two of Trump's tweets about mail-in voting has implications for the entire industry."[7]

Section 230 reform, however, has bipartisan support. While some Republicans claim that the clause allows tech companies to moderate too much, Democrats tend to think it allows them to not moderate enough. House Speaker Nancy Pelosi thinks that tech companies are not "treating [Section 230] with the respect that they should," and Democratic presidential candidate Joe Biden believes that "Section 230 should be revoked, immediately."[8] It's clear that reform is a serious possibility.

The response from the tech community has been strong, with many arguing that these reforms would be unconstitutional, fundamentally change the way the Internet works, and not have the desired results. In an *Ars Technica* article, Eric Goldman and Jess Meirs argue: "The logical consequence of 'tougher' Internet laws is clear but chilling. Google and Facebook will likely survive the regulatory onslaught, but few other user-generated content services will. Instead . . . they will shut down all user-generated content . . . [and] turn to professionally generated content. . . .

We will shift from a world where virtually everyone has global publication reach to a world where most readers will pay for access to a much less diverse universe of content."[9]

Well-intentioned regulation can often result in unintended complications. Both the European Union (EU) and Germany have come under fire for recent laws fining social media companies over content moderation. New Zealand's new law regarding "abhorrent violent material" (passed after the Christchurch shooting) will hold the "stack" of companies responsible for the presence of violent content, including the ISP, the cloud provider, and the social media platform. Technology and media analyst Ben Thompson points out an inherent problem with this approach: "The terrorist in Christchurch didn't set up a server to livestream video from his phone; rather, he used Facebook's built-in functionality. And, when it came to the video's spread, the culprit was not email or message boards, but social media generally. To put it another way, to have spread that video on the Internet would be possible but difficult; to spread it on social media was trivial."[10]

Works Used

Cox, Kate. "Biden Wants Sec. 230 Gone, Calls Tech 'Totally Irresponsible,' 'Little Creeps'." *Ars Technica*. Jan. 17, 2020. https://arstechnica.com/tech-policy/2020/01/joe-biden-is-so-mad-at-facebook-he-wants-to-revoke-sec-230-for-everyone/.

Goldman, Eric, and Jess Miers. "Why Can't Internet Companies Stop Awful Content?" *Ars Technica*. Jan. 27, 2019. https://arstechnica.com/tech-policy/2019/11/why-cant-internet-companies-stop-awful-content/.

LoMonte, Frank. "The Law That Made Facebook What It Is Today." *The Conversation*. Apr. 11, 2018. https://theconversation.com/the-law-that-made-facebook-what-it-is-today-93931.

Mohney, Gillian. "Murder on Facebook Spotlights Rise of 'Performance Crime' Phenomenon on Social Media." *ABC News*. Apr. 18, 2017. https://abcnews.go.com/US/murder-facebook-spotlights-rise-performance-crime-phenomenon-social/story?id=46862306.

Overly, Steven, and Nancy Scola. "The Trump-Twitter Fight Ropes in the Rest of Silicon Valley." *Politico*. May 30, 2020. https://www.politico.com/news/2020/05/30/trump-twitter-fight-silicon-valley-290759.

"Senator Hawley Introduces Legislation to Amend Section 230 Immunity for Big Tech Companies." June 19, 2019. https://www.hawley.senate.gov/senator-hawley-introduces-legislation-amend-section-230-immunity-big-tech-companies.

Soderberg-Rivkin, Daisy. "The Lessons of FOSTA-SESTA from a Former Content Moderator." *RStreet*. Apr. 8, 2020. https://www.rstreet.org/2020/04/08/the-lessons-of-fosta-sesta-from-a-former-content-moderator/.

Stroud, Matt. "These Six Lawsuits Shaped the Internet." *The Verge*. Aug. 14, 2019. https://www.theverge.com/2014/8/19/6044679/the-six-lawsuits-that-shaped-the-internet.

Thompson, Ben. "A Framework for Regulating the Internet." *Stratechery.* Apr. 9, 2019. https://stratechery.com/2019/a-regulatory-framework-for-the-internet/.

Wong, Julia Carrie. "Overreacting to Failure: Facebook's New Strategy Baffles Local Activists." *The Guardian.* Feb. 7, 2019. https://www.theguardian.com/technology/2019/feb/07/facebook-myanmar-genocide-violence-hate-speech.

Notes

1. LoMonte, "The Law That Made Facebook What It Is Today."
2. Stroud, "These Six Lawsuits Shaped the Internet."
3. Wong, "Overreacting to Failure: Facebook's New Strategy Baffles Local Activists."
4. Mohney, "Murder on Facebook Spotlights Rise of 'Performance Crime' Phenomenon on Social Media."
5. Soderberg-Rivkin, "The Lessons of FOSTA-SESTA from a Former Content Moderator."
6. "Senator Hawley Introduces Legislation to Amend Section 230 Immunity for Big Tech Companies."
7. Overly and Scola, "The Trump-Twitter Fight Ropes in the Rest of Silicon Valley."
8. Cox, "Biden Wants Sec. 230 Gone, Calls Tech 'Totally Irresponsible,' 'Little Creeps'."
9. Goldman and Miers, "Why Can't Internet Companies Stop Awful Content?"
10. Thompson, "A Framework for Regulating the Internet."

The Trump-Twitter Fight Ropes in the Rest of Silicon Valley

By Steven Overly and Nancy Scola
Politico, May 30, 2020

Twitter's decision to fact-check President Donald Trump's tweets has vaulted Silicon Valley's biggest players into a political fight with Washington when they least wanted it.

The deepening feud between the president and his go-to social media platform is forcing companies like Facebook and Google to gird for a lobbying battle to defend the legal protections that underpin their lucrative business models, sooner and much more publicly than they had originally expected. Those preparations accelerated this week, even as Facebook made it clear to Trump that it doesn't share Twitter's view of how online platforms should handle political speech.

Now the industry has no choice but to wade into an increasingly partisan debate over free expression, in a preelection season already torn by tensions surrounding the pandemic, mass unemployment and racial unrest.

"This is a debate that had been inside the Beltway that's now gone national, and that means that advocates of online free speech need to prepare a national response," said Carl Szabo, the vice president and general counsel at NetChoice, one of many tech industry trade groups responding to the Trump-Twitter showdown this week.

"What's the opposite of 'A rising tide lifts all boats?' That's this," said one tech company policy official, who spoke anonymously because of the sensitivities of the situation.

As Trump and Twitter sparred this week, NetChoice—whose members include Facebook, Twitter, Google and scores of other big-name online companies—rushed into an effort to convince the American public that Trump is wrong about an obscure provision of a quarter-century-old communications law.

The move, relying on Facebook posts, tweets and explainer videos, is a shift from the group's more typically insidery strategy of lobbying Hill staffers or members of Congress. And it suggests a more expansive approach to how Silicon Valley plans to engage in the messaging battle over the laws governing social media.

The rest of Silicon Valley's robust lobbying presence has kicked into higher gear as well.

> **The industry's efforts are focused mainly on the threat of legislation—and not so much on the executive order, which many legal experts say lacks the authority and conflicts with the Constitution.**

The Internet Association, which represents Twitter, Google and Facebook, among others, speedily released a video arguing that the internet depends on the liability protections at the center of the fight. The Computer and Communications Industry Association deliberated the impact of Trump's actions with its member companies. And the Consumer Tech Association says it is expecting to make a big push to the Senate's Judiciary and Commerce committees, as well as tech and business-focused caucuses among both parties—including some lawmakers they don't typically target.

Facebook, meanwhile, made a more public show of trying to stay out of this week's content moderation clash: CEO Mark Zuckerberg popped up on Fox News in mid-week to say he has a much different view from Twitter on how social media platforms should handle controversial political speech. Companies like his, Zuckerberg said, should not act as "the arbiter of truth."

Trump seized the opportunity to emphasize the divide. "@Facebook CEO Mark Zuckerberg is today criticizing Twitter," the president tweeted Friday.

But whatever public friction may exist between Zuckerberg and Twitter CEO Jack Dorsey, the fight that Twitter set off by stamping fact-check labels on two of Trump's tweets about mail-in voting has implications for the entire online industry.

Trump, Szabo said, is "using government to attack the free speech rights of internet companies." (Trump has made the opposite argument, saying Washington must protect free expression from political censorship by liberal Silicon Valley).

Trump responded to Twitter's rulings by signing an executive order Thursday that targets a law at the heart of the internet industry: Section 230 of the Communications Decency Act. The 1996 statute offers online platforms broad immunity from lawsuits over the messages, photos, videos and other content their users post—a protection that has helped companies like Facebook and Google amass some of the world's biggest corporate fortunes. It also gives sites leeway to remove content they deem objectionable, a power Trump accuses the companies of abusing for partisan ends.

In the order, Trump asks government agencies to reinterpret the law in a way that would allow them to penalize companies for content decisions they deem politically biased. He has also threatened to push Congress to pass legislation to amend or revoke Section 230, a potentially existential threat to the companies' business models.

Notably, the industry's efforts are focused mainly on the threat of legislation—and not so much on the executive order, which many legal experts say lacks authority and conflicts with the Constitution.

"If there were to be changes to Section 230, it would be coming out of Congress, not the White House," said Michael Petricone, the senior vice president of government affairs for the Consumer Tech Association. "You'll be seeing increased attention there."

Tech companies' reactions to previous government threats haven't always been industry-wide. The rest of Silicon Valley was more than happy to let Facebook bear the brunt of criticisms over data privacy and Google endure the hottest antitrust spotlight. With Twitter taking the punches, the rest of the tech world could have viewed it as a chance to breathe easy for a while. Instead, they're feeling roped into a battle triggered by Twitter.

Twitter, meanwhile, escalated its crackdown on Trump early Friday, labeling a Trump tweet containing the phrase "when the looting starts, the shooting starts" in response to protests in Minneapolis as "glorifying violence." The White House then tweeted Trump's words verbatim, prompting Twitter to append the same warning label onto the official White House account. Facebook, in contrast, announced it would take no action against a Trump post containing the identical wording.

In another test for Twitter's policies, Trump tweeted Saturday morning that the protesters who had massed outside the White House the previous night would "have been greeted with the most vicious dogs, and most ominous weapons, I have ever seen" had they breached the grounds.

While Twitter has its own policy priorities in Washington, Section 230 and other content regulations chief among them, it has fewer entanglements in the nation's capital than its Silicon Valley counterparts. It has recently been more willing to antagonize the Trump administration than some other tech companies, and has previously said that its generally hands-off approach to world leaders doesn't mean Trump's tweets can't be pulled from the platform. Twitter declined to comment for this story.

Twitter is a far smaller company than Facebook and Google, making it less of a target for federal antitrust authorities. It is largely a public platform, which leaves it out of the debate with law enforcement over encryption. And it was never the high-dollar platform for political advertising that Facebook, and as of last year it no longer accepts political ads at all.

"Twitter is acting now because they can," said Nu Wexler, a former spokesperson for Google, Facebook and Twitter. "They're not an antitrust target. They're not in China, so they don't have to worry about angering the government. And these two cases that they've chosen, voting misinformation and a direct violent threat, are good ones for them."

It's no real surprise that Trump would go after Silicon Valley as he did. The White House has for many months been mulling an executive order attempting to rein in social media that it ended up issuing this week. In mid-May, the president tweeted that the "Radical Left is in total command & control of Facebook, Instagram, Twitter and Google," urging his 80 million followers to "stay tuned."

But where some in the industry had thought Trump was likely to roll out some such order in the chaotic run-up to the November election, as part of a targeted anti-social-media appeal to his base, having this tit-for-tat escalation break out in May means the fight could suck up much more oxygen and burn longer.

"Everybody expected this fight," Wexler said. "They just thought that it would happen in September or October as part of a get-out-the-vote push."

Print Citations

CMS: Overly, Steven, and Nancy Scola. "The Trump-Twitter Fight Rages in the Rest of Silicon Valley." In *The Reference Shelf: Internet Law,* edited by Annette Calzone, 9-12. Amenia, NY: Grey House Publishing, 2020.

MLA: Overly, Steven, and Nancy Scola. "The Trump-Twitter Fight Rages in the Rest of Silicon Valley." *The Reference Shelf: Internet Law,* edited by Annette Calzone, Grey House Publishing, 2020, pp. 9-12.

APA: Overly, S., & Scola, N. (2020). The Trump-Twitter fight rages in the rest of Silicon Valley. In Annette Calzone (Ed.), *The reference shelf: Internet law* (pp. 9-12). Amenia, NY: Grey House Publishing.

The Law That Made Facebook What It Is Today

By Frank LoMonte
The Conversation, April 11, 2018

Facebook is facing a reckoning in the court of public opinion for how the social media giant and its partners handle customer data.

In the court of law, holding Facebook responsible for its actions has been quite a bit harder.

CEO Mark Zuckerberg has been hauled in front of Congress to apologize for a data scraping scandal—a scandal that quickly followed an outcry that the site had been exploited by Russia during the 2016 election.

It's rare to see a social media company pay consequences for its actions—or inactions—because of a broad immunity shield that some in Congress are rethinking.

The story starts 22 years ago. That's when a defamation suit was brought by the now-shuttered investment firm Stratton Oakmont against the operator of an online discussion board. The name Stratton Oakmont may sound familiar. That's because the brokerage was made infamous by Martin Scorsese's *The Wolf of Wall Street*. The suit prompted Congress to protect the hosts of discussion boards—and, as it now turns out, social networking sites as well.

For the past four years, I've taught a college course that considers the importance of that law, the Communications Decency Act, in making today's social media industry economically feasible. Arguably, that law created a climate in which the Facebooks of the world came to believe that anything bad happening to their users was someone else's fault.

Let's take a quick spin through the history.

"Family-friendly" Internet

In 1984, Prodigy Communications Corp. launched as a pioneering entrant into the first rudimentary wave of internet service providers. To compete with much-larger CompuServe, Prodigy promoted its services as "family-oriented," promising to moderate pornographic material.

In October 1994, a commenter on a Prodigy discussion board posted a string of accusations about fraudulent stock offerings promoted by Stratton Oakmont. The commenter called the company "a cult of brokers who either lie for a living or get fired." To anyone who has seen Scorsese's film, this seems prescient and understated. Regulators shut down Stratton in 1996, and its founder went to prison for securities fraud.

> **Congress elected to treat the Prodigies of the world, eventually including Facebook— as no more responsible for the acts of their users than the telephone company.**

Nonetheless, Stratton sued Prodigy for libel. In a 1995 ruling that shook the nascent industry, a New York judge ruled that ISPs could be held liable as "publishers" of their customers' content. The judge wrote that Prodigy "held itself out as an online service that exercised editorial control over the content of messages posted on its computer bulletin boards, thereby expressly differentiating itself from its competition and expressly likening itself to a newspaper." And like a newspaper, Prodigy could be sued over injurious material in reader submissions just as if the submissions were the company's own words.

The ruling sent a worrisome message to the industry: Stop taking down harmful or offensive material, or you'll be liable as the "publisher" of whatever remains.

Congress was alarmed.

Congress Raises the Deflector Shields

Nebraska Sen. J. James Exon, an outspoken opponent of "cyberporn," leveraged outcry over the Stratton case to help pass what became the Communications Decency Act. The CDA made it illegal to knowingly use internet services to transmit obscene material to minors. But Section 230 of the statute made two crucial concessions that – unforeseeably to Congress in 1996, seven years before the debut of MySpace—paved the way for the explosive growth of the social web.

First, the act holds only the actual creators of harmful content liable for its consequences.

Second, the act prevents liability for good-faith attempts to moderate "objectionable" material. This means immunity is not forfeited by removing offensive reader submissions. Today, this enables the *New York Times* to screen comments on its website without accepting liability for them.

In other words, Congress elected to treat the Prodigies of the world—eventually including Facebook – as no more responsible for the acts of their users than the telephone company. Just as AT&T is not liable for obscene phone calls placed by customers, neither an ISP nor any website with reader interactivity is the "publisher" of its users' submissions.

Traditional publishers are liable for the consequences of the speech they print, even if that speech comes from outsiders who were neither paid nor solicited to submit. If the *New Yorker* carries a letter to the editor falsely calling someone a criminal, the magazine can be held liable alongside the letter writer. The theory is that the editors chose the letter and had the opportunity to fact-check it.

In this way, Section 230 represents a breathtaking recalibration of liability law. In effect, the online publishing industry has convinced Congress that its capacity to distribute harmful material is so vast that it cannot be held responsible for the consequences of its own business model.

To be clear, social media sites can still be liable for how their own employees mishandle user data, or for breaching promises made to customers in their terms of service, neither of which requires treating the sites as "publishers."

The CDA is widely credited for the flourishing of YouTube, Yelp and other sites that rely on user submissions. It is also faulted for some of the social web's worst excesses. Law professor Danielle Citron, author of the influential 2014 book *Hate Crimes in Cyberspace*, highlights how CDA immunity makes "revenge porn" possible by enabling websites to refuse demands to unpublish even the most intrusive content.

Those injured by reader-submitted content may still pursue legal action directly against the authors—if they can be found. A robust body of case law governs when a website host can be forced to "unmask" the credentials of its users. But—as with the Macedonians purveying "fake news" on Facebook—those authors may be beyond the reach of American courts, or lack the capacity to pay meaningful damages. That may leave those wronged with nothing but an earnest apology from a billionaire tech entrepreneur.

Print Citations

CMS: LoMonte, Frank. "The Law That Made Facebook What It Is Today." In *The Reference Shelf: Internet Law,* edited by Annette Calzone, 13-15. Amenia, NY: Grey House Publishing, 2020.

MLA: LoMonte, Frank. "The Law That Made Facebook What It Is Today." *The Reference Shelf: Internet Law,* edited by Annette Calzone, Grey House Publishing, 2020, pp. 13-15.

APA: LoMonte, F. (2020). The law that made Facebook what it is today. In Annette Calzone (Ed.), *The reference shelf: Internet law* (pp. 13-15). Amenia, NY: Grey House Publishing.

Biden Wants Sec. 230 Gone, Calls Tech "Totally Irresponsible," "Little Creeps"

By Kate Cox
Ars Technica, January 17, 2020

Former Vice President Joe Biden is calling for one of the primary laws defining how Internet content is regulated to be "revoked," adding that the "little creeps" who run some of Silicon Valley's biggest businesses aren't the economic powerhouses they think they are.

"I've never been a fan of Facebook, as you probably know. I've never been a big [Facebook CEO Mark] Zuckerberg fan," Biden began in response to tech questions posed by the *New York Times*. "I think he's a real problem."

"He [Zuckerberg] knows better," Biden elaborated, telling the *Times*, "Not only should we be worrying about the concentration of power, we should be worried about the lack of privacy and them being exempt."

The exemption to which Biden was referring is § 230 of the Communications Decency Act. The key part of the law reads:

> No provider or user of an interactive computer service shall be treated as the publisher or speaker of any information provided by another information content provider.

At its most basic level, the law draws a line between the platform that hosts content and the generator of the content hosted on it. If something is hinky in a YouTube video, "Google" isn't the company that spoke the contents; the video creator is.

"Section 230 reform" has something of a rallying cry among the far right in recent months. Sen. Josh Hawley (R-Mo.) last year introduced legislation seeking to amend the law, revoking "the immunity big tech companies receive under Section 230 unless they submit to an external audit that proves by clear and convincing evidence that their algorithms and content-removal practices are politically neutral."

Hawley has company in both chambers of Congress. Sens. Lindsey Graham (R-S.C.) and Ted Cruz (R-Tex.) have also lent public support to the idea of Section 230 reform, as has Rep. Matt Gaetz (R-Fla.) on the House side.

The cry for reform is not limited to a single party, though. House Speaker Nancy Pelosi (D-Calif.) told Recode last April that section 230 is "a gift" to the tech firms, adding, "I don't think they are treating it with the respect that they should, and so I think that could be a question mark and in jeopardy."

Biden, however, did not call for reforms—he called for abolishing the provision entirely. "You're not exempt," he told his interviewers. "[The *Times*] can't write something you know to be false and be exempt from being sued. But he can. The idea that it's a tech company is that Section 230 should be revoked, immediately should be revoked, number one. For Zuckerberg and other platforms."

When the *NYT* pointed out that Section 230 is foundational to the modern Internet, Biden agreed, then continued:

> And it should be revoked. It should be revoked because it is not merely an internet company. It is propagating falsehoods they know to be false, and we should be setting standards not unlike the Europeans are doing relative to privacy. You guys still have editors. I'm sitting with them. Not a joke. There is no editorial impact at all on Facebook. None. None whatsoever. It's irresponsible. It's totally irresponsible.

It's Apparently Personal, but Not Criminal

Biden called particular, but oblique, attention to Facebook's decision not to block political ads that mislead users or tell outright lies, so long as those ads do not engage in obvious attempts at voter suppression. That discussion was kicked off in October, when the Trump campaign aired ads on Facebook making false accusations about Biden. The ads contained baseless claims about Biden's activities in Ukraine and elsewhere that have been repeatedly debunked by both media outlets and also other Republican politicians.

Biden suggested to the *NYT* that Facebook's choice to allow such ads could amount to defamation, saying that Zuckerberg "should be submitted to civil liability and his company to civil liability, just like you would be here at the *New York Times*" if the paper were to run demonstrably false stories. Whether Facebook should face any kind of criminal penalties, he added, is less clear.

If Zuckerberg or anyone else at Facebook "engaged in something and amounted to collusion that in fact caused harm that would in fact be equal to a criminal offense, that's a different issue," Biden added. "That's possible. That's possible it could happen. Zuckerberg finally took down those ads that Russia was running. All those bots

> **It is propagating falsehooods that they know to be false, and we should be setting standards not unlike the Europeans are doing relative to privacy.**

about me. They're no longer being run," he continued. Biden seemingly conflated action taken by an opposing campaign with the kind of foreign disinformation action that is indeed rampant across social media.

The tech sector, and Facebook in particular, is overdue for some government intervention, Biden added, drawing a line through history:

> The fact is, in every other revolution that we've had technologically, it's taken somewhere between six years and a generation for a government to come in and level the playing field again. All of a sudden, remember the Luddites smashing the machinery in

the Midlands? That was their answer when the culture was changing. Same thing with television. Same thing before that with radio. Same thing, but this is gigantic.

And it's a responsibility of government to make sure it is not abused. Not abused. And so this is one of those areas where I think it's being abused. For example, the idea that he cooperates with knowing that Russia was engaged in dealing with using the internet, I mean using their platform, to try to undermine American elections. That's close to criminal.

Intuiting that Biden was still talking about Facebook, the *Times* interviewer posited that Zuckerberg might not have known at the time how deeply involved Russia was. "He'd argue it and I don't believe him for a second," Biden replied. "Nor do you, in your heart."

Tech on Blast

Biden's antipathy for tech did not stop with Facebook; he spoke more widely of his distaste with the sector as well.

"You may recall the criticism I got for meeting with the leaders in Silicon Valley, when I was trying to work out an agreement dealing with them protecting intellectual property for artists in the United States of America," Biden said. "At one point, one of the little creeps sitting around that table, who was a multi—close to a billionaire—who told me he was an artist because he was able to come up with games to teach you how to kill people."

The interviewer asked Biden if he meant video games, and Biden agreed. He went on to say that he was "lectured" at that table by a "senior leader" who claimed that if Biden and Sen. *Patrick Leahy* (D-Vt.) moved forward with the bill in question, "they would blow up the network, figuratively speaking. Have everybody contact. They get out and go out and contact the switchboard, just blow it up."

Biden went on to say that there were representatives of seven firms sitting in that meeting, "everyone's there but Microsoft," and he found "you have fewer people on your payroll than all the losses that General Motors just faced in the last quarter, of employees. So don't lecture me about how you've created all this employment."

It is unclear which particular meeting with "little creeps" Biden was alluding to. The references to GM and to intellectual property, however, seem to indicate this meeting took place in 2008, while Biden was still representing Delaware in the Senate. Once he became Vice President in 2009, Biden continued to be deeply involved in copyright law struggles. Early in the first Obama term, Biden promised strong enforcement to the recording industries, and he was a key presence in a 2010 White House push to reform copyright enforcement.

While it's hard to work out the relative economic importance of seven unknown companies that might have been represented at an unknown meeting more than a decade ago, there is no doubt that here in 2020, the tech sector is a massive contributor to the US economy. Four publicly traded companies in US history have passed the $1 trillion valuation mark. Apple was the first to do so, in 2018. Amazon followed later that year, and Microsoft joined the club in 2019. The most recent, Google parent company Alphabet, did so earlier this week.

Print Citations

CMS: Cox, Kate, "Biden Wants Sec. 230 Gone, Calls Tech 'Totally Irresponsible,' 'Little Creeps'." In *The Reference Shelf: Internet Law,* edited by Annette Calzone, 16-19. Amenia, NY: Grey House Publishing, 2020.

MLA: Cox, Kate, "Biden Wants Sec. 230 Gone, Calls Tech 'Totally Irresponsible,' 'Little Creeps'." *The Reference Shelf: Internet Law,* edited by Annette Calzone, Grey House Publishing, 2020, pp. 16-19.

APA: Cox, K. (2020). Biden wants Sec. 230 gone, calls tech "totally irresponsible," "little creeps." In Annette Calzone (Ed.), *The reference shelf: Internet law* (pp. 16-19). Amenia, NY: Grey House Publishing.

WSJ, WaPO, NYT Spread False Internet Law Claims

By Matthew Feeney
Cato Institute, August 7, 2019

Section 230 of the Communications Decency Act is much debated and under bipartisan attack. The legislation, which includes the "26 words that created the Internet," is attacked from the right by those who complain about alleged "Big Tech" anti-conservative bias and from the left by those bemoaning the spread of extremist content. Accordingly, Section 230 has been the topic of much discussion in newspaper pages. Unfortunately, the Fourth Estate has recently allowed misinformation about Section 230 to spread, which is especially regrettable given that falsehoods about Section 230 are already ubiquitous.

The most recent example of such misinformation is an op-ed in the *Wall Street Journal* by the conservative commentator and Prager University founder Dennis Prager. The first falsehood appears in the subhead: "Big tech companies enjoy legal immunity premised on the assumption they'll respect free speech."

This is not true. Congress did not pass Section 230 on the understanding that Internet companies would engage in minimal moderation and "respect free speech." In fact, §230(c)(2)(A) of the CDA states the following:

> No provider or user of an interactive computer service shall be held liable on account of **any action** voluntarily taken in good faith to restrict access to or availability of material that **the provider or user considers** to be obscene, lewd, lascivious, filthy, excessively violent, harassing, or otherwise objectionable, whether or not such material is constitutionally protected." (emphasis mine).

This portion of Section 230 explicitly states that companies as large as Facebook and those as small as a local bakery that includes a comments section on its WordPress site can take "any action" to remove content they consider objectionable. I am at a loss trying to figure out where Prager got the idea that Section 230 was premised on Internet companies respecting "free speech." It's possible that he's considering one of Section 230's findings:

> The Internet and other interactive computer services offer a forum for a true diversity of political discourse, unique opportunities for cultural development, and myriad avenues for intellectual activity.

While this finding emphasizes the value of the Internet as an ecosystem capable of hosting a diverse range of political views, it does not encourage specific sites to adopt politically neutral content

> **Section 230 doesn't protect hate speech. Rather, it allows companies to remove speech that violates their content moderation rules without becoming liable for everything posted by users.**

moderation policies. Nor does it make such neutrality a necessary condition for Section 230 immunity.

We should keep in mind that op-ed page contributors rarely write their own subheads. But Prager makes the point explicitly in his op-ed's text:

> The clear intent of Section 230—the bargain Congress made with the tech companies—was to promote free speech while allowing companies to moderate indecent content without being classified as publishers.
>
> But Google and the others have violated this agreement. They want to operate under a double standard: censoring material that has no indecent content—that is, acting like publishers—while retaining the immunity of nonpublishers.

There was no such agreement or bargain. Section 230 was passed in an explicit attempt to encourage moderation of speech. This portion of Prager's op-ed also raises another myth that abounds in Section 230 debates: the "platform" vs. "publisher" distinction.

There is no legal difference between a "platform" and a "publisher." Indeed, publishers enjoy Section 230 protection. The *Wall Street Journal* is a publisher and can be held liable for defamatory content op-ed contributors write. But the *Wall Street Journal* also hosts moderated comment sections, which do enjoy Section 230 protection. The comments section below Prager's op-ed says as much.

When Prager writes, "But Google, YouTube and Facebook choose not to be regarded as 'publishers' because publishers are liable for what they publish and can be sued for libel" he is making a significant error. Google, YouTube, and Facebook did not "choose" to not be considered publishers. Social media sites don't "choose" not to be regarded as publishers. CDA§230(c)(1) makes the decision for them:

> No provider or user of an interactive computer service shall be treated as the publisher or speaker of any information provided by another information content provider.

These "26 words that created the Internet" include no provision that allows social media site to "choose" whether they're "publishers" or "platforms."

Section 230 was passed to encourage Internet companies to moderate user content and does not classify such companies as "publishers" or "platforms."

Prager's last important claim is that the fact that YouTube users who have opted into "restricted mode" can't access dozens of Prager U videos because of an anti-conservative bias at YouTube. This claim doesn't withstand scrutiny. Research by NetChoice demonstrates that that only 12 percent of Prager U's videos are in "restricted mode," compared to 54 percent of *Daily Show* videos and 71 percent of Young Turks videos. Prager may be correct to point out that these videos are restricted because of expletives, but expletives aren't the only kind of content that can result in videos being restricted. "Mature subjects," "violence," and "sexual situations" can also result in videos being unavailable to users in restricted mode. Anyone who takes a look at Prager U's YouTube channel can see content that would understandably put it out of reach of users who have opted into "restricted mode."

It's bad enough to get the facts of Section 230 wrong. Spreading falsehoods in pursuit of an agenda that isn't supported by what the facts reveal is worse.

Dennis Prager is the most recent proliferator of Section 230 misinformation, but he's hardly the only one.

Yesterday, the *New York Times* published a Section 230-heavy article which featured on the front page of its business section. The headline read: "Why Hate Speech on the Internet Is a Never-Ending Problem." To its credit, the *New York Times* has since issued a correction and fixed the headline. As I discussed above, Section 230 doesn't protect hate speech per se. You can thank the First Amendment for that. Rather, it allows companies to remove speech that violates their content moderation rules without becoming liable for everything posted by users. Footage of a white nationalist murdering someone would run afoul of Facebook's content moderation policy, but it might be left up by moderators of a neo-Nazi forum. Section 230 allows Facebook to remove the footage, which is legal under the First Amendment

Last month, the *Washington Post* published an op-ed by Charlie Kirk, founder of Turning Point USA. The Kirk op-ed repeats the same "publisher" v. "platform" error often seen in Section 230 debates. But it also includes the following claim:

> Social media companies have leveraged Section 230 to great effect, and astounding profits, by claiming they are platforms—not publishers—thereby avoiding under the law billions of dollars in potential copyright infringement and libel lawsuits.

Kirk's comment on Section 230's interaction with copyright law is the opposite of the truth. Section 230(e)(2) reads:

> Nothing in this section shall be construed to limit or expand any law pertaining to intellectual property.

At the time of publication neither the *Washington Post* nor the *Wall Street Journal* have issued corrections, editorial notes, or retractions related to the Prager or Kirk op-eds.

Useful policy debates only happen when participants can agree on facts. Sadly, some of the most reputable newspapers in the country have allowed for misinformation about an important piece of legislation to spread without correction. Anyone hoping for the quality of Section 230 debates to improve any time soon will be disappointed.

Print Citations

CMS: Feeney, Matthew. "WSI, WaPO, NYT Spread False Internet Law Claims." In *The Reference Shelf: Internet Law,* edited by Annette Calzone, 20-23. Amenia, NY: Grey House Publishing, 2020.

MLA: Feeney, Matthew. "WSI, WaPO, NYT Spread False Internet Law Claims." *The Reference Shelf: Internet Law,* edited by Annette Calzone, Grey House Publishing, 2020, pp. 20-23.

APA: Feeney, M. (2020). WSI, WaPO, NYT spread false internet law claims. In Annette Calzone (Ed.), *The reference shelf: Internet law* (pp. 20-23). Amenia, NY: Grey House Publishing.

The Fight Over Section 230—And the Internet as We Know It

By Matt Laslo
Wired, August 13, 2019

Few weeks have better encapsulated the whiplash-inducing discussions playing out around free speech online than the previous one. Last Monday the country was already knee-deep in questions about the internet's role in spreading hate speech—and whether platforms were doing enough to combat it—after the web forum 8chan played host once again to a hateful manifesto connected to a mass shooting. By the end of the week, however, another narrative emerged—that tech companies were policing speech too much, as reports of the White House drafting an executive order titled "Protecting Americans from Online Censorship" made the rounds.

At the center of all these debates is a bit of legislation that came into being well before Facebook and Twitter, back when the internet was plodding along at dialup speeds: Section 230 of the 1996 Communications Decency Act.

Section 230, as it's commonly known, provides "interactive computer services"—that is, anything from web hosts to websites to social media companies—with broad immunity from civil cases over the content users publish on their platforms. (Companies can still be held liable under federal criminal law and for intellectual property violations.) Among other things, this protection allowed social media companies to flourish without worrying about each and every post bringing about some potential, ruinous lawsuit. But it's also come under increasing scrutiny, with some critics arguing that tech firms need more accountability.

"Something tech companies have really gotten wrong—they've proceeded for years basically treating Section 230 like it's a right that's enshrined in the Constitution, and I think, frankly, some of the large platforms in particular have gotten incredibly arrogant," says Jeff Kosseff, who wrote a book about Section 230 called *Twenty-Six Words That Created the Internet*. "And now what you're seeing is a backlash to that arrogance."

Nowhere, perhaps, is that backlash bigger or more consequential than in Washington, DC. In Congress, both parties have singled Section 230 for attack, with some Democrats saying it allows tech companies to get away with not moderating content enough, while some Republicans say it enables them to moderate too much. So far this hyper-partisan divide on the exact nature of Section 230's shortcomings has precluded any meaningful progress on reform. But lawmakers from both parties keep signaling that they're serious about changing the status quo.

Just last week, Representatives Frank Pallone (D-New Jersey) and Greg Walden (R-Oregon) publicly criticized the inclusion of a Section 230–like provision in a trade agreement with Mexico and Canada.

"As you may know, the effects of Section 230 and the appropriate role of such a liability shield have become the subject of much debate in recent years," they wrote, citing a 2017 *Wires* story. "While we take no view on that debate in this letter, we find it inappropriate for the United States to export language mirroring Section 230 while such serious policy discussions are ongoing."

Is Section 230 Safe?

The recent mass shootings added another edge to an already multilayered and contentious debate in the nation's capital. Congress is now on its month-long August recess, but just before lawmakers headed out of the swamp, *Wired* caught up with many of the key players.

"The world has changed," Senator Josh Hawley (R-Missouri) told *Wired*. "The internet has changed, and I think we need to keep pace with change. The dominant, monopoly-sized platforms that exist today didn't exist then. The business model they employ today wasn't employed then."

Hawley, like many of his colleagues in the GOP, has accused social media companies of censoring conservative voices—a charge those companies have repeatedly denied. In June, he introduced a bill in the Senate that would require the FTC to certify that companies like Facebook, Twitter, and Google do not "moderate information provided by other information content providers in a politically biased manner" in order for Section 230 immunity to apply. (Republican representative Paul Gosar, of Arizona, announced he was introducing a similarly minded bill in the House a few weeks ago.) But the constitutional questions it raises, along with the lack of support from Democrats, makes it seem unlikely to succeed.

"It creates a government kind of information police—censorship, information police," Senator Ron Wyden (D-Oregon) told *Wired*. "A government-established neutrality board is a 180-degree departure of everything conservatives have stood for for years."

Republicans who support Hawley's act claim it's the lesser of two evils.

"I'm a conservative. I don't want Washington running my life, but I sure as hell don't want Silicon Valley running my life," Representative Matt Gaetz (R-Florida) told *Wired*. Last year, Gaetz claimed to be "shadow banned" by Twitter, after a Vice report found a handful of accounts for conservative figures weren't surfacing in some search results. At the time, Twitter told *Wired* that this was an error, and not based on the political content of tweets. But the incident didn't improve tech companies' standing with Gaetz, who already had been a vocal critic of Section 230 in hearings on the Hill.

Gaetz says he has semi-frequent cell calls with the president, and says he's discussed this issue with senior Trump officials, including "what we can do in the absence of legislation." While Gaetz won't divulge the details of those private talks, he supports reining in tech companies.

"There is no First Amendment right for online platforms to have a unique shield from liability that is not enjoyed by newspapers, magazines, or television stations," Gaetz told *Wired*. "That is an extraconstitutional privilege that is statutory in nature,

> **It must be noted that there's scant evidence that social media companies are systematically suppressing conservative content because of users' political views.**

enshrined in The Communications Decency Act." (Newspapers, magazines, and TV stations can enjoy Section 230 protections, too, for example if their websites have comments sections for users.)

If Congress doesn't move the needle on Section 230 reform, the president has indicated he's willing to take up the torch. Late last week, Politico was first to report that the White House is in the early stages of drafting an executive order to deal with what it claims is anti-conservative bias in Silicon Valley. Similar to Hawley's bill, it would have government agencies oversee how social media companies moderate their sites, according to a summary of a draft order obtained by CNN.

It must be noted that there's scant evidence that social media companies are systematically suppressing conservative content because of users' political views. In fact, social media analytics companies like NewsWhip routinely find outlets like Fox News and Breitbart in the top 10 or 20 publishers on sites like Facebook. But persnickety facts don't really matter in today's Washington.

An Often Misunderstood Law

Senator Wyden helped pen Section 230 while serving in the House back in the '90s, along with conservative former California congressperson Chris Cox. Section 230 wasn't crafted to shield companies for the heck of it. The fear was that if companies could be held responsible for *all* the content its users posted simply because they moderated some of it—as had happened to Prodigy in 1995—they wouldn't moderate anything at all. Or so the argument went.

Since then, Section 230 has become sacrosanct in the eyes of Silicon Valley executives and free speech advocates. It is also frequently misunderstood or misportrayed, including by lawmakers.

"I hear constantly about how the law is about neutrality. Nowhere, nowhere, nowhere does the law say anything about that," an animated Wyden said. He brushes aside contemporary Republican cries of "censorship" as mere hollow talking points. Wyden is open to tweaking the law he helped write, but for him the debate in Washington needs to go beyond issues of content moderation.

Not all Republicans are on board with "the fix" Hawley and Gaetz are peddling in the marble halls of the Capitol and on conservative cable outlets, either.

"I'm generally supportive of the Section 230, because without it you don't have the Internet," Senator Ron Johnson (R-Wisconsin) told *Wired*. "Sen. Hawley's bill—I think the concern about that is, well who's going to be able to judge whether a company is or isn't showing bias? Then all the sudden take away that 230 protection—I don't know, I've got my doubts on that one."

For Democrats, there are no doubts.

"I have to say, I have not seen evidence of political bias," Senator Mark Warner (D-Virginia), the ranking member on the Intelligence Committee, told *Wired*. "I think the bias they [tech companies] have is they want to make as much money as possible."

That's not to say Warner is opposed to changes to Section 230, but he urges caution. "The idea that this is simply a totally unregulated square is simply not accurate, because we already have put in certain regulations," Warner said, and added that the issue needs more debate.

What's Next?

For years, the very business models of platforms like Facebook and YouTube have come under fire for prioritizing whatever grabbed their users' attention, often leading to feeds full of content that shocks or stokes outrage or divides. And Section 230 has enabled those business models, by shielding companies from responsibility for their users' behavior at its most extreme. Just last month, an appeals court used the provision to rule that Facebook couldn't be sued for providing a platform for terrorists, throwing out a lawsuit from the families of American citizens killed in Hamas attacks.

But in terms of solutions, Section 230 still might not be the right lever to pull.

"I think there definitely is a big problem with hate speech and all sorts of absolutely vile content online," Kosseff, the author, says. "The question is how do changes to Section 230 address that."

In 22 years, there's only been one real update to Section 230. The Fight Online Sex Trafficking Act and the Stop Enabling Sex Traffickers Act, or Fosta-Sesta, was signed into law last year, removing Section 230 immunity for services that "promote and facilitate prostitution." The controversial amendment led to broad self-censorship by many sites, and some sex workers say the fallout has made their lives more dangerous, not less.

When Congress returns from recess in September, all signs point to lawmakers taking up the Section 230 debate where they left off. But gutting Section 230 could have other unintended effects, some experts fear. As distasteful as many parts of the web may be, they say, policing speech that is, after all, protected by the First Amendment could blow up in lawmakers' faces.

"Maybe the internet companies could have been better at foreseeing where the problems would arise, but I think they're quickly realizing they don't have the right policy yet and they're going to keep working towards it," Eric Goldman, a Section 230 expert at the Santa Clara University School of Law, told *Wired*. "And that's the beauty of Section 230."

Content moderation is hard to get right, and examples of companies getting it wrong abound. Goldman contends the statute is what gives tech firms the power and freedom to explore what works and what doesn't.

"Section 230 allows the internet companies to make those decisions confidently without fearing their liability," Goldman said. "The basis of those decisions are, 'What's in the best interest of my audience? What can I do to facilitate my audience's needs?' So Section 230 is—in that part—is unquestionably a part of the solution."

Print Citations

CMS: Laslo, Matt. "The Fight Over Section 230—And the Internet as We Know It." In *The Reference Shelf: Internet Law,* edited by Annette Calzone, 24-28. Amenia, NY: Grey House Publishing, 2020.

MLA: Laslo, Matt. "The Fight Over Section 230—And the Internet as We Know It." *The Reference Shelf: Internet Law,* edited by Annette Calzone, Grey House Publishing, 2020, pp. 24-28.

APA: Laslo, M. (2020). The fight over Section 230—and the internet as we know it. In Annette Calzone (Ed.), *The reference shelf: Internet law* (pp. 24-28). Amenia, NY: Grey House Publishing.

2
Net Neutrality

Columbia University law professor Tim Wu, who coined the term "net neutrality" in 2003, maintains that the 2017 repeal of net neutrality laws upends a long history. Above, Wu at Wikipedia Day in 2017.

Should the Internet Be a Public Utility?

Network neutrality—more commonly net neutrality—is the principle that Internet service providers (ISPs) should treat access to all data equally, regardless of its source or destination, and not slow down delivery, block content, or charge different prices for different services. The idea is borrowed from the "common carrier" classification given to the Bell telephone system (later AT&T) under the Mann-Elkins Act and codified by the Communications Act of 1934. The intent was to impose neutrality rules similar to those of the transportation industry on electronic communications. Just as a railroad company cannot discriminate against or charge higher fares for different types of passengers, the government ensured that AT&T's prices were the same for all Americans. AT&T also had to interconnect with smaller rural services and let competitors use their infrastructure. To ensure "universal service," being a common carrier under Title II of the 1934 act "meant (and still means) that they must be end-to-end neutral for the transportation of data; the service provider cannot change their service based on the person dialing the number, the person being dialed, or the content of the conversation."[1]

If the Section 230 debate is about striking a balance between accountability and free speech, the debate over net neutrality seeks a balance between the free flow of information and the costs necessary to maintain that flow. Advocates of net neutrality argue that the Internet is too important to leave unregulated and that neutrality would promote the free flow of information and innovation and keep data transmission at an acceptable level. They point to the rise of corporate monopolies—the 1934 act was in part designed to break up the monopoly of the Bell system—with periods of reduced regulation. Opponents say it reduces investment in infrastructure and innovation and raises costs for ISPs and telecom equipment manufacturers, which may then have to be passed along to consumers. Some also argue that if ISPs can charge more for certain web services, typically those that use more bandwidth such as video streaming, this will allow them to charge end users less.

Common Carrier Laws and the Internet

With the advent of the Internet in the 1980s, digital subscriber line (DSL)—a technology that allowed digital data to travel on the same copper wire as voice by using a higher frequency—providers were still subject to common carrier rules, as they used telephone wires to carry data. The Telecommunications Act of 1996 made a distinction between traditional telephone/telecommunications services and information services, reserving strict common carrier rules only for the telephone industry, and excluding cable broadband services (which transmits data using space on a designated television channel) from this category. This bifurcation resulted in many legal battles over the next several years. Some believe that investment by telephone companies was hampered by the 1996 telecom act, which required them to share their copper phone lines at a regulated price. According to a 2014 Progressive Policy Institute report, "This put the phone companies in a Catch-22. They had to sell the most important component of DSL service—the network that conveys it—to their competitors. But if they made the significant investments needed to offer a better product . . . they could find themselves forced to resell that improved capacity to competitors as well."[2]

As Internet technologies developed, the designation of broadband as an information service exempt from common carrier rules was challenged, and it was reversed in 2015 under Barack Obama's administration. In sum, the 400-page document set forth by the Federal Communications Commission (FCC) contained three key rules:

1. No blocking—providers cannot block lawful content or non-harmful devices.
2. No throttling—providers cannot slow down specific applications or services based on who sends it, who receives it, and what its content is.
3. No paid prioritization—providers cannot accept fees for creating an Internet "fast lane."[3]

The FCC did include some modifications for Internet providers of the strict controls that normally apply to utilities, but a provision requiring "just and reasonable conduct" left room for the FCC to make case-by-case judgments. Anticipating appeals to the ruling, Northwestern University law professor James B. Speta noted in a 2015 *New York Times* article that the challenges would focus on the classification itself, that is, on whether "the companies [are] more defined by their infrastructure, qualifying them as telecommunications services, or by what is transmitted over it."[4]

In 2017, the Republican-led FCC under Donald Trump repealed the net neutrality rules, and even sought to throw out a 2016 U.S. Court of Appeals for the District of Columbia Circuit ruling upholding the Obama-era policy. The U.S. Supreme Court refused, leaving a legal precedent in place for future attempts to pass net neutrality legislation.[5] A notable difference in this round of debate was the absence of Big Tech companies pushing for net neutrality. Before the 2015 ruling, companies like Netflix lobbied against the fees charged by ISPs. But Georgetown University's Larry Downes explains that many tech companies have simply grown too big for net neutrality to matter to them: "From [these companies'] standpoint, it doesn't really matter who's enforcing net neutrality, or if there's net neutrality at all—they don't need it. . . . They have all the leverage they need to make sure their content gets delivered as best it can be."[6]

Net neutrality has been in the news again in relation to Covid-19, as advocacy groups point out the need for oversight during a public health crisis, when Internet access is critical. In February 2020, a federal appellate court upheld the repeal but instructed the FCC to look into its effect on public safety, including the Lifeline program, which subsidizes broadband. The FCC issued a call for comments, and in response Public Knowledge and other advocacy groups wrote: "Without the tools afforded to the FCC via Title II, the FCC lacks the ability to respond to unexpected contingencies, ensure continuous service to users, gather the data it needs about network performance, or even to ensure that smaller ISPs can continue to interconnect with the broader network despite temporary liquidity problems."[7] As voice and video calls have skyrocketed, video streaming services like YouTube, Netflix, and Facebook have voluntary reduced bandwidth consumption during the pandemic, and AT&T, Comcast, and Verizon have pledged to waive late fees, open up Wi-Fi hotspots, and not terminate service for customers and businesses unable to keep up with their bills. But with the net neutrality repeal, the FCC's ability to intervene if needed is ambiguous.[8] In June AT&T was accused of violating net neutrality rules by not counting the use of its own HBO Max streaming service against customer data caps while counting usage of competitors such as Netflix and Disney+.[9]

The Future, the Past

Columbia University law professor Tim Wu, who coined the term net neutrality in 2003, contends that the 2017 repeal upends a long history of neutrality. Wu explains the issue as a simple question of how a network's owner should treat its traffic and what rights the network's users have. Although the concept has been applied to medieval bridges and railroad networks, Wu considers that the modern debate has two "ancestors," both from the 1970s. The first was the development of a new group of businesses that ran "over the top" of AT&T's nationwide network—precursors of operations like Netflix, Wikipedia, and Google. These businesses were vulnerable to what Wu calls AT&T's "legendary jealousy." The FCC began putting rules in place to protect over-the-top services, both basic and enhanced (the equivalent of applications like Skype). These rules are the "first" net neutrality rules. The second ancestor of the modern debate concerns the main operating protocols of the Internet, which were designed to be neutral in terms of carriers and content and to follow an "end-to-end" principle of network design, which roughly translates as the "ends," or the users of the network, deciding "what the network was for rather than the network operators." This end-to-end philosophy favored outsiders and startups rather than AT&T, resulting in the creation of such important applications as the World Wide Web, email, streaming video, and social networking. When high-speed DSL and broadband were deployed in the 1990s, both telecom and cable carriers tried to block or otherwise restrict (through terms of service) access to gaming applications and voice-over Internet protocol (VoIP) services like Skype. In response to the rise in broadband restrictions, in 2004 FCC chair Michael Powell delineated "Four Internet Freedoms" (modeled after Franklin Delano Roosevelt's "Four Freedoms):

1. Freedom to access content
2. Freedom to use applications
3. Freedom to attach personal devices
4. Freedom to obtain service plan information

The following year these basic rules became legal precedent when the FCC fined a small DSL provider (North Carolina-based Madison River) for blocking then-popular VoIP program Vonage. The FCC under presidents as disparate as George W. Bush and Barack Obama continued to step in to ensure compliance to net neutrality rules. According to Wu, the repeal put in place by current FCC Commissioner Ajit Pai is more radical than simply tinkering with rules that have been in place in one form or another since the 1970s. Pai rescinded net neutrality rules in their entirety and placed oversight in the hands of the Federal Trade Commission (FTC), essentially giving up the FCC's role in monitoring telephone and cable carriers. Wu believes that future legal challenges will rely on questioning such a complete reversal of course.[10]

Works Used

Bettilyon, Tyler Elliot. "Network Neutrality: A History of Common Carrier Laws 1884–2018." *Medium*. Dec. 12, 2017. https://medium.com/@TebbaVonMathenstien/network-neutrality-a-history-of-common-carrier-laws-1884-2018.

Davis, Wendy. "Covid-19 Crisis Shows Need for Net Neutrality Rules, Advocates Say." *Digital News Daily*. Apr. 20, 2020. https://www.mediapost.com/publications/article/350285/covid-19-crisis-shows-need-for-net-neutrality-rule.html

Ehrlich, Ev. "A Brief History of Internet Regulation." Progressive Policy Institute. 2014. https://www.progressivepolicy.org/wp-content/uploads/2014/03/2014.03-Ehrlich_A-Brief-History-of-Internet-Regulation.pdf.

Hersko, Tyler. "AT&T Ignores Net Neutrality: HBO Max Won't Hit Data Caps but Competing Streamers Will." *IndieWire*. June 4, 2020. https://www.indiewire.com/2020/06/att-net-neutrality-hbo-max-no-data-caps-1202235538/.

Hurley, Lawrence. "U.S. Supreme Court Ends Fight over Obama-Era Net Neutrality Rules." *Reuters*. Nov. 5, 2018. https://www.reuters.com/article/us-usa-court-netneutrality/u-s-supreme-court-ends-fight-over-obama-era-net-neutrality-rules-idUSKCN1NA1UW.

Makena, Kelly. "Self-Isolation Has Stressed Networks, and No One Knows if the FCC Can Step In." *The Verge*. Mar. 31, 2020. https://www.theverge.com/2020/3/31/21200992/fcc-coronavirus-net-neutrality-networks-att-comcast-carriers.

Pinsker, Joe. "Where Were Netflix and Google in the Net-Neutrality Fight?" *The Atlantic*. Dec. 20, 2017. https://www.theatlantic.com/business/archive/2017/12/netflix-google-net-neutrality/548768/.

Reardon, Marguerite. "What You Need to Know about the FCC's 2015 Net Neutrality Regulation." *CNET*. Mar. 14, 2015. https://www.cnet.com/news/13-things-you-need-to-know-about-the-fccs-net-neutrality-regulation/.

Ruiz, Rebecca R. "F.C.C. Sets Net Neutrality Rules." *The New York Times*. Mar. 12, 2015. https://www.nytimes.com/2015/03/13/technology/fcc-releases-net-neutrality-rules.html.

Wu, Tim. "How the FCC's Net Neutrality Plan Breaks with 50 Years of History." *Wired*. Dec. 6, 2017. https://www.wired.com/story/how-the-fccs-net-neutrality-plan-breaks-with-50-years-of-history/.

Notes

1. Bettilyon, "Network Neutrality: A History of Common Carrier Laws 1884–2018."
2. Ehrlich, "A Brief History of Internet Regulation."
3. Reardon, "What You Need to Know about the FCC's 2015 Net Neutrality Regulation."
4. Ruiz, "F.C.C. Sets Net Neutrality Rules."
5. Hurley, "U.S. Supreme Court Ends Fight over Obama-Era Net Neutrality Rules."
6. Pinsker, "Where Were Netflix and Google in the Net-Neutrality Fight?"
7. Davis, "Covid-19 Crisis Shows Need for Net Neutrality Rules, Advocates Say."
8. Makena, "Self-Isolation Has Stressed Networks, and No One Knows if the FCC Can Step In."
9. Hersko, "AT&T Ignores Net Neutrality: HBO Max Won't Hit Data Caps but Competing Streamers Will."
10. Wu, "How the FCC's Net Neutrality Plan Breaks with 50 Years of History."

The Wired Guide to Net Neutrality

By Klint Finley
Wired, May 5, 2020

Net neutrality is the idea that internet service providers like Comcast and Verizon should treat all content flowing through their cables and cell towers equally. That means they shouldn't be able to slide some data into "fast lanes" while blocking or otherwise discriminating against other material. In other words, these companies shouldn't be able to block you from accessing a service like Skype, or slow down Netflix or Hulu, in order to encourage you to keep your cable package or buy a different video-streaming service.

The Federal Communications Commission spent years, under both the Bush and Obama administrations, trying to enforce net neutrality protections. After a series of legal defeats at the hands of broadband providers, the FCC passed a sweeping net neutrality order in 2015. But in December 2017, the now Republican-controlled FCC voted to jettison that order, freeing broadband providers to block or throttle content as they see fit unless Congress or the courts block the agency's decision.

Net neutrality advocates have long argued that keeping the internet an open playing field is crucial for innovation. If broadband providers pick favorites online, new companies and technologies might never have the chance to grow. For example, had internet providers blocked or severely limited video streaming in the mid-2000s, we might not have Netflix or YouTube today. Other advocates highlight the importance of net neutrality to free expression: a handful of large telecommunications companies dominate the broadband market, which puts an enormous amount of power into their hands to suppress particular views or limit online speech to those who can pay the most.

Most large broadband providers promised not to block or throttle content ahead of the ruling, but all four major mobile carriers began slowing down at least some video content before the FCC had fully repealed the rules. Net neutrality advocates worry things could get worse. A broadband provider might, for example, allow some companies to pay for priority treatment on broadband networks. The fear is that, over time, companies and organizations that either can't afford priority treatment, or simply aren't offered access to it, will fall by the wayside.

The History of Net Neutrality

Columbia University law professor Tim Wu coined the term "network neutrality" in a 2003 paper about online discrimination. At the time, some broadband providers, including Comcast, banned home internet users from accessing virtual private networks (VPNs), while others, like AT&T, banned users from using Wi-Fi routers. Wu worried that broadband providers' tendency to restrict new technologies would hurt innovation in the long term, and called for anti-discrimination rules.

The Bush-era FCC took a first pass at anti-discrimination rules for the internet in a policy statement in 2005. It prohibited internet service providers from blocking legal content or preventing customers from connecting the devices of their choosing to their internet connections. Under this policy, the FCC ordered Comcast in 2008 to stop slowing connections that used the peer-to-peer file-sharing software BitTorrent, which was often used for digital piracy but also had legitimate uses. Comcast sued the FCC, arguing the agency had overstepped its bounds. A federal court agreed, ruling that the FCC had failed to make the legal case that it had the authority to enforce the 2005 policy statement.

Wait, What's a Common Carrier Again?

Certain services and businesses have been seen as so crucial to the functioning of society and the economy that governments dating back to Ancient Rome have passed special laws to ensure open access to them. In exchange for serving the entire public, as opposed to being able to pick and choose customers, common carriers were often rewarded with legal benefits, such as special access to public property. For example, railroads—long treated as common carriers in the US—are allowed to lay tracks across public land. Today, telephone providers are classified as common carriers, and in the dialup era internet providers were considered to be their customers. If it hadn't been for their common carrier status, telcos might have gotten away with charging customers more to access the internet than to make traditional voice calls, as they tried to do in the 1990s.

In 2010, the Obama-era FCC passed a more detailed net neutrality order that it hoped would stand up to legal scrutiny. But the agency was sued again, this time by Verizon, and in 2014 the same court ruled the agency didn't have the authority to impose net neutrality regulations on services that weren't considered common carriers under Title II of the Communications Act, like traditional telephone services.

> **Outright blocking a competitor may well be an antitrust violation, but creating fast lanes for companies that pay extra for special treatment might not be.**

Later that year, the FCC floated a new proposal that net neutrality proponents worried would allow internet "fast lanes." The idea drew the ire of comedian John Oliver, who encouraged viewers of his show *Last Week Tonight* to file comments to express their support for net neutrality. The flood of comments crashed the FCC's website. The agency eventually received 21.9 million comments on the issue, shattering the record previously held by Janet Jackson's 2004 Super Bowl "wardrobe malfunction."

Then-FCC chair Wheeler eventually changed tack and decided to reclassify broadband providers as Title II carriers, though with fewer obligations than landline telephone operators. The FCC passed its sweeping net neutrality order in 2015, and was again sued by telecommunications firms. The same federal court that shot down the FCC's previous attempts at net neutrality rules finally sided with the agency, ruling that the 2015 rules were legal. An industry group appealed that decision to the Supreme Court, which has yet to hear the case.

Meanwhile, control of the FCC changed as a result of the 2016 election. In January 2017, President Trump appointed Republican FCC Commissioner Ajit Pai as the agency's new chair. In April, he announced a plan to reverse the 2015 net neutrality order. The FCC website was once again flooded with comments. But this time, observers noticed that a huge number of comments, many of which opposed net neutrality, were filed not by people but by bots.

The December 2017 FCC vote effectively threw out the 2015 rules in their entirety. The FCC's new rules drop the common-carrier status for broadband providers, as well as any restrictions on blocking or throttling content. In place of those restrictions, the new rules only require that internet service providers disclose information about their network-management practices. It will now be up to the Federal Trade Commission to protect consumers from alleged net neutrality violations. But the FTC is only an enforcement agency: It can't create new rules. That means that unless a net neutrality violation is also illegal under existing fair-competition laws, there's not much the agency can do about it. Outright blocking a competitor may well be an antitrust violation, but creating fast lanes for companies that pay extra for special treatment might not be.

The Future of Net Neutrality

The future of net neutrality is now in the hands of Congress, the courts, and the states. Twenty-one state attorneys general sued the FCC in January 2018 to block the new rules and restore the old ones; so did several consumer-advocacy groups. A federal court decided mostly in the FCC's favor in 2019 but ruled that the agency couldn't override state-level net neutrality laws.

Past Net Neutrality Violations

Early 2000s

A few internet providers, including Cox and Comcast, banned some customers from using virtual private networks (VPNs) and asked users to upgrade to professional or business accounts if they wanted access. The practice was short lived, but it helped inspire the net neutrality movement.

Early 2000s

Today we think about net neutrality mostly in terms of access to content, but in the early 2000s advocates were also worried that broadband providers would block customers from using some devices. AT&T, for example, used to ban customers from setting up their own Wi-Fi routers.

2005

North Carolina internet service provider Madison River blocked Vonage, a service for making telephone calls over the internet. The FCC fined Madison River in 2005 and ordered it to stop blocking, marking one of the first efforts to enforce net neutrality rules.

2008

The FCC ordered Comcast to stop throttling BitTorrent connections on its network in 2008. Comcast denied that it throttled BitTorrent but sued the FCC, successfully arguing it had no authority to stop Comcast from slowing down connections if it wanted to.

2009

Apple was caught blocking iPhone users from making Skype calls at the request of AT&T. The companies eventually relented under pressure from the FCC.

Several states have already passed such laws. Washington became the first in March 2018, and Oregon followed soon after. California passed one of the most comprehensive net neutrality laws of all, but the rules are currently on hold amidst a legal challenge from the federal government. Governors of Hawaii, Montana, New Jersey, New York, and Vermont have passed executive orders banning state agencies from doing business with broadband providers that don't uphold the principles of net neutrality.

In the meantime, you can expect broadband providers to slowly take advantage of their new freedom. They probably won't take big overt steps to slow down or block competing services, especially not while courts are still deliberating the FCC's latest decision. But you can expect to see more of the practices that carriers already employ, like letting their own content bypass data limits. For example, AT&T lets you watch its DirecTV Now video service without having it count against your data plan, but watching Netflix or Hulu still chews through your limit.

Print Citations

CMS: Finley, Klint. "The Wired Guide to Net Neutrality." In *The Reference Shelf: Internet Law,* edited by Annette Calzone, 37-41. Amenia, NY: Grey House Publishing, 2020.

MLA: Finley, Klint. "The Wired Guide to Net Neutrality." *The Reference Shelf: Internet Law,* edited by Annette Calzone, Grey House Publishing, 2020, pp. 37-41.

APA: Finley, K. (2020). The wired guide to net neutrality. In Annette Calzone (Ed.), *The reference shelf: Internet law* (pp. 37-41). Amenia, NY: Grey House Publishing.

FCC Chairman: Our Job Is to Protect a Free and Open Internet

By Ajit Pai
CNET, June 10, 2018

I support a free and open internet. The internet should be an open platform where you are free to go where you want, and say and do what you want, without having to ask anyone's permission. And under the Federal Communications Commission's Restoring Internet Freedom Order, which takes effect Monday, the internet will be just such an open platform. Our framework will protect consumers and promote better, faster internet access and more competition.

Our approach includes strong consumer protections. For example, we empower the Federal Trade Commission to police internet service providers for anticompetitive acts and unfair or deceptive practices. In 2015, the FCC stripped the FTC—the nation's premier consumer protection agency—of its authority over internet service providers. This was a loss for consumers and a mistake we have reversed. Starting Monday, the FTC will once again be able to protect Americans consistently across the internet economy, and the FCC will work hand-in-hand with our partners at the FTC to do just that.

Transparency is also a critical part of our framework. In the Restoring Internet Freedom Order, the FCC strengthened its transparency rule so that internet service providers must make public more information about their network management practices. They are required to make this information available either on their own website or on the FCC's website. This information will allow consumers to make an informed decision about which internet service provider is best for them and give entrepreneurs the information they need as they develop new products and services. Our transparency rule will also help ensure that any problematic conduct by internet service providers is quickly identified and corrected.

Why am I confident that this approach will work? Because it was a tremendous bipartisan success for two decades. At the dawn of the commercial internet, President Clinton and a Republican Congress agreed on a light-touch framework to regulating the internet. Under that approach, the internet was open and free. Network investment topped $1.5 trillion. Netflix, Facebook, Amazon, and Google went from small startups to global tech giants. America's internet economy became the envy in the world.

But then in 2015, the FCC chose a different course and slapped heavy-handed regulations from 1934—known as "Title II"—on the internet. This was the wrong decision. Rules designed for the Ma Bell monopoly during the era of rotary phones were a poor fit for the greatest innovation of our time, the internet. Following the FCC's decision, network investment fell by billions of dollars—the first time that had happened outside of a recession in the broadband era.

> **The FCC strengthened its transparency rule so that internet service providers must make public more information about their network management practices.**

The impact was especially harmful for smaller internet service providers who didn't have the means to withstand a regulatory onslaught. These providers often serve rural and lower-income areas where better internet access and competition are most desperately needed. But they were forced to spend scarce funds on regulatory compliance rather than building out broadband to more Americans.

Monday, we are ending this flawed approach and allowing smaller internet service providers to focus their efforts on deploying more broadband, connecting more Americans with digital opportunity, and offering more competition in the marketplace.

That approach will be very positive for consumers. For instance, recently I heard from a rural broadband provider in Vermont called VTel. VTel wrote to say that "regulating broadband like legacy telephone service would not create any incentives for VTel to invest in its network. In fact, it would have precisely the opposite effect." The company went on to say that it's now "quite optimistic about the future, and the current FCC is a significant reason for our optimism." Indeed, VTel just announced that it has committed $4 million to upgrade its 4G LTE service and to begin rolling out faster mobile broadband that will start its transition to 5G, the next generation of wireless connectivity.

The bottom line is that our regulatory framework will both protect the free and open internet and deliver more digital opportunity to more Americans. It's worked before and it will work again. Our goal is simple: better, faster, cheaper internet access for American consumers who are in control of their own online experience. And that's what the FCC's Restoring Internet Freedom Order will deliver.

Print Citations

CMS: Pai, Ajit. "FCC Chairman: Our Job Is to Protect a Free and Open Internet." In *The Reference Shelf: Internet Law,* edited by Annette Calzone, 42-43. Amenia, NY: Grey House Publishing, 2020.

MLA: Pai, Ajit. "FCC Chairman: Our Job Is to Protect a Free and Open Internet." *The Reference Shelf: Internet Law,* edited by Annette Calzone, Grey House Publishing, 2020, pp. 42-43.

APA: Pai, A. (2020). FCC chairman: Our job is to protect a free and open internet. In Annette Calzone (Ed.), *The reference shelf: Internet law* (pp. 42-43). Amenia, NY: Grey House Publishing.

What the Microsoft Antitrust Case Taught Us

By Richard Blumenthal and Tim Wu
The New York Times, May 18, 2018

Twenty years ago today, Microsoft was sued by the Department of Justice and a coalition of 20 state attorneys general (including one of us, Mr. Blumenthal, of Connecticut) for violating federal antitrust law.

Microsoft, the world's dominant software firm, and Bill Gates, the world's richest man, faced a challenge from the upstart company Netscape and its internet browser, Netscape Navigator. The suit accused Microsoft of illegally protecting its operating-system monopoly and seeking a new monopoly for its own browser, Internet Explorer. The fear was that Microsoft would kill Netscape, monopolize the browser market and use that point of control to dominate the coming age of the web.

After a tough fight, the government won the case. There is now no browser monopoly, and the world has come to rely on the many apps, firms and ideas that were born after Microsoft's control was broken. Microsoft has become a gentler giant, and Mr. Gates has become a philanthropist.

Yet it is worth remembering that at the time, challenging Microsoft was not a popular decision. Microsoft was a well-liked company and Mr. Gates was widely heralded as a visionary genius. Many, Microsoft most of all, argued that enforcing the antitrust laws against Microsoft would damage innovation and impede the economic growth fueled by the technology sector.

This view turned out to be wrong. Innovation surged in the newly opened markets and the United States continued to spearhead growth in the technological world. The enduring lesson of the Microsoft case was that keeping markets open can require a trustbuster's courage to take decisive action against even a very popular monopolist.

Imagine a world in which Microsoft had been allowed to monopolize the browser business. Holding a triple monopoly (operating system, major applications and the browser), Microsoft would have controlled the future of the web. Google, the tiny start-up, would have faced an unfair fight against Bing. Microsoft-MySpace might have become the default social network instead of Facebook. And who knows whether Netflix or any other online video service would have been started?

It took the power of law enforcement to rebut Microsoft's claims that everything it was doing was pro-competitive, innovative and innocent. The discovery of candid internal company memos, a famously revealing deposition of Bill Gates and a full trial made it clear that Microsoft saw the internet as a major threat to its monopoly rule and was seeking to tame it.

The presiding judge, Thomas Penfield Jackson of the United States District Court for the District of Columbia, was right to propose that Microsoft be broken into two companies—one for the Windows operating system, one for other products. In the end, unfortunately, Microsoft was kept whole.

Some limitations were placed on Microsoft's behavior, such as a requirement that it share certain programming information with third-party companies. The appropriateness of that remedy is still debated. But what we do know is that the remedy pushed Microsoft to act with more caution, creating an essential opening for a new generation of firms.

It might seem like a cruel irony that the immediate beneficiaries of the Microsoft antitrust case—namely, Google, Facebook and Amazon—have now become behemoths themselves. But this is how the innovation cycle works: It creates room for saplings to grow into giants, but then prevents the new giants from squashing the next generation of saplings. (Microsoft was itself, in the early 1980s, the beneficiary of another antitrust case, against IBM, the computing colossus of its time.)

> **Holding a triple monopoly (operation system, major applications, and the browser), Microsoft would have controlled the future of the web.**

Which takes us to the present day. Unfortunately, ever since the Microsoft case there has been remarkably little oversight of the technology sector, despite the obvious signs of corporate consolidation and outsize market power. Enforcement of the antimonopoly laws has fallen: Between 1970 and 1999, the United States brought about 15 monopoly cases each year; between 2000 and 2014 that number went down to just three.

Antitrust efforts have become too fixated on the idea that the only real harm consists of raising of prices for consumers. Yet in the Microsoft case, Internet Explorer was "free," even though Microsoft was bent on destroying competition with it. Today, both Google and Facebook offer products that are free. Society has grown to rely on them, but because they have no dollar price, antitrust regulators have been hesitant to take action.

Any American can tell you that there is no free lunch. Everything has a price. We pay for these products and services with our time and our data. And like Microsoft, these firms have come to exert too much control over our shared technological future.

At a hearing before the Senate, Mark Zuckerberg, the chief executive of Facebook, was asked to name Facebook's biggest competitor—a company providing a similar service that consumers can go to if they are unhappy with Facebook. Mr. Zuckerberg could not name one. Part of the reason for this is that Facebook bought its most obvious competitors, Instagram and WhatsApp, and continues to acquire upstart companies before they can reach that point.

The pattern is familiar. And if the Microsoft case showed us anything, it is that we should not trust any one company to decide our future.

Print Citations

CMS: Blumenthal, Richard, and Tim Wu. "What the Microsoft Antitrust Case Taught Us." In *The Reference Shelf: Internet Law,* edited by Annette Calzone, 44-46. Amenia, NY: Grey House Publishing, 2020.

MLA: Blumenthal, Richard, and Tim Wu. "What the Microsoft Antitrust Case Taught Us." *The Reference Shelf: Internet Law,* edited by Annette Calzone, Grey House Publishing, 2020, pp.44-46.

APA: Blumenthal, R., & Wu, T. (2020). What the Microsoft antitrust case taught us. In Annette Calzone (Ed.), *The reference shelf: Internet law* (pp. 44-46). Amenia, NY: Grey House Publishing.

How the Loss of Net Neutrality Could Change the Internet

Margaret Harding McGill

Politico, December 14, 2017

The repeal of net neutrality ushers in a new chapter of the internet that could eventually transform the way Americans communicate, shop and consume information online.

The Federal Communications Commission's party-line vote Thursday to dump the Obama-era rules, which required internet service providers to treat all Web traffic equally, opens the door for companies like Verizon and AT&T to experiment with new business models free from government regulation.

ISPs point to an array of possible pro-consumer outcomes like "family friendly" broadband packages that block content not suitable for children, or guaranteed fast speeds for health-related mobile applications. But net neutrality advocates paint an array of troubling scenarios—from smaller websites like the crafts marketplace Etsy and streaming service Vimeo forced to pay tolls to reach consumers, to cable giants like Comcast blocking or slowing disfavored sites while giving priority to their own content.

"You will see fast lanes and slow lanes. You can't have fast lanes without slow lanes," said Gigi Sohn, a net neutrality advocate who worked as an FCC aide when the rules were passed in 2015. "That will mean some of your websites are going to load slower, and some you like, mainly the smaller ones, may cease to exist because they can't pay to get to customers faster."

Thursday's move comes amid a rapidly changing media environment in which the internet is hotly contested turf. Big media companies like Disney, which just announced plans to acquire 21st Century Fox film and TV assets in a $52 billion deal, will still have the resources to negotiate deals with internet providers for preferential access to consumers—but net neutrality advocates fear that smaller competitors and innovative startups will find themselves priced out.

"As a result of today's misguided action, our broadband providers will get extraordinary new powers. They will have the power to block websites, the power to throttle services, and the power to censor online content," Democratic FCC Commissioner Jessica Rosenworcel said at Thursday's meeting. "They will have the right to discriminate and favor the internet traffic of those companies with whom they have pay-for-play arrangements and the right to consign all others to a slow and bumpy road."

The FCC's Republican majority, led by Chairman Ajit Pai, and the major internet providers are adamant that the regulatory rollback won't change things for Americans.

Claims that the net neutrality repeal will destroy the internet are "a scary bedtime story for the children of telecom geeks," GOP Commissioner Mike O'Rielly said Thursday. ISPs say they have no plans to engage in some of the nefarious practices the activists are warning about.

"It is not going to end the internet as we know it. It is not going to kill democracy. It is not going to stifle free expression online," Pai said. "If stating these propositions alone doesn't demonstrate their absurdity, our internet experience before 2015, and our internet experience tomorrow, once this order passes, will prove them so."

The hype around net neutrality "has given the public an over-exaggerated and catastrophic image of what is likely and is going to happen," said Michael Powell, head of the cable industry trade group NCTA and himself a former Republican FCC chairman.

But critics foresee an eventual fracturing of the internet, as some websites and streaming services get a speed advantage over others. And they fear the internet will someday look more like cable TV, with providers acting as gatekeepers, channeling people into bundled packages of websites, apps and services rather than offering unfettered access to the Web.

Such changes could take years to become apparent, said Andrew Schwartzman, senior counselor at Georgetown University Law School's Institute for Public Representation, who supports the now-repealed net neutrality rules.

The big internet providers will be on their "good behavior" in the short term, as expected litigation over the FCC's order plays out, he said. But over the long term he expects them to start making changes, like charging websites to upgrade "interconnection" points between networks or extracting fees from sites for faster access to their online customers—all shielded by nondisclosure agreements.

"This is no longer a debate among tech nerds," he said. "Over the last few years, as more and more consumers have come to realize the importance of an open Internet, a broad pro-net neutrality consensus has emerged."

The wireless industry has already flirted with preferential treatment of some Web traffic, in the form of so-called zero-rating or sponsored data programs. They offer customers a way to stream video content and access other services without it counting against their monthly data caps. For example, T-Mobile customers can use the company's "Binge On" program to stream Netflix videos. The previous, Democratic-led FCC warned that some of these practices violate net neutrality principles, a stance that Pai rejected when he took over as chairman earlier this year.

While most of the major internet providers have said they have no intention of blocking or throttling Web traffic, the companies are more vague on the issue of "paid prioritization," or creating fast lanes for businesses that pay more.

Verizon supports a ban on the practice in situations where there is "harm to

> **Critics foresee an eventual fracturing of the internet, as some websites and streaming services get a speed advantage over others.**

competition or consumers." AT&T says it will not "unfairly discriminate in our treatment of internet traffic." Charter says it's never included internet fast lanes in its business plans and has no plans change course. Comcast also has "no plans" to enter into paid prioritization agreements but did not address whether such plans could change in the future.

The FCC, in its repeal order, argues that eliminating the ban on fast lanes could spur innovation in the marketplace. O'Rielly on Thursday said he thinks such arrangements could be useful to some kinds of driverless cars, which need to transmit and receive data to communicate with transportation infrastructure like stoplights and potentially other vehicles.

"Clearly, there are cases today and many more that will develop in time in which the option of a paid prioritization offering would be a necessity based on either technology or needs of consumer welfare," he said.

But advocates of the 2015 rules believe the repeal is the beginning of a darker phase of the internet.

"The loss of net neutrality means the loss of your fundamental rights," said Matt Wood, policy director of advocacy group Free Press. "ISPs shouldn't discriminate against internet content and your choices online. Now they can."

Print Citations

CMS: McGill, Margaret Harding. "How the Laws of Net Neutrality Could Change the Internet." In *The Reference Shelf: Internet Law,* edited by Annette Calzone, 47-49. Amenia, NY: Grey House Publishing, 2020.

MLA: McGill, Margaret Harding. "How the Laws of Net Neutrality Could Change the Internet." *The Reference Shelf: Internet Law,* edited by Annette Calzone, Grey House Publishing, 2020, pp. 47-49.

APA: McGill, M.H. (2020). How the laws of net neutrality could change the internet. In Annette Calzone (Ed.), *The reference shelf: Internet law* (pp. 47-49). Amenia, NY: Grey House Publishing.

Net Neutrality May Be Dead in the US, but Europe Is Still Strongly Committed to Open Internet Access

Saleem Bhatti
The Conversation, January 5, 2018

The belief that unrestricted internet access is vital to modern life is not necessarily a view held by all businesses that provide internet services. And now that net neutrality—the equal treatment of all data sent and received without differential charges and service quality—has come to an end in the US, how will this affect the rest of the world?

The idea that all internet service providers (ISPs) treat all data and users equally is, in theory, the best deal for customers as well as for businesses. Net neutrality allows businesses to compete on service quality, and provides users with a choice across the range of all providers.

But on December 14, 2017, the US Federal Communications Commission (FCC) effectively reneged on its own 2015 Open Internet Order, which was devised to allow open and fair access to the internet. This decision was made even though users and many technology companies and content providers such as Google, Facebook and Netflix remained strongly in favour of net neutrality.

The Loss of Net Neutrality

At the time, pioneering internet tech experts warned against removing net neutrality rules, effectively accusing the FCC of not understanding how the internet works. This ruling means that in the US, providers will be able to slow down data traffic to and from certain websites, give preferential treatment to other websites and charge differently for different types of content, such as web access, video streaming, social media and so on.

Former counsel for communications giant Verizon, Ajit Pai is now Chairman of the FCC which voted in December to abolish net neutrality in America. Wikipedia, CC BY-SA

With net neutrality gone, there are fears that some content, services and applications may be completely blocked by some ISPs. Not everyone in the US has a wide choice of broadband providers, so it is not easy for some citizens to "take their business elsewhere" if they are not satisfied with their provider.

Among other things, supporters of net neutrality fear a loss of consumer protection. However, supporters of the FCC ruling say that it could encourage ISPs to invest in new infrastructure by allowing them more flexibility in the services they offer. This could enable improved access for many, as well as increased competition that would benefit users.

Impact Beyond the US

So how does this decision in the US affect the UK and continental Europe? In the UK, net neutrality is currently protected by EU policy 2015-2120 in support of a Digital Single Market—Brexit fallout aside. Potentially, after Brexit, the UK government could choose to revoke this policy, although this is unlikely because it has already committed to a Universal Service Obligation (USO), effectively making broadband access a legal requirement, as it has been in Finland for many years.

Additionally, ISPs are held to account by the UK communications regulator OFCOM, which is tasked with ensuring fair play and protecting consumers from poor service. There has been widespread criticism that OFCOM has been slow and ineffective in persuading big players such as BT/Openreach to act responsibly in the past, though it has made progress recently.

OFCOM also has proposals for punitive fines for those who provide poor service. Meanwhile, OFCOM's own December 2017 report states that millions of UK households and businesses still lack decent broadband access.

Even with the EU policy and OFCOM in place, many users in the UK and continental Europe experience huge variation in broadband access speeds, quality of connection and customer service. Various providers also have preferential deals already in place with specific content providers, such as the recent deal between BT and Sky for certain TV channels. Which goes to show that the existence of net neutrality does not stop content providers and ISPs making mutually beneficial business arrangements.

> **Not everyone in the US has a wide choice of broadband providers, so it is not easy for some citizens to "take their business elsewhere" if they are not satisfied with their provider.**

However, current EU policy does prevent blocking and slow-down of any content, services and applications. Now, hot on the heels of the FCC ruling, there are calls in the US for "no blocking, no slow-down" regulation to counter the loss of net neutrality rules.

But there is concern that the FCC ruling in the US could pave the way for similar moves in other countries. The greatest negative impact could be on those who are already digitally impoverished, with poor access to knowledge and information, or where governments could impose access restrictions more easily.

Taking a Lead from Finland

But while things look encouraging with the UK government's Finnish-style commitment to a Universal Service Obligation, access speeds will need to keep increasing. While Finland's groundbreaking national USO was a great step forward, the requirement is for only a 2Mbps service. Most people would consider that inadequate for modern uses, especially for streaming video.

The UK's USO aims for at least 10Mbps for all citizens by 2020 which, considering the current average UK internet speed is 16.51 Mbps, seems a bit paltry. Of course, we shall have to wait and see how far the UK actually progresses towards rolling out 10Mbps for the entire country.

Given the demand for net neutrality among users, as well as support from many technology companies and content providers, there would seem to be a business opportunity for ISPs to offer a net-neutrality service to attract customers, as much as there might be to make deals with content providers.

Users' need for global and open access is clearly visible. Currently there is a global research community promoting access for all, as well as initiatives by users themselves in local communities. These are cooperative schemes facilitating high-speed, unconstrained internet access like B4RN in the north of England and RemIX in the Scottish Highlands and Islands.

The Global View

In terms of global scope, the UN has recognised that internet access is a vital enabler for realising its own Sustainable Development Goals, designed to address inequality and improve the everyday lives of millions around the world.

So, while the FCC ruling may be a blow for those wanting unrestricted access to the internet in the US, there is plenty of activity worldwide which supports users of open internet access. But complacency would be unwise; it would be preferable to have net neutrality support from national governments, and there are many parts of the world—the US and the UK included—where internet access could be improved.

However, one of the most attractive attributes of internet access—empowerment—means that the internet itself remains the most effective platform for users to communicate, coordinate and pursue improved open access to information, now and for the future.

Print Citations

CMS: Bhatti, Saleem. "Net Neutrality May Be Dead in the US, but Europe Is Still Strongly Committed to Open Internet Access." In *The Reference Shelf: Internet Law,* edited by Annette Calzone, 50-53. Amenia, NY: Grey House Publishing, 2020.

MLA: Bhatti, Saleem. "Net Neutrality May Be Dead in the US, but Europe Is Still Strongly Committed to Open Internet Access." *The Reference Shelf: Internet Law,* edited by Annette Calzone, Grey House Publishing, 2020, pp. 50-53.

APA: Bhatti, S. (2020). Net neutrality may be dead in the US, but Europe is still strongly committed to open internet access. In Annette Calzone (Ed.), *The reference shelf: Internet law* (pp. 50-53). Amenia, NY: Grey House Publishing.

3
Digital Copyright Law and Open-Source Software

Activist and EFF founder John Perry Barlow, whose 1996 "Declaration of the Independence of Cyber-space" is still influential, predicted that copyright on the Internet would have legal implications. Above, Barlow at the European Graduate School in Switzerland in 2006.

The End of Private (Digital) Ownership?

Electronic Frontier Foundation (EFF) founder John Perry Barlow thought at the very least that copyright was unenforceable on the Internet. Perry wrote his anti-regulatory "A Declaration of the Independence of Cyberspace" primarily in response to the 1996 Telecommunications Act, but his opinion on digital copyright was also radical: "I said this whole notion of property [in cyberspace] is going to get hammered. . . . It has been hammered."[1]

In 1999 the file-sharing network Napster revolutionized digital music piracy—and was used by an estimated 80 million people— before it was sued by recording artists like Metallica and Dr. Dre and ultimately shut down in 2001. While Napster unquestionably had an impact on artists' revenue, it also exposed people all over the world to every kind of music, and eventually served as a business model for modern streaming services (Napster is now owned by Rhapsody). As tech writer Abhimanyu Ghoshal recalls of his experience: "What struck me was that these people sharing music had nothing to gain except goodwill, and perhaps some notoriety in an anonymous chat room. . . . I was probably around 12 or 13 at the time, and I was just getting into modern rock and nu-metal. It wasn't always easy to find that sort of stuff in India as it hit the airwaves."[2]

Enter the DMCA

The Digital Millennium Copyright Act (DMCA) was signed into law by President Bill Clinton in 1998 and took effect in 2000. The DMCA made the United States compliant with the 1996 World Intellectual Property Organization (WIPO) Copyright Treaty and the WIPO Performances and Phonograms Treaty, which mandated legal remedies against circumventing technological protection measures against copyright infringement.[3] The DMCA also attempted to address digital piracy, which seemed to grow with every new technological development. Artists, software creators, and other copyright holders wanted a means of legal redress when their work was shared on the Internet without consent or payment. End users, especially schools and libraries, countered that it narrowed fair use and hampered copying works for educational purposes. And researchers engaged in finding and fixing vulnerabilities in programs found themselves without legal standing to bypass protective hardware or software encryption.

A 2001 Brookings article by Jonathan Band, which questioned whether the DMCA would survive constitutional challenges, noted a "paradox . . . rooted in a mismatch between the stated ends of the content community and the means employed to reach them. . . . The problem with piracy is not the inadequacy of existing laws, but the high cost of enforcing any law against the large universe of infringers." While libraries, universities, and other large institutions would follow the rules, individuals would not. "Put differently, the DMCA would do little to deter unlawful conduct, but much to deter conduct that is otherwise lawful."[4]

SpongeBob and Safe Harbor

Two sections of the DMCA have created controversy. One is Section 512, which contains safe harbor protections that limit online service provider liability for copyrighted works uploaded to sites by users. To qualify for these protections, companies must have adequate takedown mechanisms to remove copyrighted material once they are notified of infringement. These safe harbor rules are credited with the development of the Internet as we know it in much the same way as Section 230 of the Communications Decency Act (DCA), which protects tech companies from lawsuits over user content. There has been a host of legal action over Section 512. An example of the kinds of issues digital copyright law addresses can be found in *Viacom Inc. v. YouTube, Google Inc.* (2007), in which media conglomerate Viacom sued YouTube over users' uploading of Viacom content, including videos of Nickelodeon's *SpongeBob Squarepants*. Can YouTube be held responsible when users click on hyperlinks and SpongeBob videos begin streaming? What about YouTube's creation of hyperlinked thumbnails of those videos to aid users in searching for them? Users are uploading the videos, but YouTube is converting the files into Flash—does this constitute illegal copying? Since YouTube is clearly aware that SpongeBob videos are copyrighted, is it encouraging infringement? Should YouTube be proactively enforcing copyright restrictions since it is knowingly profiting from SpongeBob traffic on its site?[5] Ultimately, because of the DMCA's safe harbor provisions, judgment was found in favor of YouTube in 2013.

In a June 2020 Senate subcommittee hearing on the viability of the DMCA, former Eagles frontman Don Henley testified that the notice and takedown system of Section 512 does not work for artists, especially individual creators without the resources to fight infringement. He went on to explain that entire teams of people are devoted to sending takedown notices of his work, only to have it show up again immediately online.[6]

Takedown notices can also be used to discredit competitors or to suppress political speech; the Ecuadorian political news website "4Pelagatos" was shut down by a series of undue takedown notices sent by the government of Ecuador in 2017, forcing the site's creators to move it from Amazon Web Services (AWS) to another hosting service.[7] Though there are penalties associated with false takedown notices, larger companies will often err on the side of caution when it comes to copyright infringement.

The EFF takes a different stand, focusing on end-users, whose experience of the Web might be severely limited if Section 512 is reformed. The organization cautions that the debate is not "Big Content v. Big Tech." Harvard law professor Rebecca Tushnet testified at the Senate hearing that "the system is by no means perfect, there remain persistent problems with invalid takedown notices used to extort real creators or suppress political speech, but like democracy, it's better than most of the alternatives that have been tried . . . . The numbers of independent creators and the amount of money spent on content is growing every year. Changes to 512 are likely to make things even worse."[8]

A 2018 law signed by President Trump, the Music Modernization Act, is an effort to fix some loopholes for streaming music in existing copyright law. The law created a nonprofit collection agency, the Mechanical Licensing Collective (MLC), to ensure that songwriters get paid when streaming services use their work. It also mandates payment for sound recordings made before 1972. The MLC began operating in 2020 and is scheduled to begin paying royalties in January 2021.[9]

Circumvention Prevention

Section 1201, which contains anti-circumvention regulation, is one of the DMCA's most controversial parts; it:

> prohibits the circumvention of technological measures employed by or on behalf of copyright owners to protect access to their works (also known as "access controls"), as well as the trafficking in technology or services that facilitate such circumvention. It also prohibits trafficking in technologies or services that facilitate circumvention of technological measures that protect the exclusive rights granted to copyright owners under title 17 (also known as "copy controls"). In addition, Section 1201 establishes a triennial rulemaking process through which the Librarian of Congress, following a public proceeding conducted by the Register of Copyrights in consultation with the National Telecommunications and Information Administration of the Department of Commerce ("NTIA"), may grant limited exceptions to the bar on circumventing access controls.[10]

Designed to prevent copyright infringement that bypasses technological safeguards built into a device or software, the DMCA has resulted in some strange instances of copyright overreach, which the triennial exceptions that the Librarian of Congress allows do not always address well. For instance, the librarian's 2013 decision to make it illegal to unlock smartphones to use different carriers resulted in a public petition to the White House that garnered over 100,000 signatures (Barack Obama reversed this in 2014). Every three years organizations like the American Foundation for the Blind must renew an exemption to use adaptability technology to make e-books accessible to the blind. As Derek Khana, one of the smartphone petition's organizers, said in a 2013 *Forbes* article:

1. Why do the blind have to ask for an exception to use adaptability technology for e-books? Why is developing, trafficking, or selling that technology still illegal?

2. In a world where we can't unlock our own phones—who really owns our phones?[11]

Restrictions still exist for things as wide-ranging as cellphones, automotive repair, and tractors. But because of rising complaints about harassment and political polarization, Adi Robertson reports in a 2020 Verge article that the recent DMCA hearings are not "taking place in a landscape where 'internet freedom' [is] . . . as compelling a rallying cry as it once seemed, and copyright could join everything from sex work to social media bias as a potential reason to place heavier restrictions on the web. But it also offers an opportunity to rewrite some truly broken rules—as long as they're rewritten to benefit users, not just punish platforms."[12]

Open Source Software and Copyright

Free and open-source software (FOSS), broadly speaking, is software that makes its code available and allows modification and redistribution. Like Section 512 of the DMCA and Section 230 of the CDA, FOSS is considered instrumental to the development of the Internet as we know it. It is not necessarily free in terms of price, and it can be, and has been, commercialized. Hacker and activist Richard Stallman pioneered the open-source movement in the early 1980s in an effort to preserve the cooperative spirit of the Internet's early days, which he believed was being eroded by developers of proprietary, or closed, software. Stallman developed a complete free software system, GNU, in 1983, and created a nonprofit organization and a "copyleft" license to help sustain the movement. Stallman delineated "four freedoms" for open-source:

1. the freedom to run the program as you wish;
2. the freedom to copy the program and give it away to your friends and coworkers;
3. the freedom to change the program as you wish, by having full access to the source code; and
4. the freedom to distribute an improved version and thus help build the community.[13]

Open-source companies often rely on charging for installation and support, upgrades, or selling a licensed version of their software for income; a more recent revenue stream is selling software as a service (SaaS). Big companies like Amazon Web Services, Google Cloud, and Microsoft Azure have taken innovations from the FOSS community to repackage and sell in direct competition, forcing a shift toward licenses with more restrictions, which are not true open-source. As Scott Gilbertson explains in a 2019 *Ars Technica* article, "Open source licenses vary, but the gist since the 1998 founding of OSI has generally been as follows: you can take this code and do what you want with it, but you can't make the code proprietary, and if you use it in another project, then that project can't be proprietary either. These licenses were written this way to prevent companies from taking open source code, using it in their own code, and not sharing any of that work back to the original project."[14] This dilemma is not new to the open-source community—in fact, it's one of the reasons open source was created—but the development of the cloud has arguably made the situation more dire.

AWS in particular has come under a lot of scrutiny. A recent *New York Times* article by Daisuke Wakabaya describes Amazon's tactics as "strip-mining" software, forcing tech companies to rethink how they conduct business. The potential effect on society is pervasive:

A.W.S. is just one prong of Amazon's push to dominate large swaths of American industry. The company has transformed retailing, logistics, book publishing and Hollywood. It is rethinking how people buy prescription drugs, purchase real estate, and build surveillance for their homes and cities.

But what Amazon is doing through A.W.S. is arguably more consequential. The company is the unquestioned market leader—triple the size of its nearest competitor, Microsoft—in the seismic shift to cloud computing. Millions of people unknowingly interact with A.W.S. every day when they stream movies on Netflix or store photos on Apple's iCloud, services that run off Amazon's machines.[15]

But some argue that the *Times* article misunderstands the idea of open source. Abby Kearns replies in a *Medium* article:

> Think of it this way: when you post your secret apple pie recipe online, it's not a secret anymore.

> AWS has not violated any rule in the open source community. What it has done is take advantage of the superb code and talented engineers in the open source ecosystem. I won't comment on AWS' . . . alleged poaching of engineers from . . . companies. I don't agree with all of Amazon's business tactics, but I can't let the *New York Times* deliver such a gross misrepresentation of open source software to such a broad audience. (And shame on you *New York Times* for making me defend Amazon.)[16]

Works Used

Band, Jonathan. "The Copyright Paradox: Fighting Content Piracy in the Digital Era." *Brookings*. Dec. 1, 2001. https://www.brookings.edu/articles/the-copyright-paradox-fighting-content-piracy-in-the-digital-era/.

Band, Jonathan. "The Digital Millennium Copyright Act." *ALA Washington Office*. Nov. 25, 1998. http://www.ala.org/advocacy/sites/ala.org.advocacy/files/content/copyright/dmca/pdfs/dmcaanalysis.pdf.

Brodsky, Rachel. "The Music Modernization Act, One Year Later." *Advocacy*. Oct. 11, 2019. https://www.grammy.com/advocacy/news/music-modernization-act-one-year-later.

"Complicit in Censorship? Amazon and the Suppression of Online Expression in Ecuador." George Washington University Law School. International Human Rights Clinic. Apr. 2017. https://www.law.gwu.edu/sites/g/files/zaxdzs2351/f/downloads/GWU-Amazon-Ecuador-Report-Final.pdf.

"The Digital Arts: Web, Internet, and Software." Copyright website. https://www.benedict.com/.

Ghoshal, Abhimanyu. "A Nostalgic Look Back at Digital Music Piracy in the 2000s." *TNW*. Dec. 28, 2018. https://thenextweb.com/insights/2018/12/28/a-nostalgic-look-back-at-digital-music-piracy-in-the-2000s/.

Gilbertson, Scott. "In 2019, Multiple Open Source Companies Changed Course—Is It the Right Move?" *Ars Technica*. Oct. 16, 2019. https://arstechnica.com/

information-technology/2019/10/is-the-software-world-taking-too-much-from-the-open-source-community/.

Greenberg, Andy. "It's Been 20 Years Since This Man Declared Cyberspace Independence." *Wired*. Feb. 8, 2016. https://www.wired.com/2016/02/its-been-20-years-since-this-man-declared-cyberspace-independence/.

Kearns, Abby. "How the New York Times Got Open Source Wrong." *Medium*. Dec. 19, 2019. https://medium.com/@ab415/how-the-new-york-times-got-open-source-wrong-e67bf1283988.

Khana, Derek. "White House Petition on Cellphone Unlocking Receives over 100,000 Signatures." *Forbes*. Feb. 25, 2013. https://www.forbes.com/sites/derekkhanna/2013/02/25/white-house-petition-on-cellphone-unlocking-receives-over-100000-signatures/#1dda62c536bd.

Madigan, Kevin. "Senators and Creators Say Notice and Takedown System Is Broken, While Platforms Blame the Systems' Failures on Creators." *Copyright Alliance*. June 4, 2020. https://copyrightalliance.org/ca_post/senators-and-creators-say-notice-and-takedown-system-is-broken-while-platforms-blame-creators/.

"Overview of the GNU System." *GNU Operating System*. https://www.gnu.org/gnu/gnu-history.en.html#:~:text=Overview%20of%20the%20GNU%20System,GNU%20Project%20in%20September%201983.

Robertson, Adi. "Copyright Could Be the Next Way for Congress to Take on Big Tech." *The Verge*. Feb. 13, 2020. https://www.theverge.com/2020/2/13/21133754/congress-dmca-copyright-reform-hearing-tillis-coons-big-tech.

"Section 1201 Study." Copyright.gov. June 22, 2017. https://www.copyright.gov/policy/1201/#:~:text=Enacted%20in%201998%20as%20part,in%20technology%20or%20services%20that.

Trendacosta, Katherine. "Reevaluating the DMCA 22 Years Later: Let's Think of the Users." *Electronic Frontier Foundation*. Feb. 12, 2020. https://www.eff.org/deeplinks/2020/02/reevaluating-dmca-22-years-later-lets-think-users.

Wakayaba, Daisuke. "Prime Leverage: How Amazon Wields Power in the Technology World." *The New York Times*. Dec. 15, 2019. https://www.nytimes.com/2019/12/15/technology/amazon-aws-cloud-competition.html.

Notes

1. Greenberg, "It's Been 20 Years Since This Man Declared Cyberspace Independence."
2. Ghoshal, "A Nostalgic Look Back at Digital Music Piracy in the 2000s."
3. Band, "The Digital Millennium Copyright Act."
4. Band, "The Copyright Paradox: Fighting Content Piracy in the Digital Era."
5. "The Digital Arts: Web, Internet, and Software."
6. Madigan, "Senators and Creators Say Notice and Takedown System Is Broken, While Platforms Blame the Systems' Failures on Creators."
7. "Complicit in Censorship?" GWU Law School.
8. Trendacosta, "Reevaluating the DMCA 22 Years Later: Let's Think of the Users."

9. Brodsky, "The Music Modernization Act, One Year Later."
10. "Section 1201 Study," Copyright.gov.
11. Khana, "White House Petition on Cellphone Unlocking Receives over 100,000 Signatures."
12. Robertson, "Copyright Could Be the Next Way for Congress to Take on Big Tech."
13. "Overview of the GNU System," *GNU Operating System.*
14. Gilbertson, "In 2019, Multiple Open Source Compaines Changed Course— Is It the Right Move?"
15. Wakayabe, "Prime Leverage: How Amazon Wields Power in the Technology World."
16. Kearns, "How the New York Times Got Open Source Wrong."

A Brief History of Open Source Software

By Andy Updegrove
ConsortiumInfo.org, **December 27, 2019**

Everybody uses open source software (OSS) today. Millions of people contribute to the code itself. Indeed, a substantial percentage of the users and creators of OSS today are young enough to have never known a world that didn't rely on OSS. In other words, it's very easy to take this remarkable product of open collaboration for granted.

But that would be a mistake, especially given how unlikely it was that such a unique phenomenon could ever have taken hold. If you've never had reason to wonder how all this came about, this three part series is for you. In it, I'll review how remote developers began to collaborate to create OSS, how the legal tools to make its distribution possible evolved, and how the world came to embrace it.

* * *

In the early days of information technology (IT), computers were delivered with operating systems and basic application software already installed, without additional cost, and in editable (source code) form. But as software emerged as a stand-alone product, the independent software vendors (ISVs) that were launched to take advantage of this commercial opportunity no longer delivered source code, in order to prevent competitors from gaining access to their trade secrets. The practice also had the (intended) result that computer users became dependent on their ISVs for support and upgrades.

Due to the increasingly substantial investments computer users made in application software, they also became "locked in" to their hardware, because of the high cost of abandoning, or reconfiguring, their existing application software to run on the proprietary operating system of a new vendor. In response, a movement in support of distributing human-readable source code as well as the legal right to modify, share and distribute that code, together with the usual, machine-readable object code, emerged in the mid-1980s. The early proponents of such "free software" regarded the right to share source code as an essential freedom and created licenses—notably, the GNU General Public Licenses—that required vendors to give back their own innovations to the project community. Those who espoused this view are usually referred to as being part of the "free software movement." A later faction focused only on the practical advantages of freely sharable code, which they called "open source software" (OSS), leading to adherents of that group becoming known as the "open source movement."[i]

Concurrently, the Internet enabled a highly distributed model of software development to become possible, based upon voluntary code contributions and globally collaborative efforts. The combined force of these developments resulted in the rapid proliferation of millions of both free software and OSS development projects that have created many "best of breed" operating system and application software products. Today, virtually all proprietary software includes open source software, and an increasingly large percentage of crucial software platforms and programs are entirely open source.

While terms like "free software" and "open source software" may sound innocuous, when properly understood they imply elements of political philosophy, revolutionary zeal, technical development methodologies, traditional as well as radical legal theories, and cold, hard business pragmatism. Needless to say, such a rich stew of attributes is likely to present something of a challenge to anyone interested in gaining a quick understanding of exactly what this phenomenon is all about.

The reasons for investing the time to gain a better understanding of free and open source software (FOSS) are several. From a socio-political point of view, the FOSS movement is part of a broader, socio-political initiative, energized in part by the ability of the Internet to enable the sharing of information and the active collaboration of people on a global basis. In the case of the free software movement, that movement questions the utility and fairness of many traditional copyright and patent-based legal restrictions, and seeks to liberate software for the benefit of all. [iii] Unlike proponents of OSS, who primarily wish to permit open source software to be freely available without traditional proprietary constraints, free software advocates support a set of ethical rules intended not only to foster free access, but also to inspire—and in some cases require—those that benefit from such access to contribute their own modifications and additions back to the community of developers as well.

From an economic point of view, the OSS development model has reordered the business realities of software development in multiple ways. For a software vendor or user, the per-business costs of development of a given piece of software can be radically reduced by participating in a development project in which many others contribute their efforts as well. For an end user, access to the source code of an OSS product grants independence from a proprietary vendor, since the end user can adapt the code, or put development work out for competitive bidding. For commercial intermediaries, efforts can be directed towards developing value added services on top of core code that is available for free and maintained by a community of developers. For policy makers, OSS offers opportunities to level the playing field for domestic vendors while lowering costs of procuring public IT systems. From a marketplace perspective, the OSS model presents a disruptive force that offers opportunities for both existing as well as new businesses to attack the dominance of entrenched market participants whose advantages rest on proprietary development and sales models.

Today, FOSS has become so pervasive that effective IT procurement and management requires a working knowledge of what FOSS is all about. Active participants in the development and use of FOSS products additionally need to know how FOSS can be

> **The early proponents of such "free software" regarded the right to share source code as an essential freedom and created licenses—notably, the GNU General Public License—that required vendors to give back their own innovations to the project community.**

expected to evolve in the future, and how the legalities of FOSS apply to anyone that participates in the development of FOSS, uses a FOSS product, or embeds a FOSS code in their own products for resale.

In this article, I will provide an overview of the history of FOSS and its champions, the major philosophical differences that differentiate free software from other open source software, the multiple licenses under which FOSS is made available, and the principal non-profit institutions that support and promote FOSS. I will conclude with a brief bibliography of primary FOSS sources for those that wish to learn more than this necessarily superficial review can hope to provide regarding such a rich and complex topic.

OSS: The Basics

What exactly does someone mean when they speak of free or open source software?

What it is (and what it isn't): The answer is not only "it depends," but that it depends a lot more than one might think. Depending on the context, it may imply a broad spectrum of information, covering topics as varied as legal rights and obligations, affiliation with social movements, and mode of development. In other words, the words "open source", and in particular, "free software", may mean many things at once.

At the most basic level, the term OSS is sometimes used to refer, albeit incorrectly, to a piece of software for which both machine readable (object) and human readable (source) code is supplied to the user.[iii] And sometimes, this is all the person using the term intends, as when a single developer creates a piece of code and then posts it to the Internet at a public site with few, or no, restrictions on its reuse.

A popularly used OSS program, however, is likely to have additional attributes that differentiate it from proprietary software. Most likely, it will have been developed and be maintained at a public web site that allows any interested programmer to sign up and offer to help, whether by pointing out bugs and suggesting ways to fix them, by actively participating in development of additional code, or by helping document or promote the ongoing work of others as it happens.

The project in question may have been started by a single individual, or by a group of individuals, or it might have been launched when a proprietary vendor released the object and source code to a product that it had developed, concluding that it would gain greater benefit as a result of doing so (e.g., by having continuing access to the same code at a lower cost, due to the labor contributed by non-employees, or by selling support services to the users that download the program for free).

Frequently, multiple projects will collaborate to create software "stacks" that together provide an essential service. When they do, each project creates a single layer while coordinating in real time to ensure that each layer is technically interoperable and tightly integrated with the others.[iv]

Until FOSS became ubiquitous, most computer users spent their entire lives in the locked-in "Win-Tel" platform world that sprang from the marriage of Microsoft operating systems with Intel processors. In the realm of application software, most of the same users still live (when it comes to office productivity tools) in the same convenient, but constrained world of Microsoft Office.[v] Convenient, because almost everyone else continues to use Office, and text documents and spreadsheets can therefore be easily exchanged among other Office users. But constrained, because once a user enters the world of Office, it is difficult to leave.

Legally, the term OSS at minimum implies that anyone can download the code with the freedom to do whatever they want with it, so long as they do not try to sue the developer for any flaw in the code or infringement of the rights of any third party and acknowledge the copyright of the original code author in her code. The "copyleft" software licenses (described in greater detail below) generally associated with the free software movement have additional, more restrictive terms. Anyone that changes copyleft-licensed code and sells the modified version must make their modifications available to all under the same copyleft license terms as a matter of ethics and morality, as well as in response to a legal obligation.

What OSS is *not* is an infringement on any developer's rights, a second-best alternative to proprietary code, or a security risk to the enterprise.

And it certainly isn't a passing fad. OSS is here to stay.

The value proposition: While the value of free software for the customer sounds obvious, there are benefits beyond the lack of a license fee. Briefly stated, they are as follows:

For the customer: Under the traditional consumer software licensing model, individuals typically incurs a one-time cost to acquire proprietary software and are then on their own, whereas commercial customers are likely to make a more substantial investment in additional services, such as purchasing training for their employees to learn how to use the new software, and also ongoing "support" services (i.e., ensuring that there is someone at the end of the phone if problems are encountered installing, integrating, or operating the software on complex enterprise systems), as well as "maintenance" rights to ensure that they will get updates (e.g., bug fixes and improvements) after the software has been installed. They may also need to pay for hardware upgrades in order to be able to run new software, and pay consultants and other service providers to plan and complete the upgrade.

The aggregate of all of these fees is the "total cost of ownership" of a given software package, and the sum of these additional costs can be substantial. Similarly, while some FOSS may be free (e.g., the OpenOffice and LibreOffice productivity suites), a customer may decide to buy a proprietary product instead.

While the total cost of ownership of a FOSS product will generally be cheaper, there are other advantages to using FOSS instead of proprietary products. They include:

- *Access to code:* When a customer installs proprietary software, it becomes entirely dependent on the vendor for the code's improvement and performance, because the customer has neither the technical means (access to source code) nor the right (legal permission) to alter the code. If the customer needs new or different features, or needs an update to maintain compatibility when switching or upgrading other systems, the vendor may or may not be willing to customize the program (either at all or at a price the customer is willing to pay). If the vendor discontinues support for the product, or goes out of business, the customer is stranded. In contrast, a customer with a FOSS alternative has the ability as well as the legal right to change the code any time it wants to. It can also hire anyone it wishes to help it change or maintain the program. If the project that created the code goes dormant, a customer may be disappointed, but it won't be stranded.

- *Freedom from lock in:* While open standards increasingly give customers protection from "lock in" (i.e., dependency on a single vendor, and the certainty of significant switching costs if they wish to change vendors), changing from one product to another can still be difficult and expensive. In the case of systems based on Linux, the OSS operating system that has become predominant in use cases as diverse as telecommunications, automobiles and nuclear power plants, there are multiple independent "distributions," all based on the same core software (the Linux kernel).

Release cycles and bug fixes: Well-run OSS projects are in constant motion, upgrading and fixing bugs in real time. Customers can access this work on a far more frequent basis than users of proprietary products, who must wait until the vendor decides to incur the costs of making a minor or major release. Because the source code to OSS is available to the customer, popular OSS software also generates a flood of bug reports and suggested fixes, which are evaluated on a constant basis and implemented as appropriate.

Or, as stated in what is often referred to as "Linus's Law" (as in Linus Torvalds, the originator and ongoing leader of Linux kernel development): "Given enough eyeballs, all bugs are shallow." In contrast, proprietary vendors who receive complaints from customers must seek to replicate and diagnose the problem before they can fix it.[vi]

Security: While it may seem counterintuitive that code visible to anyone anywhere would be safer to use, popular OSS programs are in general acknowledged to be more secure, largely for the same reasons just stated: because anyone can see the code, anyone can track down the source of a vulnerability, let project managers know of the cause of concern, and/or propose a fix herself. As a result, security issues can typically be identified, fixed, and propagated to all users faster than flaws in proprietary code. As a result, OSS is increasingly being used by defense, financial and other users who place the highest priority on security. That said, where the numbers of eyes are small, open source can be as vulnerable as proprietary code.[viii] The Linux Foundation (LF) is currently working to identify similar situations and provide funding to correct them.

For the developer: It is important to note that much of the code contained in many FOSS products is created by individuals participating on a volunteer basis rather than at the instruction of their employers. Such individuals participate without compensation for many reasons, including enjoyment, challenge, gaining status within the project community, and gaining valuable job skills that enhance marketability and compensation potential. Individuals that rise through the ranks of prominent FOSS projects can dramatically enhance their professional credentials, as corporations are also major contributors to FOSS projects and skilled FOSS developers are in high demand.

Points of origin: Those learning about FOSS for the first time are often puzzled that there is usually no physical "there" there, in the sense of a central development facility. This is hardly surprising, because in most cases there is no person or legal entity that owns more than a small percentage of the code in an OSS product, or that is responsible for creating or maintaining the code (the Linux kernel, which is created by a global network of thousands of individual developers, is a prime example). Instead, the code may simply be hosted in the cloud, usually for free, by an organization formed for that purpose, which also provides a variety of supporting tools and services.

Other projects are supported by non-profit foundations formed to support them (e.g., the Mozilla Foundation, which supports the Firefox web browser), or by so-called "umbrella organizations," such as the Apache, Eclipse, and Linux Foundations, which host from scores to hundreds of FOSS projects. A small number of FOSS projects is supported by for-profit corporations, such as Red Hat and Micro Focus International, which host the Fedora and SUSE Linux distributions, respectively. They profit by offering paid support services along with these unique Linux-kernel based distributions.

While selling services on top of FOSS (or increasing profits as a result of using FOSS) are popular ways to benefit from FOSS economically, they are not the only ones. Simply sharing the development costs of software with other companies needing the same software tools and platforms lowers the overhead per vendor. And, just as collaboratively developed open standards permit competitors to vie with each other in other ways (e.g., by developing and selling proprietary features and services offered above the level of standardization), FOSS can enable entirely new and competitive business opportunities. A current example can be found in the mobile device marketplace, where the majority of mobile phones today run on variations of the Google-developed Android operating system, which is itself based on the Linux kernel. Google profits from its ability to ensure that mobile platforms can attractively display Google ads and support other Google software and services; mobile device manufacturers can sell more phones at lower prices due to greatly reduced software development costs; and silicon vendors can sell far more chips due to the rapidly expanding number of people who own mobile devices.

---

[i] In this article, I use the word FOSS to mean (a) software delivered in both machine-readable object code and human-readable source code, together with (b) the rights to modify, copy and distribute that under any license that complies with the "free software" OR the "open source" definitions that are discussed further below. When necessary, I use "free software" to refer to software that complies with the free software definition created by Richard Stallman and "OSS" to refer to any other software made available under a license approved by the Open Source Initiative as an "open source license."

[ii] Richard Stallman laid out the foundation for the concept of free software in 1981 in the GNU Manifesto, Stallman codified the definition of free software in 1986 in what he refers to as "the four essential freedoms." They are:
A program is free software if the program's users have the four essential freedoms: [1]

- The freedom to run the program as you wish, for any purpose (freedom 0).

- The freedom to study how the program works, and change it so it does your computing as you wish (freedom 1). Access to the source code is a precondition for this.

- The freedom to redistribute copies so you can help others (freedom 2).

- The freedom to distribute copies of your modified versions to others (freedom 3). By doing this you can give the whole community a chance to benefit from your changes. Access to the source code is a precondition for this.

Importantly, Stallman's use of the word "free" in the definition is not meant to have economic significance, although free software is usually available without cost. Rather, "free," as Stallman explains, is meant to be "free as in speech, not as in beer."

[iii] While the term open source software is sometimes used in connection with code that is licensed under terms that don't meet the Open Source Initiative FOSS definition, this usage is incorrect. The correct way to refer to such code is "source available" rather than "open source."

[iv] The prototypical example is the "LAMP" server stack, comprising Linux kernel, Apache HTTP server, MySQL relational database management system, and the PHP programming language.

[v] Today, most still do, notwithstanding the availability of free tools like Google Docs and the LibreOffice suite.

[vi] While the output of the global team of developers led by Linus Torvalds is often referred to simply as "Linux," this is misleading. What they produce is correctly referred to as the Linux kernel. While a kernel program forms the core of a computer operating system – and in the case of the Linux kernel comprises many millions of lines of code – the operating system upon which a computer relies includes additional important code as well.

[vii] As was famously proven in the case of the massively consequential "Heartbleed" attacks that exploited a security flaw in the OpenSSL code incorporated in products everywhere. That code was famously maintained by two woefully overworked and underpaid programmers. See, *The Internet Is Being Protected By Two Guys Named Steve*, https://www.buzzfeed.com/chris-stokelwalker/the-internet-is-being-protected-by-two-guys-named-st. All footnote links in this article were last accessed on June 24, 2019.

Andrew Updegrove is a founding partner of Boston law firm Gesmer Updegrove LLP. This article first appeared at *The Standards Blog* https://www.consortiuminfo.org/standardsblog/.

Print Citations

CMS: Updegrove, Andy. "A Brief History of Open Source Software." In *The Reference Shelf: Internet Law,* edited by Annette Calzone, 65-72. Amenia, NY: Grey House Publishing, 2020.

MLA: Updegrove, Andy. "A Brief History of Open Source Software." *The Reference Shelf: Internet Law,* edited by Annette Calzone, Grey House Publishing, 2020, pp. 65-72.

APA: Updegrove, A. (2020). A brief history of open source software. In Annette Calzone (Ed.), *The reference shelf: Internet law* (pp. 65-72). Amenia, NY: Grey House Publishing.

Reevaluating the DMCA 22 Years Later: Let's Think of the Users

By Katherine Trendacosta
EFF, February 12, 2020

The Digital Millennium Copyright Act (DMCA) is one of the most important laws affecting the Internet and technology. Without the DMCA's safe harbors from crippling copyright liability, many of the services on which we rely, big and small, commercial and noncommercial, would not exist. That means YouTube, but also Wikipedia, Etsy, and your neighborhood blog. At the same time, the DMCA has encouraged private censorship and hampered privacy, security, and competition.

The DMCA is 22 years old this year and the Senate Subcommittee on Intellectual Property is marking that occasion with a series of hearings reviewing the law and inviting ideas for "reform." It launched this week with a hearing on "The Digital Millennium Copyright Act at 22: What is it, why was it enacted, and where are we now," which laid out the broad strokes of the DMCA's history and current status. In EFF's letter to the Committee, we explained that Section 1201 of the DMCA has no redeeming value. It has caused a lot of damage to speech, competition, innovation, and fair use. However, the safe harbors of Section 512 of the DMCA have allowed the Internet to be an open and free platform for lawful speech.

This hearing had two panels. The first featured four panelists who were involved in the creation of the DMCA 22 years ago. The second panel featured four law professors talking about the current state of the law. A theme emerged early in the first panel and continued in the second: the conversation about the DMCA should not focus on whether it is and is not working for companies, be they Internet platforms, major labels and studios, or even, say, car manufacturers. Users—be they artists, musicians, satirists, parents who want to share videos of their kids, nonprofits trying to make change, repair shops or researchers—need a place and a voice.

The intent of the DMCA 22 years ago was to discourage copyright infringement but create space for innovation and expression, for individuals as well as Hollywood and service providers. Over the course of the last two decades, however, many have forgotten who is supposed to occupy that space. As we revisit this law over the course of many hearings this year, we need to remember that this is not "Big Content v Big Tech" and ensure that users take center stage. Thankfully, at least at this hearing, there were people reminding Congress of this fact.

Section 512: Enabling Online Creativity and Expression

The DMCA has two main sections. The first is Section 512, which lays out the "safe harbor" provisions that protect service providers who meet certain conditions from monetary damages for the infringing activities of their users and other third parties on the net. Those conditions include a notice and takedown process that gives copyright holders an easy way to get content taken offline and, in theory, gives users redress if their content is wrongfully targeted. Without the safe harbor, the risk of potential copyright liability would prevent many services from doing things like hosting and transmitting user-generated content. Thus, the safe harbors, while imperfect, have been essential to the growth of the Internet as an engine for innovation and free expression.

In the second part of the hearing, Professor Rebecca Tushnet, a Harvard law professor and former board member of the Organization for Transformative Works (OTW), stressed how much that the safe harbor has done for creativity online. Tushnet pointed out that OTW runs the Archive of Our Own, home to over four million works from over one million users and which receives over one billion page views a month. And yet, the number of DMCA notices averages to less than one per month. Most notices they receive are invalid, but the volunteer lawyers for OTW must still spend time and expense to investigate and respond. This process—small numbers of notices and individual responses—is how most services experience the DMCA. A few players—the biggest players—however, rely on automated systems to parse large numbers of complaints. "It's important," said Tushnet, "not to treat YouTube like it was the Internet. If we do that, the only service to survive will be YouTube."

> **(Section) 1201 covers pretty much anything that has a computer in it. In 1998, that meant a DVD, in 2020, it means the Internet of Things, from TVs to refrigerators to e-books to tractors.**

We agree. Almost everything you use online relies in some way on the safe harbor provided by section 512 of the DMCA. Restructuring the DMCA around the experiences of the largest players like YouTube and Facebook will hurt users, many of which would like more options rather than fewer.

"The system is by no means perfect, there remain persistent problems with invalid takedown notices used to extort real creators or suppress political speech, but like democracy, it's better than most of the alternatives that have been tried," said Tushnet. "The numbers of independent creators and the amount of money spent on content is growing every year. Changes to 512 are likely to make things even worse."

Section 1201: Copyright Protection Gone Horribly Wrong

On the other hand, the DMCA also includes Section 1201, the "anti-circumvention" provisions that bar circumvention of access controls and technical protection measures, i.e., digital locks on software. It was supposed to prevent copyright "pirates" from defeating things like digital rights management (DRM is a form of access control) or building devices that would allow others to do so. In practice, the DMCA anti-circumvention provisions have done little to stop "Internet piracy." Instead, they've been a major roadblock to security research, fair use, and repair and tinkering.

Users don't experience Section 1201 as a copyright protection. They experience it as the reason they can't fix their tractor, repair their car, or even buy cheaper printer ink. And attempts to get exemptions to this law for these purposes—which, again, are unrelated to copyright infringement and create absurd conditions for users trying to use things they own—are always met with resistance.

Professor Jessica Litman, of University of Michigan Law School, laid out the problem of 1201 clearly:

> The business that make products with embedded software have used the anti-circumvention provisions to discourage the marketing of compatible after-market parts or hobble independent repair and maintenance businesses. Customers who would prefer to repair their broken products rather than discard and replace them face legal obstacles they should not. It's unreasonable to tell the owner of a tractor that if her tractor needs repairs, she ought to petition the Librarian of Congress for permission to make those repairs.

1201 covers pretty much anything that has a computer in it. In 1998, that meant a DVD; in 2020, it means the Internet of Things, from TVs to refrigerators to e-books to tractors. Which is why farmers trying to repair, modify or test those things—farmers, independent mechanics, security researchers, people making e-books accessible to those with print disabilities, and so on—either have to abandon their work, risk being in violation of the law (including criminal liability), or ask the Library of Congress for an exemption to the law every three years.

Put simply, the existing scheme doesn't discourage piracy. Instead, it prevents people from truly owning their own devices; and, as Litman put it, "prevents licensed users from making licensed uses."

The DMCA is a mixed bag. Section 512's safe harbor makes expression online possible, but the specific particulars of the system have failures. And section 1201 has strayed far away from whatever its original purpose was and hurts users far more than it helps rightsholders. To see why, the DMCA hearings must include testimony focused needs and experiences of all kinds of users and services.

Print Citations

CMS: Trendacosta, Katherine. "Reevaluating the DMCA 22 Years Later: Let's Think of the Users." In *The Reference Shelf: Internet Law,* edited by Annette Calzone, 73-75. Amenia, NY: Grey House Publishing, 2020.

MLA: Trendacosta, Katherine. "Reevaluating the DMCA 22 Years Later: Let's Think of the Users." *The Reference Shelf: Internet Law,* edited by Annette Calzone, Grey House Publishing, 2020, pp. 73-75.

APA: Trendacosta, K. (2020). Reevaluating the DMCA 22 years later: Let's think of the users. In Annette Calzone (Ed.), *The reference shelf: Internet law* (pp. 73-75). Amenia, NY: Grey House Publishing.

To Save Pepe the Frog from the Alt-Right, His Creator Has Invoked Copyright Law's Darker Side

By Aja Romano
Vox, September 21, 2017

Matt Furie, the creator of Pepe the Frog, has made numerous attempts over the past two years to reclaim the good-natured cartoon amphibian from the alt-right meme makers who adopted him and turned him into a hate symbol.

But his latest attempt marks a surprising departure from his previous, more remix-friendly tactics to deal with the widespread memeing of Pepe. Furie is now turning to US copyright laws to challenge the legal right of alt-right websites to distribute Pepe's image. That's a bold, decisive move for Furie—and one that carries unfortunate implications for the reach of US copyright law as it pertains to what does and does not fall under the umbrella of fair use.

Furie Is on the Copyright Warpath against Several Major Alt-Right Figures

Furie has issued Digital Millennium Copyright Act (DMCA) takedowns to Google, Reddit, Redbubble, and Amazon, alleging infringement for the spread of Pepe's image hosted on their platforms. Additionally, he has issued cease-and-desist orders to the notorious alt-right subreddit r/The_Donald; the website AltRight.com, which is owned and run by the white nationalist leader Richard Spencer; and several public figures known for spreading Pepe's image, including social media personality and right-wing commentator Mike Cernovich and Tim Gionet, a.k.a. the alt-right YouTube personality Baked Alaska. Some of Furie's cease-and-desist orders have been published by *Motherboard*, revealing that he's charging each recipient with different misuses of Pepe, some of them clearly for profit.

A few of the more blatant examples that Furie cites include dozens of Pepe-themed items being peddled by various Redbubble sellers, a now-yanked Android game developed by Gionet (the same game was denied release on iOS because of its allusions to Pepe), and a book that Gionet self-published about alt-right memes. The book, which has since been removed from Amazon in response to Furie's DMCA claims, frequently discusses Pepe; Gionet even devotes a chapter to explaining the rise of the frog as an alt-right symbol and credits Pepe's creation to "Matt Furey."

Tim Gionet a.k.a. Baked Alaska's book about alt-right memes credits the creation of Pepe to "Matt Furey."

Tim Gionet, a.k.a. Baked Alaska, wrote a book about alt-right memes that credits the creation of Pepe to "Matt Furey." Amazon

Though so far the targets of Furie's complaints have mostly complied by removing images and allegedly infringing works from various platforms, not all of them have done so quietly. In an incendiary Medium essay, Cernovich in particular invited Furie and his lawyers to engage, with his own lawyers claiming, "Should you file a suit against Mr. Cernovich, we will be delighted to embarrass the fuck out of you."

Furie's Decision to Invoke The DMCA Is Part of an Intensifying Fight between Copyright Holders and the Alt-Right

Furie's move to issue DMCA takedown notices comes after Furie successfully sicced his lawyers on a for-profit "children's book" called *The Adventures of Pepe and Pede* in August. The book, written by an assistant principal at a Texas middle school who's since been fired, contained alt-right and Islamophobic symbols and themes within its story, including a prominent emphasis on a green frog named Pepe. Furie reached a settlement with the author that resulted in the author handing over his meager profits of $1,500 to the Council on American-Islamic Relations (CAIR).

Furie's crackdown also follows a similar recent turn to copyright enforcement by a game developer who'd grown sick of the "humor" of YouTube star PewDiePie, the staggeringly popular gaming vlogger whose political views appear to lean toward the alt-right despite his frequent denials. After PewDiePie (whose real name is Felix Kjellberg) dropped a racial slur during a recent gaming live stream, a developer named Sean Vanaman issued DMCA takedowns against all of PewDiePie's videos

> **Fair use is shorthand for the fair use clause of U.S. copyright law, which allows a copyrighted work to be remixed or reproduced as long as it's for a "transformative" purpose like commentary, education, or parody.**

that feature games made by Vanaman's creative studio, Campo Santo. On Twitter, Vanaman issued a plea for other creators to follow suit, hoping to essentially forcibly separate PewDiePie's incendiary views from the games around which his commentary is built:

> I'd urge other developers & will be reaching out to folks much larger than us to cut him off from the content that has made him a milionaire
>
> — Sean Vanaman (@vanaman) September 10, 2017

But using DMCA takedowns to suppress alt-right content carries some concerning implications, no matter what you think of the content itself. In fact, Vanaman has since quickly backtracked from his fight against PewDiePie, telling *BuzzFeed* that he regrets turning to the DMCA to enforce a copyright claim—a practice many internet creators staunchly oppose. This is because strictly applying the DMCA in these situations restricts the idea of fair use.

Pepe Memes Are Generally Allowed to Exist Because of the "Fair Use" Doctrine of US Copyright Law

Fair use is shorthand for the fair use clause of US copyright law, which allows a copyrighted work to be remixed or reproduced as long as it's for a "transformative" purpose like commentary, education, or parody. Thus, fair use is the protection under which memes and remixes of other people's work are able to flourish online. But what constitutes an allowable remix or transformative use of the original work under fair use is essentially anybody's guess. For years, court rulings have been inconsistent when it comes determining what is and isn't a "fair" use of someone else's copyright.

Inch by inch, various rulings have established that the most common examples of fair use in modern contexts—remixes, sampling, memes, fanfiction, fan art, and brief clips and citations of someone else's work in commentary and reviews—are all standard exceptions to copyright law that fall under the umbrella of fair use.

But there's still a large gray area surrounding what, exactly, constitutes fair use, and the clause is frequently enforced in a way that puts the impetus on remixers to defend the transformative qualities of their works, rather than on copyright holders to acknowledge that the remixers' works are examples of fair use.

What usually happens—as anyone who's ever been unfairly hit with a DMCA takedown notice knows all too well—is that remixers are issued scary cease-and-desist orders first, and are then expected to argue their case before a corporation or legal body that may or may not believe them. If the original copyright holder, or the platform hosting the remixer's work, doesn't agree that fair use applies, the remixer's only recourse is usually to take down their content, even if that content is extremely popular. (The main exception: If the remixer happens to have a lot of time and money to spend arguing the point in a courtroom, they're free to do so.)

For a prime example, witness the recent case of the popular *McMansion Hell* parody blog, which briefly deleted all its content in June upon receiving a DMCA takedown notice. It was only restored once news of its case went viral and notable copyright defense lawyers stepped in to shepherd the owner through the ins and outs of arguing that the blog constituted fair use.

The Practice of Invoking the DMCA to Fight the Alt-Right Should Concern Anyone Who Makes Stuff on the Internet

In issuing DMCA takedown notices and cease-and-desist orders, Furie has mainly targeted prominent alt-right creators who are directly profiting from Pepe the Frog's image. These are generally clear-cut examples of copyright infringement, since fair use is harder to prove in instances where a person is making money off someone else's work.

But not all of the examples Furie has cited—like simply using an image of Pepe on a website—are quite as straightforward. The key criteria of whether a work constitutes fair use of an existing copyright is that it be "transformative." The alt-right's use of Pepe has been to transform him from Furie's original comic character—a stoner frog living with his bro roommates—into a reincarnated Egyptian god who holds the key to all modern-day politics. In terms of the basic concept of fair use, few things seem more clearly transformative (much as many might hate to admit it). Thus, in leaning on the DMCA to pursue the makers of art he doesn't like, Furie (like Vanaman before him) is taking regressive steps in interpreting what fair use is and what it means for anyone who creates original work.

Applying a moral limitation to the idea of what is and isn't fair use is extremely risky. For one thing, fair use limitations are already frustratingly ambiguous, even without introducing a moral component. For another, pursuing a DMCA takedown, even where the use is clearly an infringing for-profit use, sets a precedent for allowing the kind of countercultural ideas that flourish in meme culture and remix culture to be threatened purely because a creator doesn't like them.

If anything, the move shows how desperate Furie is to salvage Pepe the Frog from the alt-right. After trying everything from working with the Anti-Defamation League to reclaim Pepe from his official status as a hate symbol to ceremonially killing off and then reviving the character, Furie seems to have fallen back on the last best hope afforded by the DMCA: good old-fashioned censorship.

"The truth is I've made all the Pepes on the internet," Furie said in a 2016 interview. "They are all mine. I made them and I own them all!" While his frustration with the alt-right's adoption of Pepe is understandable, this is a suppressive view of remix culture that the doctrine of fair use is designed to withstand, not capitulate to. As Michael Lee, an internet lawyer specializing in copyright, previously told *Motherboard* regarding Vanaman's DMCA takedowns, "[T]he biggest issue here [is] that the DMCA is being used to stop the expression of free speech."

(Furie has not responded to *Vox*'s request for comment.)

But meme culture itself—heck, even the endless examples that Furie cites in his "inexhaustive" list of Pepe-infringing items on Redbubble—illustrates how futile this effort is. Memes by their very nature are unstoppable, and the only way to really counter them is to dilute them with more, not fewer, mutations of the original.

In 2016, the artist Leon Chang (literally) illustrated this idea when he drew a comic in response to alt-right-leaning Dilbert creator Scott Adams participating in the memeing of Pepe. Chang's comic remixed one of Adams's Dilbert comic strips in order to discuss the complexity and importance of supporting remix culture, even though it means your work could fall into the wrong hands. Chang acknowledged that because memes fall under fair use by default, the only real way to fight the ones we don't like is by generating counter-memes. "There's one thing you can do," he wrote in his comic. "Take some asshole's art and make it good."

Print Citations

CMS: Romano, Aja. "To Save Pepe the Frog from the Alt-Right, His Creator Has Invoked Copyright Law's Darker Side." In *The Reference Shelf: Internet Law,* edited by Annette Calzone, 76-80. Amenia, NY: Grey House Publishing, 2020.

MLA: Romano, Aja. "To Save Pepe the Frog from the Alt-Right, His Creator Has Invoked Copyright Law's Darker Side." *The Reference Shelf: Internet Law,* edited by Annette Calzone, Grey House Publishing, 2020, pp. 76-80.

APA: Romano, A. (2020). To save Pepe the Frog from the alt-right, his creator has invoked copyright law's darker side. In Annette Calzone (Ed.), *The reference shelf: Internet law* (pp. 76-80). Amenia, NY: Grey House Publishing.

Twitter Blocks EFF Tweet That Criticized Bogus Takedown of a Previous Tweet

By Jon Brodkin
Ars Technica, April 15, 2019

Twitter and Starz have given us a new example of how copyright enforcement can easily go overboard.

At Starz's request, Twitter blocked an April 8 tweet by the news site *TorrentFreak*, which had posted a link to one of its news articles about piracy. News coverage about piracy is obviously not the same thing as piracy, and the article contained only still images from pirated TV shows and did not tell readers where pirated content could be downloaded. Despite that, Twitter blocked access to the tweet in response to the copyright takedown request by Starz, whose show *American Gods* was mentioned in the *TorrentFreak* article.

Here's what the tweet looked like before the takedown:

TF
@torrentfreak

Pirated Promo Screeners of 'American Gods' and Other TV-Shows Leak Online

Promo Screeners of 'American Gods' and Other TV-Shows ...
Unreleased episodes of several high-profile TV-shows including American Gods, The 100, Bless This Mess, and Knightfall have leaked online. The leaks appear to come from promotional scr...
torrentfreak.com

9:54 AM - 8 Apr 2019

Screenshot of a TorrentFreak tweet from before it was removed by Twitter. TorrentFreak

On April 11, hours after the tweet was blocked, *TorrentFreak* wrote an article about the takedown and quoted an Electronic Frontier Foundation (EFF) attorney as saying that the takedown was inappropriate because news coverage about piracy is not illegal. The EFF then posted a tweet that included a link to the new *TorrentFreak* article and a portion of the EFF quote from the article. Twitter then blocked that EFF tweet in response to another Starz request, even though the EFF tweet merely linked to the new *TorrentFreak* article about the takedown and criticized Twitter's decision to block the first tweet.

Here's a look at the EFF tweet:

EFF ● @EFF · Apr 12

Your Tweet has been withheld in response to a report from the copyright holder. **Learn more**

Screenshots are important parts of reporting that validate the facts being reported—the article reported that there are people on the Internet infringing copyright, but that is a far cry from being an infringement itself.

Promo Screeners of 'American Gods' and Other TV...
Unreleased episodes of several high-profile TV-shows including American Gods, The 100, Bless This Mess, and Knightfall have leaked online. The leaks appear t...
torrentfreak.com

♡ 2   ↺ 16   ♡ 28   ⌁

Screenshot of an EFF tweet that was blocked by Twitter.

"Get ready for a tale as good as anything you'd see on television," EFF Policy Analyst Katharine Trendacosta wrote yesterday. "Here's the sequence of events: the website *TorrentFreak* publishes an article about a leak of TV episodes, including shows from the network Starz. *TorrentFreak* tweets its article, Starz sends a copyright takedown notice. *TorrentFreak* writes about the takedown, including a comment from EFF. EFF tweets the article about the takedown and the original article. EFF's tweet... gets hit with a takedown."

The tweets were still inaccessible this morning and early afternoon but are now visible again here and here. When contacted by *Ars*, Twitter said it was restoring the tweets that it previously removed because of the Starz takedown notices. Starz apologized for the incorrect takedown notices, *Variety* reported today.

The *TorrentFreak* tweet was blocked for four days before being restored. The EFF tweet was blocked for about one day.

Starz deserves blame for sending bogus takedown notices. But Twitter could have avoided the mess by performing even a cursory review of Starz's requests, which offered no evidence of copyright infringement.

DMCA Takedowns

Like other online platforms that rely on user-generated content, Twitter offers copyright owners a simple way to report content that infringes copyright. This type of process protects websites from legal action by providing a "safe harbor" under the Digital Millennium Copyright Act (DMCA).

Starz used a third-party agency called *The Social Element* to send DMCA takedown requests on its behalf. Starz's vendor sent the first takedown request to Twitter after *TorrentFreak* posted a tweet consisting only of the headline and link to its April 8 article, which was titled, "Pirated Promo Screeners of *American Gods* and Other TV-Shows Leak Online." The *TorrentFreak* article describes a recent increase in leaks of promotional copies of episodes, which are generally sent to reviewers and are supposed to be kept confidential, suggesting that "a serious security hole has been exploited."

"According to the takedown notice, Starz argues that the tweet is infringing because it links to an article where people can see 'of images of the unreleased episode" and find more 'information about their illegal availability,'" *TorrentFreak* wrote on April 11, hours after the tweet was blocked by Twitter.

TorrentFreak continued:

> For the record, our article only includes a single identifiable frame from a leaked American Gods episode, to show the screener watermarks, which are central to the story. That's just 0.001 percent of the episode in question, without audio, which is generally seen as fair use, especially in a news context.
>
> As for the claim that the article includes information about the shows' "illegal availability," we only mention that they are being shared on pirate sites, without giving any names or links. That's no ground for a takedown request.

EFF Senior Staff Attorney Kit Walsh agreed, saying in the article that "Starz has no right to silence *TorrentFreak*'s news article or block links to it. The article reports that there are people on the Internet infringing copyright, but that is a far cry from being an infringement itself'"

Walsh further argued that "The screenshots are important parts of the reporting that validate the facts being reported. Starz should withdraw its takedown and refrain from harassing journalists in the future."

EFF Tweet Blocked

When the EFF used its official Twitter account to post a link to the new *Torrent-Freak* article and included a snippet from Walsh's quote, its tweet was also suppressed.

"A few days later, we also received a takedown and our tweet was blocked," Trendacosta wrote. "At this point, you may have noticed just how far removed we are from anything that remotely resembles copyright infringement."

Twitter acted on Starz's DMCA notice even though it didn't present a convincing case that the EFF's tweet violated Starz's copyright.

"In the field labeled 'links to original work,' Starz wrote 'n/a,'" Trendacosta wrote. "To reiterate: in the field about where the original work being infringed on can be located, the answer is 'not applicable.' Under 'Description of infringement,' it says, 'Link to bootleg.' There's no bootleg link in any of the articles or tweets."

The EFF challenged Twitter directly. "The DMCA process allows us to send a counterclaim,

Twitter could have avoided the mess by performing even a cursory review of Starz's requests, which offered no evidence of copyright infringement.

explaining that the tweet is not infringement and directing Twitter to restore the tweet, barring a copyright infringement lawsuit being filed by Starz. We have done so," Trendacosta wrote yesterday. Twitter's decision to restore the tweets came after that challenge.

Twitter's copyright policy says it will respond to reports of copyright infringement about "tweets containing links to allegedly infringing materials." But the policy also notes that "not all unauthorized uses of copyrighted materials are infringements," and it advises copyright holders to consider whether a tweet is fair use before submitting a copyright complaint.

We contacted Starz this morning and haven't heard back yet. But Starz explained itself in its statement to Variety, saying that it hired a third-party vendor to conduct copyright enforcement after a recent security breach.

Starz told Variety:

> The techniques and technologies employed in these efforts are not always perfect, and as such it appears that in this case, some posts were inadvertently caught up in the sweep that may fall outside the DMCA guidelines... That was never our intention and we apologize to those who were incorrectly targeted. We are in the process of reviewing all of the impacted posts as well as the scope and procedure for the previous takedowns and are working with our vendors to reinstate any such content that was inappropriately targeted for removal.

Print Citations

CMS: Brodkin, Jon. "Twitter Blocks EFF Tweet That Criticized Bogus Takedown of a Previous Tweet." In *The Reference Shelf: Internet Law*, edited by Annette Calzone, 81-84. Amenia, NY: Grey House Publishing, 2020.

MLA: Brodkin, Jon. "Twitter Blocks EFF Tweet That Criticized Bogus Takedown of a Previous Tweet." *The Reference Shelf: Internet Law*, edited by Annette Calzone, Grey House Publishing, 2020, pp. 81-84.

APA: Brodkin, J. (2020). Twitter blocks EFF tweet that criticized bogus takedown of a previous tweet. In Annette Calzone (Ed.), *The reference shelf: Internet law* (pp. 81-84). Amenia, NY: Grey House Publishing.

In 2019, Multiple Open Source Companies Changed Course—Is It the Right Move?

By Scott Gilbertson
Ars Technica, October 16, 2019

Free and open source software enables the world as we know it in 2019. From Web servers to kiosks to the big data algorithms mining your Facebook feed, nearly every computer system you interact with runs, at least in part, on free software. And in the larger tech industry, free software has given rise to a galaxy of startups and enabled the largest software acquisition in the history of the world.

Free software is a gift, a gift that made the world as we know it possible. And from the start, it seemed like an astounding gift to give. So astounding in fact that it initially made businesses unaccustomed to this kind of generosity uncomfortable. These companies weren't unwilling to use free software, it was simply too radical and by extension too political. It had to be renamed: "open source."

Once that happened, open source software took over the world.

Recently, though, there's been a disturbance in the open source force. Within the last year, companies like Redis Labs, MongoDB, and Confluent all changed their software licenses, moving away from open source licenses to more restrictive terms that limit what can be done with the software, making it no longer open source software.

The problem, argue Redis Labs, MongoDB and others, is a more modern tech trend: hosted software services. Also known as, "the cloud." Also known as Amazon AWS.

Amazon, for its part, came out swinging, releasing its own version of the code behind Elasticsearch this spring in response to licensing changes at Elastic (the company behind Elasticsearch). And besides a new trademark dispute over Amazon's naming convention, Elastic has a very different response from that of MongoDB and Redis—it hasn't said a word in protest.

MongoDB the company is built around the open source "NoSQL" database of the same name. MongoDB's database is useful for storing unstructured data, for example images, which it can handle just as well as it handles more traditional data types. Data is stored in JSON-like documents rather than the columns and rows of a relational database. Since there's no structured tables there's no "structured query language" for working with the data, hence the term "NoSQL."

MongoDB is not the only NoSQL database out there, but it's one of the most widely used. According to industry aggregator, DB Engines, MongoDB is the fifth most popular database, with everyone from Google to Code Academy to Foursquare using MongoDB.

MongoDB is also leading the charge to create a new kind of open source license, which CTO Eliot Horowitz believes is necessary to protect open source software businesses as computing moves into the new world of the cloud.

The cloud, argue Horowitz and others, requires the open source community to re-think and possibly update open source licenses to "deal with new challenges in a new environment." The challenges are, essentially, AWS, Google Cloud and Microsoft Azure, which are all capable of taking open source software, wrapping it up as a service, and reselling it. The

> **These licenses were written this way to prevent companies from taking open source code, using it in their own code, and not sharing any of that work back to the original project.**

problem with AWS or Azure wrapping up MongoDB and offering it as part of a software as a service (SaaS) is that it then competes with MongoDB's own cloud-based SaaS—MongoDB Atlas. What's threatened then is not MongoDB's source code, but MongoDB's own SaaS derived from that source code, and that happens to be the company's chief source of revenue.

To combat the potential threat to its bottom line, MongoDB has moved from the GNU General Public License (GPL) to what it calls the Server Side Public License, or SSPL. The SSPL says, in essence, you can do anything you want with this software, except use it to build something that competes with MongoDB Atlas.

Originally MongoDB submitted the SSPL to the Open Source Initiative (OSI), the organization that oversees and approves new open source licenses. But after seeing the writing on the wall—discussion on the OSI mailing lists, combined with the wording of the license made it unlikely the SSPL would ever be approved by the OSI—MongoDB withdrew the SSPL from consideration earlier this year. The SSPL is not an open source license and it never will be.

To understand why, it helps to realize that MongoDB is not the first open source business to run into this situation. In fact, part of this problem—companies taking software, using it as they please, and contributing nothing back to the open source community—is the entire reason open source software exists at all.

Open source licenses vary, but the gist since the 1998 founding of OSI has generally been as follows: you can take this code and do what you want with it, but you can't make the code proprietary, and if you use it in another project, then that project can't be proprietary either. These licenses were written this way to prevent companies from taking open source code, using it in their own code, and not sharing any of that work back to the original project.

But the concept of SaaS didn't exist two decades ago. And today, Horowitz argues that wrapping a piece of code in a SaaS offering is the modern equivalent of using it in an application.

It is a novel argument, but it's in defense of a very old problem that goes well beyond licensing. It's a problem that goes all the back to the beginning of free software long before the OSI—how do you make money off software if you give it away for free?

One traditional answer has been that you sell services around your open source software. But for Horowitz that's not good enough. "Monetizing open source with support contracts has never been a great business model," he tells *Ars*. Red Hat would likely disagree, but Horowitz believes that more protective licenses would bring more venture capital investment and spawn more software businesses based on the open model MongoDB has used. "We're unique," he says, "I want us to be less unique."

He may be correct. A more protective license could induce more venture capital investment because there's (arguably) a greater likelihood of return on their investment. But if that capital did come, it wouldn't be investing in open source because that kind of restriction on the software means it no longer fits the definition of open source.

The Counterargument

Quite a few open source advocates have already made the counter argument to what MongoDB's Horowitz believes. The current set of licenses are fine, others say, it's the business models that need work.

Bruce Perens, co-author of the original open source definition, says the SSPL is incompatible with the OSI's open source definition number nine, which says that the "license must not restrict other software." Since the SSPL forces any SaaS software that is aggregated with the covered software, but not a derivative of it, to nevertheless be open source, it fails this test. "I wrote number nine into the OSD to prohibit exactly this sort of conduct," says Perens. "The text is really clear."

MongoDB is far from the only one complaining that the cloud is raining on its profits. Redis Labs, another data storage company, was the first to sound the alarm about cloud providers threatening its business, and Redis Labs may have the better solution in the end. Redis Labs initially changed its license to include something called the Common Clause sublicense, which forbids anyone from selling any software it covers. Software licensed with the Common Clause is not, by anyone's definition, open source, which Redis Labs acknowledged. It has never described those portions of its software as open source.

But this spring, Redis Labs made yet another licensing change—in essence dropping all pretense of being open source software and adopting a homegrown proprietary license for some of its modules. To be clear, most of Redis is governed by the three-clause BSD license, but some modules are not, namely RedisJSON, RedisSearch, RedisGraph, RedisML and RedisBloom.

The license Redis Labs applies to these modules says that while users can view and modify the code or use it in their applications, it restricts which types of applications they can build. With Redis Labs' new license, you are not free to build anything you want. You cannot build database products, a caching engine, a processing engine, a search engine, an indexing engine or any kinds of ML or AI derived serving engine. You cannot in other words use Redis Labs' code to compete with Redis Labs. This violates one of the core tenets of open source licensing—that there be no restrictions on derivative software.

Unfortunately for both Redis Labs and MongoDB, it doesn't make sense to simultaneously say that you are open source and that only you should profit from your open source software. There is a business model where that does make sense: proprietary software.

That's a path that Elastic.co has hewed for some time. While part of the problem here is that there is no playbook set in stone yet, some companies have managed to prosper with both open source and proprietary code. Elastic is one such example; it has faced the exact competition from AWS and soldiered on.

Not only has Amazon for years offered Elasticsearch on AWS (ostensibly competing with Elastic's own offerings), Amazon recently packaged up its own version of the Elasticsearch codebase, extending it to offer for free several of the services Elastic hasn't released as open source. Elastic's response has been little more than the corporate equivalent of a shrug.

Print Citations

CMS: Gilbertson, Scott. "In 2019, Multiple Open Source Companies Changed Course—Is It the Right Move?" In *The Reference Shelf: Internet Law,* edited by Annette Calzone, 85-88. Amenia, NY: Grey House Publishing, 2020.

MLA: Gilbertson, Scott. "In 2019, Multiple Open Source Companies Changed Course—Is It the Right Move?" *The Reference Shelf: Internet Law,* edited by Annette Calzone, Grey House Publishing, 2020, pp. 85-88.

APA: Gilbertson, S. (2020). In 2019, multiple open source companies changed course—is it the right move? In Annette Calzone (Ed.), *The reference shelf: Internet law* (pp. 85-88). Amenia, NY: Grey House Publishing.

With Friends Like AWS, Who Needs an Open Source Business?

By Cliff Saran
Computer Weekly, January 7, 2020

In December, a *New York Times* article suggested that Amazon Web Services (AWS) was strip-mining open source projects by providing managed services based on open source code without contributing back to the community.

In response to the article, Andi Gutmans, vice-president of analytics and ElastiCache at AWS, wrote a blog post claiming that customers have repeatedly asked AWS to offer managed services for Elasticsearch and other popular open source projects.

"A number of maintainers of open source projects build commercial companies around the open source project," he said.

"A small set of outliers see it as a zero-sum game and want to be the only ones able to freely monetise managed services around these open source projects. As such, they have gone back and altered the open source licensing terms, co-mingled truly open source with proprietary code."

Open source licensing aims to encourage innovation by enabling contributors to build new functionality as a branch of the core open source code. The project maintainer can then choose to incorporate this contribution into the core code.

In open source business models, some pieces of functionality are left out of the core code to enable the developer behind the original project to charge for enhancements, such as those that offer functionality required by enterprise customers.

Some companies have also tried to offer managed services for their open source products to provide their products as software as a service (SaaS) for enterprise customers.

Commenting on the *New York Times* article, Abby Kearn, executive director at Cloud Foundry Foundation, said: "When the software behind a commercial product is open source, there's nothing to stop someone from building another commercial software offering.

"I won't argue that many of the companies mentioned in the article have changed their business strategy since AWS began using their open source code," she said. "But ignoring the open source method by which these individuals created code and built companies around it is missing the bigger picture. And AWS is using what this open source ideology has afforded them in the form of really good code.

"As my colleague Chip Childers, CTO [chief technology officer] of Cloud Foundry Foundation, recently wrote, open source works best for a technology company when it's adopted as a series of strategies and tactics that support an otherwise sound business model—not the other way around."

Is Proprietary Open Source Viable?

In March 2019, Sid Sijbrandij, CEO and co-founder of open source DevOps tools company GitLab, warned that the biggest challenge commercial open source faces is how to deal with hybrid cloud providers.

"Commercial open source companies such as Confluent, which makes Kafka, then the hybrid cloud providers take the Kafka open source code and offer that as a service, competing with the SaaS services these companies were betting on to generate revenue.

"This has led a number of open source companies, such as Redis, MongoDB, Elastic and Confluent, to introduce non-competing licences, in which managed services are required to pay a licence fee."

But, according to Sijbrandij, this change in licence means the code is no longer open source. "We want these companies to do well, but we also love the lack of lock-in that comes with open source."

He described how AWS directly went after the value people pay Elasticsearch for, in the enterprise version of its open source product, by creating a fork of the open source project and commoditising the enterprise add-ons by making them freely available. He suggested that it is much easier for an open source project to become commoditised if the code offers open APIs.

Targeting Different Types of Buyer

GitLab's approach has been to target different types of buyer, as Sijbrandij said: "If your customer is much more price-sensitive, they are more likely to go with an open source offering, than your paid-for product."

The company offers is a free version of GitLab based on the core open source code for individuals; managers pay a small monthly subscription for additional features, while the most expensive version of GitLab, provides full oversight of the DevOps lifecycle across multiple projects in an organisation.

Business models do need to evolve, and some experts warn this is something open source companies must now face.

"You are less likely to become commoditised if you have more proprietary functionality," said Sijbrandij.

This model has evolved over time and is currently, the way GitLab commercialises its open source product. But business models do need to evolve, and some experts warn that this is something open source companies must now face. But how open source businesses can continue to generate commercial value in the intellectual property in their open source projects has become a hotly debated topic.

"In my opinion, capitalism and open source function best when there's robust competition based on equal access to opportunity," said Mark Collier, chief operating officer at Openstack Foundation.

"While I can sympathise with companies who are under threat from large, dominant cloud platform companies, restricting competition through license changes to ensure your own monopoly is unlikely to produce a great outcome for the market or open source."

Print Citations

CMS: Saran, Cliff. "With Friends Like AWS, Who Needs an Open Source Business?" In *The Reference Shelf: Internet Law,* edited by Annette Calzone, 89-91. Amenia, NY: Grey House Publishing, 2020.

MLA: Saran, Cliff. "With Friends Like AWS, Who Needs an Open Source Business?" *The Reference Shelf: Internet Law,* edited by Annette Calzone, Grey House Publishing, 2020, pp. 89-91.

APA: Saran, C. (2020). With friends like AWS, who needs an open source business? In Annette Calzone (Ed.), *The reference shelf: Internet law* (pp. 89-91). Amenia, NY: Grey House Publishing.

4
Privacy and Cybercrime

A screenshot of the 2017 WannaCry ransomware attack, ultimately traced to North Korea, which affected hundreds of thousands of computers globally.

Hackers, User Rights, and Government Surveillance

Like all things from the early days of the Internet, hacking began with the impulse to create a free and open environment focused on innovation, to harness the Internet's profound uniqueness for the good of all. But hacking developed a dark side. The term "hack" comes from the tinkering of a group of toy train enthusiasts in Massachusetts Institute of Technology's (MIT's) Tech Model Railroad Club in 1961. They transferred their efforts to computers and in the process expanded the limits of what computers could do. Traditional hackers were primarily interested in testing and improving existing technology. In the 1970s "phreakers" (phone hackers) emerged after John Draper famously discovered that he could use a toy whistle from a Cap'n Crunch cereal box to trick the telephone network into allowing him to make free long-distance calls. When personal computers became readily available in the 1980s, hacking—including criminal activity like creating viruses and stealing personal information— also increased, eventually leading to the 1986 passage of the Computer Fraud and Abuse Act (CFAA).[1]

Hackers in the Public Mind

The negative image of the hacker began to form in the public mind in the 1980s with the publication of "The Hacker Papers" in *Psychology Today*, an article about the addictive nature of computers. Movies like 1983's *War Games*—in which a teenager hacks into the North American Aerospace Defense Command (NORAD) system—cemented the image of the lone-wolf hacker capable of wreaking havoc on society. Image turned into reality when a group of teenagers breached Los Alamos National Laboratory, Sloan-Kettering Cancer Center, and Security Pacific Bank that same year. A subsequent *Newsweek* cover featuring one of the hackers was the first mainstream media use of the term "hacker" in a derogatory manner. As the U.S. Congress worked to pass legislation to deal with computer crime, the hacking community continued to form groups and publish guides. Hacking grew to encompass individual crime for financial gain or notoriety, corporate espionage, and finally state-sponsored campaigns aimed at disrupting other nation-states and sowing confusion within them.[2]

Hacking has become simultaneously both more and less difficult: new generations must contend with antivirus programs and firewalls, but also have access to a robust community and open source tools that were once the province of skilled hackers. As hacker-turned-security-consultant Danny Moules says, "IT crime is now an outlet for criminal activity of all stripes, no longer the preserve of the technical elite." Moules goes on to explain that this has shifted the focus of hacking from a desire to master the technology to a variety of different motives, from "hacktivists" with a political agenda like Anonymous to individuals motivated by revenge to "project-managed crime" designed by teams of IT professionals like 2017's WannaCry ransomware.[3]

State-Sanctioned "Cybercrime"

While governments have been the target of many cyberattacks, nation-states have increasingly become agents of cyberwarfare. In 2010 the U.S.-Israel backed Stuxnet worm caused a malfunction at an Iranian nuclear facility. North Korean hackers stole $13.5 million in 2018 from India's Cosmos Bank by using unauthorized ATM withdrawals, and the United Nations (UN) Security Council claims that North Korea has stolen $670 million in foreign and cryptocurrency between 2015 and 2018. A Russian cyberattack took Ukraine's power grids offline for several hours in 2015.[4] Russia's recent interference in the Olympics and U.S. elections is well-documented, and fears around the 2020 elections are significant. Cybersecurity journalist Patrick Howell O'Neill explains in an *MIT Technology Review* article that hackers have become the "weapon of choice" for governments: "Cyber capabilities are expanding and transforming the old game of statecraft. The Russians are playing right alongside the Americans, Chinese, Iranians, North Koreans, and others in using hackers to shape history and try to bend geopolitics to their will."[5]

The Computer Fraud and Abuse Act (CFAA)

The CFAA, the law that most hackers run afoul of, was passed in 1986 as an amendment to the Comprehensive Crime Control Act of 1984, the first U.S. law passed to deal with the emerging field of computer crime. The CFAA has in turn been amended to what many consider a significant overreach of the law's original intent. While it has been used to prosecute notorious hackers, it has also been used to prosecute opening fake user accounts and downloading open source software. Researchers exploring vulnerabilities in programs have also been threatened with lawsuits under the CFAA, making some reluctant to disclose their findings. Critics claim that is not truly effective at preventing cybercrime, and that it has resulted in extreme punishments for even minor transgressions. As originally passed, the CFAA protected computers networked to the federal government and criminalized distribution of malicious code, denial-of-service attacks, and trafficking in passwords. Amendments to the CFAA added tampering and extortion and taking information off of systems, and the definition of a protected computer eventually reached almost any computer in the United States. One of the law's most controversial provisions was a 1994 clause that allowed civil action, where the burden of proof is much lower and does not always entail the involvement of law enforcement, as well as criminal prosecution. This provision gave corporations leverage in fighting legitimate cyberattacks but also gave software and hardware companies undue influence over cybersecurity researchers. The Electronic Frontier Foundation (EFF) and the American Civil Liberties Union (ACLU) have pushed for changes to the CFAA, and attempts have been made to pass the Aaron's Law Act of 2013 to remove terms-of-service violations (Hactivist Aaron Swartz committed suicide after facing $1 million in fines and 35 years in federal prison for violating JSTOR's terms of service by downloading academic journal articles to an MIT guest account.)[6]

In 2020 a federal court ruled that violating terms of service (in this case for creating fake user accounts) is not a crime under the CFAA.[7] And the U.S. Supreme Court has agreed to hear a case in fall 2020 involving a former Georgia police officer convicted in 2017 after he allegedly sold information from a police database. Critics say the CFAA does not apply because Nathan Van Buren only misused his access to the database but did not actually hack it. The Justice Department counters that only prosecuting hacking cases is too narrow a definition of cybercrime, and that there are already directives in place for prosecutors to consider whether actions have caused major economic damage or are a part of a larger criminal enterprise. Georgia State University law professor Jeffrey L. Vagle says, "This is important because the law either says very few people are criminals under CFAA or almost everyone is a criminal under CFAA. . . . This question has been unanswered for years."[8]

Hacking Back

Another legal concept that often surfaces around hacking is the idea of "hacking back." The Active Cyber Defense Certainty Act (ACDC) was proposed in 2017 as an amendment to the CFAA in response to ransomware (such as the WannaCry attack, which impacted hundreds of thousands of computers in 150 countries), data dumps, and foreign hackers from North Korea, Iran, and Russia. The law would allow cybercrime victims to break into the systems of organizations that they suspect the hackers used to carry out a cyberattack. Under existing law, only government agencies like the Federal Bureau of Investigation (FBI) can track down suspected hackers like this. Supporters claim that the FBI and other government agencies are overwhelmed and cannot keep up with cyberattacks, and also that the law would only allow a "qualified defender" to mount a counterattack, which would then be monitored by the FBI. Detractors believe the law could make the problem much worse. They point out that most companies are not sophisticated enough to take on hackers, it's really difficult to tell where hacks originate, the law does not clearly define what a "qualified defender" is, such action would result in damaging reprisals, and private companies could inadvertently confront nation-states and escalate political situations.[9]

The Internet of Things (IoT)

As more devices become connected to the Internet of Things, the dangers of such interconnectedness are becoming increasingly apparent. Past examples of IoT hacking could come straight out of a dystopian science fiction novel: sensitive high-roller data at a casino was accessed through a thermometer in a lobby aquarium; hackers have gotten into wireless baby monitor systems; CNN was able to access footage from cameras located in people's homes; hackers launched a Distributed Denial of

Service (DDoS) attack on the environmental control system of a Finland apartment complex, leaving residents without heat for a week; the Food and Drug Administration (FDA) confirmed that certain implantable cardiac devices and insulin pumps can be hacked and remotely controlled; Germany banned an interactive doll, "My Friend Cayla," because it allowed hackers to see and hear children playing with it while the companion app encouraged them to share where they lived and attended school; and a team of researchers was able to take control of a Jeep SUV.[10] Lawyers are struggling to add language about IoT technology to restraining orders as thermostats, doorbells, radios, and front-door locks are being used to harass individuals in domestic abuse cases.[11]

A current debate centers on whether or not the CFAA applies to voting machines, which are usually not connected to the Internet. A July 2018 U.S. Department of Justice (DoJ) report found that "in general, the CFAA only prohibits hacking computers that are connected to the Internet (or that meet other narrow criteria for protection). In many conceivable situations, electronic voting machines will not meet those criteria, as they are typically kept off the Internet." Some are pressing for updates to the CFAA that would include voting machines as protected computers.[12]

A recent *Forbes* article warns of the dangers of writing government regulations directly into software, which might include things like monitoring water usage or automatically deactivating drones if they fly into restricted areas. Warns Competitive Enterprise Institute policy director Clyde Wayne Crews Jr. "The same IoT that animates objects can also mean instantaneous nanny-state regulation from a distance—of drones, vehicles, buildings, social media use, schooling and more."[13]

Privacy and the Encryption Debate

Striking a balance between public safety and government and law enforcement overreach is not always easy, and it is behind the continued refusal of tech companies like Apple to build a "back door" to access locked devices in criminal investigations, which they maintain would leave all devices open to hacking. The development of the dark web—so called not because of its criminal activity but because of the anonymity of its users—has afforded individuals freedom from the ubiquitous scrutiny of search engines and ad trackers. This is essential to journalists, citizens of totalitarian states, and businesses that need to keep legal matters private, to name a few legitimate uses. The dark web is also the home of drug trafficking, child pornography, and the infamous Silk Road, an online black market in the 2010s that operated as a Tor hidden service.

The FBI broke Tor's encryption in the 2013 capture of dark web tycoon Eric Marques and refused to reveal how they accomplished it, worrying activists and lawyers. "The overarching question is when are criminal defendants entitled to information about how law enforcement located them?" asks Mark Rumold, a staff attorney at the Electronic Frontier Foundation.[14] That same year Edward Snowden exposed the vast surveillance powers granted to the federal government with USA Patriot Act, passed just days after the 9/11 World Trade Center attacks.

The Patriot Act updated the Electronic Communications Privacy Act (ECPA), passed in 1986, which updated the Federal Wiretap Act of 1968 to include restrictions on how the government could intercept computer and other digital and electronic communications. Title I, often called the Wiretap Act, prohibits intentional interception of electronic communication and prevents such illegally obtained information from being used as evidence. The Stored Communications Act (SCA), or Title II, protects the contents of files stored by internet service providers and of any associated records, such as subscriber name, billing records, or Internet protocol (IP) addresses. Title III states that government entities must obtain a warrant for pen register and trap and trace devices, both of which do not intercept actual communications but only numbers and related information about incoming and outgoing calls. The Patriot Act eased controls on law enforcement access. States also have laws relating to legal wiretapping; some require the consent of all parties concerned, but some only require the consent of one party.[15] The EFF contends that the ECPA has not kept pace with technological developments like cloud computing, and does not consider geolocation tracking.[16]

Consumer Privacy

Tech companies and web service providers legally monetize data through selling information, algorithms, advertising revenue, and web scraping. In many instances, consumers have to proactively opt out of data sharing; vital information about how personal data will be used is often buried in hard-to-understand terms-of-service agreements. While states have instituted consumer protections for digital privacy, the federal government has not. There is a proposed law in the works, the Online Privacy Act, which would create a comprehensive set of rules and establish a new federal agency, the U.S. Digital Privacy Agency, to enforce them.[17] To date California is leading the way. The new California Consumer Privacy Act went into effect in January of 2020 and has other states and the federal government looking at passing similar legislation. The California law gives consumers the right to know what personal information is being collected; they can also demand that their data be deleted and not sold. The Internet Association, a trade group that represents big tech companies like Google parent Alphabet, Inc., spent half a million dollars in 2019 to try to weaken the law and effectively blocked provisions that would have allowed consumers to pursue legal action and automatically opt out of personal information collection. Alastair McTaggart, who implemented the state ballot initiative that led to the law, plans to push for further privacy protections in the coming year, including creating a state enforcement agency and limiting geolocation-based targeted advertising.[18]

Works Used

Ahasker, Abhijit. "How Cyberattacks Are Being Used by States against Each Other." *Livemint*. June 21, 2019. https://www.livemint.com/technology/tech-news/how-cyberattacks-are-being-used-by-states-against-each-other-1561100711834.html.

Bowles, Nellie. "Thermostats, Locks, and Lights: Digital Tools of Domestic Abuse." *The New York Times*. June 23, 2018. https://www.nytimes.com/2018/06/23/technology/smart-home-devices-domestic-abuse.html.

Cope, Sophia. "EFF Supports Senate Email and Location Privacy Bill." *Electronic Frontier Foundation*. July 27, 2017. https://www.eff.org/deeplinks/2017/07/eff-applauds-senate-email-and-location-privacy-bill#:~:text=ECPA%20was%20first%20passed%20in,and%20the%20habits%20of%20users.

Crews, Clyde Wayne, Jr. "Helicopter Government? How the Internet of Things Enables Pushbutton Regulation from a Distance." *Forbes*. Nov. 11, 2019.

"Electronic Communications Privacy Act." *ScienceDirect*. https://www.sciencedirect.com/topics/computer-science/electronic-communications-privacy-act.

Giles, Martin. "Five Reasons 'Hacking Back' Is a Recipe for Cybersecurity Chaos." *MIT Technology Review*. June 21, 2019. https://www.technologyreview.com/2019/06/21/134840/cybersecurity-hackers-hacking-back-us-congress/.

Herrera, Sebastian. "Activist Behind California's New Privacy Law Already Wants to Improve It." *The Wall Street Journal*. Dec. 29, 2019. https://www.wsj.com/articles/activist-behind-californias-new-privacy-law-already-wants-to-improve-it-11577615401.

Johnson, Derek B. "Does the CFAA Apply to Voting Machine Hacks?" *FCW*. Aug. 30, 2018. https://fcw.com/articles/2018/08/30/cfaa-voting-hacks-johnson.aspx.

Lee, Timothy B. "Court: Violating a Site's Terms of Service Isn't Criminal Hacking." *Ars Technica*. Mar. 30, 2020. https://arstechnica.com/tech-policy/2020/03/court-violating-a-sites-terms-of-service-isnt-criminal-hacking/.

Marks, Joseph. "The Cybersecurity 202: There's Finally a Supreme Court Battle over the Nation's Main Hacking Law." *The Washington Post*. Apr. 24, 2020. https://www.washingtonpost.com/news/powerpost/paloma/the-cybersecurity-202/2020/04/24/the-cybersecurity-202-there-s-finally-a-supreme-court-battle-coming-over-the-nation-s-main-hacking-law/5ea1ade6602ff140c1cc5f51/.

Moules, Danny. "A History of Hacking and Hackers." *Computer Weekly*. Oct. 25, 2017. https://www.computerweekly.com/opinion/A-history-of-hacking-and-hackers.

O'Neill, Patrick Howell. "A Dark Web Tycoon Pleads Guilty: But How Was He Caught?" *MIT Technology Review*. Feb. 8, 2020. https://www.technologyreview.com/2020/02/08/349016/a-dark-web-tycoon-pleads-guilty-but-how-was-he-caught/.

———. "Hackers Will Be the Weapon of Choice for Governments in 2020." *MIT Technology Review*. Jan. 2, 2020. https://www.technologyreview.com/2020/01/02/23/hackers-will-be-the-weapon-of-choice-for-governments-in-2020/.

Power, Katrina. "The Evolution of Hacking." *Tripwire*. Aug. 17, 2016. https://www.tripwire.com/state-of-security/security-data-protection/cyber-security/the-evolution-of-hacking/.

"What Is Hacking?" *Malwarebytes*. https://www.malwarebytes.com/hacker/.

"What Is the Computer Fraud and Abuse Act?" *Cybersecurity Masters Degree.org*. n.d. https://www.cybersecuritymastersdegree.org/what-is-the-computer-fraud-and-abuse-act/.

"The Worst and Weirdest IoT Hacks of All Time." *Finance Monthly*. Sept. 2019. https://www.finance-monthly.com/2019/09/the-worst-and-weirdest-iot-hacks-of-all-times/.

Zhang, Wendy. "Comprehensive Federal Privacy Law Still Pending." *JD Supra*. Jan. 10, 2020. https://www.jdsupra.com/legalnews/comprehensive-federal-privacy-law-still-66167/#:~:text=Online%20Privacy%20Act%3A%20This%20act,enforce%20the%20rights%20and%20requirements.

Notes

1. Power, "The Evolution of Hacking."
2. "What Is Hacking?" *Malwarebytes*.
3. Moules, "A History of Hacking and Hackers."
4. Ahaskar, "How Cyberattacks Are Being Used by States against Each Other."
5. O'Neill, "Hackers Will Be the Weapon of Choice for Governments in 2020."
6. "What Is the Computer Fraud and Abuse Act?" *Cybersecurity Masters Degree.org*.
7. Lee, "Court: Violating a Site's Terms of Service Isn't Criminal Hacking."
8. Marks, "The Cybersecurity 202: There's Finally a Supreme Court Battle Coming over the Nation's Main Hacking Law."
9. Giles, "Five Reasons 'Hacking Back' Is a Recipe for Cybersecurity Chaos."
10. "The Worst and Weirdest IoT Hacks of All Time," *Finance Monthly*.
11. Bowles, "Thermostats, Locks, and Lights: Digital Tools of Domestic Abuse."
12. Johnson, "Does the CFAA Apply to Voting Machine Hacks?"
13. Crews, "Helicopter Government? How the Internet of Things Enables Push-button Regulation from a Distance."
14. O'Neill, "A Dark Web Tycoon Pleads Guilty: But How Was He Caught?"
15. "Electronic Communications Privacy Act," *ScienceDirect*.
16. Cope, "EFF Supports Senate Email and Location Privacy Bill."
17. Zhang, Wendy. "Comprehensive Federal Privacy Law Still Pending."
18. Herrera, "Activist Behind California's New Privacy Law Already Wants to Improve It."

Senate Republicans Unveil COVID-19-Specific Privacy Bill

National Law Review, **May 26, 2020**

On April 30, 2020, Senator Roger Wicker (MS), Chairman of the Senate Commerce Committee, along with Senators John Thune (SD), Jerry Moran (KS) and Marsha Blackburn (TN), announced plans to introduce the COVID-19 Consumer Data Protection Act of 2020 ("the bill"), which would put temporary rules in place regarding the collection, processing and transfer of data used to combat the spread of the coronavirus. The bill would only apply during the course of the COVID-19 Public Health Emergency as declared by the Secretary of Health and Human Services, and would only apply to specific uses of certain personal data.

In particular, the bill would only apply to precise geolocation data, proximity data and personal health information used for the following purposes: (1) to track the spread, signs or symptoms of COVID-19; (2) to measure compliance with social distancing guidelines or other COVID-19-related requirements imposed by federal, state or local

> **The bill would put temporary rules in place regarding the collection, processing, and transfer of data used to combat the spread of the coronavirus.**

governments; or (3) to conduct contact tracing for COVID-19 cases. It would require that covered entities provide individuals with notice prior to the collection, processing and transfer of such data for those purposes, and that individuals give affirmative express consent for that collection, processing or transfer unless they are otherwise necessary to comply with a legal obligation.

Additionally, the bill would require the following of covered entities:

Make a privacy policy available to the public and publish a report every 30 days containing the aggregate number of individuals whose data has been collected, processed or transferred for a covered purpose, as well as the categories of data and specific purpose for which the data was collected, processed or transferred and to whom it was transferred;

- Provide a mechanism for individuals who have given consent to revoke that consent or opt out;

- Delete or deidentify all covered data when it is no longer being used for a purpose covered by the bill;

- Limit collection, processing and transfer of data to what is reasonably necessary, proportionate and limited to carry out the covered purpose; and

- Establish, implement and maintain reasonable data security policies and practices to protect against risks to confidentiality, security and integrity of the covered data.

The bill would be enforced by both the Federal Trade Commission and state attorneys general, and would prevent states from adopting or enforcing any laws or regulations related to the collection, processing or transfer of covered data used for purposes covered in the bill.

Print Citations

CMS: "Senate Republicans Unveil COVID-19-Specific Privacy Bill." In *The Reference Shelf: Internet Law,* edited by Annette Calzone, 103-104. Amenia, NY: Grey House Publishing, 2020.

MLA: "Senate Republicans Unveil COVID-19-Specific Privacy Bill." *The Reference Shelf: Internet Law,* edited by Annette Calzone, Grey House Publishing, 2020, pp. 103-104.

APA: National Review. (2020). Senate Republicans unveil COVID-19-specific privacy bill. In Annette Calzone (Ed.), *The reference shelf: Internet law* (pp. 103-104). Amenia, NY: Grey House Publishing.

Mixed Messages: Encryption Fight Pits Security Against Privacy

By Mark Scott
Politico, December 23, 2019

Just in time for the holiday season, European and American officials are putting aside their differences over tech.

What's fueling this festive bonhomie is growing transatlantic pressure on Big Tech to loosen its grip on encryption—technology that makes it almost impossible for anyone, including law enforcement, to read messages or documents held on people's smartphones or other digital devices.

Officials in Brussels, Washington and other capitals are flexing their muscles. They're warning companies like Facebook and Apple that if they don't allow government agencies to access this material—especially when it comes to law enforcement investigations—they'll introduce a slew of new laws that will force firms to do just that.

In recent months, the drumbeat for action has been growing louder.

U.S., British and Australia officials published an open letter to Mark Zuckerberg, Facebook's chief executive officer, calling on him call off plans to encrypt the company's messaging service. U.S. senators railed on big Tech in early December, threatening to pass legislation that would strong-arm companies into giving access to encrypted information under a court order.

Some European Union governments are mulling a revisit of so-called data retention rules, requirements that telecom providers keep hold of people's online messages for a set period of time in case law enforcement agencies need to access them.

And senior American and European officials, including William Barr, the U.S. attorney general, and Didier Reynders, the newly appointed European Commissioner for Justice, recently met in Washington to figure out how to crack the encryption problem.

Here's some advice: This Christmas, be careful what you wish for.

Backdoor Men

For years, Western officials have, unsuccessfully, demanded so-called backdoors to encrypted messaging services like WhatsApp and Telegram in order to allow law

---

enforcement to keep tabs on potential terrorist activity and gather evidence in criminal cases.

> **It's hard to claim that you're an advocate for tough privacy rules while also demanding access to people's digital messages.**

Lawmakers cite failures by authorities to get their hands-on data connected to high-profile crimes like child exploitation as evidence that tech companies are dragging their heels. Noting that traditional telecoms operators routinely hand over information on their subscribers, under a court order, officials complain that Big Tech wants to play by different rules.

Silicon Valley (along with privacy and freedom of expression advocates) has cried foul.

Big Tech firms argue that encryption does more good than harm by protecting vulnerable groups from having their data misused and warn that harmful actors, including authoritarian governments, would inevitably get their hands on backdoors.

Tech executives also say they already provide law enforcement with reams of information (though not encrypted data) when it comes through the right legal channels.

In a recent open letter, more than 100 civil society groups said weakening encryption would put the security and privacy of billions of people at risk. They called on Washington, London and Canberra to back down from efforts to water down the technology.

Several Western national security officials, who spoke on the condition of anonymity, acknowledged to *Politico* that the creation of digital backdoors could affect companies' ability to keep users' information safe.

But they also argued that tech firms were overplaying the danger. In particular, officials said compromises—including the ability to decrypt the contents of devices, and not necessarily online messages—could give law enforcement access to life-saving information without putting the wider population at risk because any decryption efforts would be limited to specific smartphones, and would not involve bulk collection of people's online conversations.

Pandora's Box

It's a sign of how important politicians are taking encryption that transatlantic tensions over tech—including ongoing EU-U.S. spats over digital tax, competition policy, and online policy—have been put aside to present a united front on the issue. The latest move: U.K. officials giving evidence to the U.S. Congress last week on why existing encryption standards were flawed.

The push comes at a time when public sympathy for Big Tech is at an all-time low, and companies like Facebook and Apple find themselves in the unenviable position of protecting would-be criminals in high-profile cases that involve law enforcement trying to break into people's devices or messages in search of evidence.

But if encryption is compromised, it'll be hard to put the genie back in the bottle.

The battle pits governments' responsibility to keep people safe from harm against fundamental rights like the freedom of expression (and, at least in Europe, the right to privacy).

Many of the officials who are calling on Big Tech to create digital backdoors are the same ones who have accused tech firms of not doing enough to protect online privacy. It's hard to claim that you're an advocate for tough privacy rules while also demanding access to people's digital messages.

Existing national efforts, including the U.K.'s Investigatory Powers Act—which already includes provisions that call on companies to remove encryption if ordered to do so—have remained mothballed despite growing clamor by politicians to weaken global encryption.

And in Australia, the Western country that has gone the farthest with its domestic data retention rules, the government is routinely criticized for using those rules to access data held by journalists—a direct threat to freedom of expression and other civil liberties.

No one is saying that law enforcement should be hamstrung in their fight against online criminals. But when those efforts would likely harm the wider public's fundamental rights, policymakers should move carefully.

In their push for backdoors, they risk undermining the inalienable freedoms at the heart of Western society.

Print Citations

CMS: Scott, Mark. "Mixed Messages: Encryption Fight Pits Security Against Privacy." In *The Reference Shelf: Internet Law,* edited by Annette Calzone, 105-107. Amenia, NY: Grey House Publishing, 2020.

MLA: Scott, Mark. "Mixed Messages: Encryption Fight Pits Security Against Privacy." *The Reference Shelf: Internet Law,* edited by Annette Calzone, Grey House Publishing, 2020, pp. 105-107.

APA: Scott, M. (2020). Mixed messages: Encryption fight pits security against privacy. In Annette Calzone (Ed.), *The reference shelf: Internet law* (pp. 105-107). Amenia, NY: Grey House Publishing.

One Man's Obsessive Fight to Reclaim His Cambridge Analytica Data

By Issie Lapowsky
Wired, **January 25, 2019**

It's 8 on a Wednesday morning in January, and David Carroll's Brooklyn apartment, a sunny, wood-beamed beauty converted from an old sandpaper factory, is buzzing.

His 10-year-old daughter, dressed in polka-dot pants, dips out the front door and off to school, Jansport backpack slung over her shoulders. His 5-year-old son darts into the living room in a luchador mask he picked up on the family's holiday trip to Mexico. (His wrestling name, he tells me, is Diablo.) Carroll's wife, Alex, who was unaware a reporter was coming to interview her husband this morning, hurries around picking up the detritus any family of four might leave behind in the morning rush and tucking away product samples from her job as a market researcher. There's a crayon drawing on the coffee table, an intricate toy camping scene set up on the floor. And on the refrigerator, someone—I suspect the boy—has spelled out the word POOP in multicolored alphabet magnets.

For most everyone in Carroll's bustling household, today is a morning like any other. Not for Carroll. This morning, he rolled out of bed at 6 am to news that the parent company of Cambridge Analytica, the now defunct international conglomerate, had pled guilty to criminal charges of disobeying a British data regulator.

The story of how the data analytics firm and former Trump campaign consultant misappropriated the Facebook data of tens of millions of Americans before the 2016 election is by now well known. But the company's guilty plea wasn't really about all those headlines you've seen splattered in the news over the past year. Instead, their crime was defying a government order to hand over all of the data they had ever collected on just one person: David Carroll.

For more than two years, Carroll, a professor of media design at The New School in Manhattan, has been on an obsessive, epically nerdy, and ultimately valuable quest to retrieve his data from Cambridge Analytica. During the 2016 election, when the firm worked for both the Trump campaign and senator Ted Cruz's campaign, its leaders bragged openly about having collected thousands of data points to build detailed personality profiles on every adult in the United States. They said they used these profiles to target people with more persuasive ads, and when President Trump won the White House, they hungrily accepted credit.

A year ago, Carroll filed a legal claim against the London-based conglomerate, demanding to see what was in his profile. Because, with few exceptions, British data protection laws allow people to request data on them that's been processed in the UK, Carroll believed that even as an American, he had a right to that information. He just had to prove it.

Carroll shuffles past me barefoot, a mug of coffee in one hand, his phone in the other. "Enjoy the moment," he says, reading a message from his lawyer, Ravi Naik, who's been feeding him updates from London all morning. About an hour later, an email floats into Carroll's inbox from the British Information Commissioner's Office, the regulator that brought the charges. Carroll turns his phone toward me to reveal the news. Cambridge Analytica's parent company, SCL, is being fined the equivalent of roughly $27,000. Carroll's cut? About $222.

He couldn't help but laugh. The sum is insignificant. The moment, anything but.

When he started out, Carroll was an underdog, facing off against a corporation with ties to the president of the United States and backed by billionaire donor Robert Mercer. If he lost, Carroll would be on the hook for the opposing team's legal fees, which he wasn't quite sure how he'd pay.

But if he won, Carroll believed he could prove an invaluable point. He could use that trove of information he received to show the world just how powerless Americans are over their privacy. He could offer up a concrete example of how one man's information—his supermarket punch card, his online shopping habits, his voting patterns—can be bought and sold and weaponized by corporations and even foreign entities trying to influence elections.

But more importantly, he could show what's possible in countries like the UK where people actually have the right to reclaim some of that power. He could prove why people in the United States, who have no such rights, deserve those same protections.

Much has changed since David Carroll picked this fight with Goliath. Following a relentless flood of scandals last spring, SCL shuttered and is now going through insolvency proceedings in the UK. The Cambridge Analytica scandal spurred just the kind of privacy awakening in the US that Carroll was seeking. Facebook tightened its hold on user data and has been increasingly asked to answer for all the ways it gave that data away in the first place. A strict data protection law passed unanimously in California last summer, and members of Congress have begun floating plans for broader federal privacy legislation.

Carroll, meanwhile, has emerged as a cult hero of privacy hawks, who follow every turn in his case, Twitter fingers itching. This week, he'll become a movie star, appearing as a central character in a feature-length documentary called *The Great Hack*, premiering at the Sundance Film Festival. "We hope this film sheds light on what it means to sign the terms and conditions that we agree to every day," the filmmakers, Jehane Noujaim and Karim Amer, explained in an email. "What does it mean when we actually become a commodity being mined?"

But for all that's changed during these past two years, so much has stayed the same. Despite SCL's guilty plea, Carroll still hasn't gotten his data. And Americans today have no more legal rights to privacy than they did when Carroll's crusade began two years ago. That could change this year. With a strict data protection law set to go into effect in California next January, even tech giants have begun pushing for federal regulation that would set rules for businesses across the country. Now more than ever, Carroll says, having that information in hand could help illustrate exactly how this new economy—so often misunderstood and discussed in the abstract—works. Which is why, nearly a year after the Cambridge Analytica story broke, and many months after its name has fallen out of the daily headlines, Carroll keeps fighting.

If you know Carroll from Twitter—where, as @profcarroll, he spends his days tweeting bombastically about Facebook's duplicity or stridently skewering obscure figures from the Trump campaign in long, snarky, and inscrutable threads—then you couldn't possibly imagine the nervous, affable guy I first met in a downtown Manhattan coffee shop back in 2017.

He looked exactly the way I expected a tenured liberal arts professor to look: gray stubble on his face, a disarming smile. I could easily imagine him in tweed. It was November 8, a year to the day since Donald Trump was elected president of the United States. That evening, Carroll sat across the table from me, a lit tea light casting his face in a film noir glow, and told me what he knew so far of his story.

Carroll hadn't always been in academia. During the dotcom boom and bust, he worked in digital marketing and watched as advertising evolved from the sort of broad branding exercise that had been the dominion of television and print to an industry dominated by Google, which used infinite quantities of user data to hypertarget ads. When he left his marketing career to teach full time, Carroll, who has an MFA in design and technology, transformed from an industry participant to a chief critic, lecturing students on what he calls the "myth" that advertising doesn't work if it's not targeted.

In 2014, while he was on sabbatical, Carroll began working on a startup called Glossy, which integrated with Facebook to recommend articles from magazine archives based on users' interests. The idea never took off; Carroll couldn't get funding, and his early employees got quickly poached by tech giants. But he got just far enough to see how much user data Facebook was willing to give away in the name of growth. At the time, the social networking giant allowed developers to slurp up data not just from their own users but from their users' friends, all without their friends' awareness or explicit consent. Facebook didn't officially end this policy until April 2015, and continued to give some developers access even after that.

"I saw how the sausage got made and how easy it was to amass data and create a surveillance infrastructure," Carroll says.

Around that same time, across the Atlantic Ocean, another young professor at the University of Cambridge named Aleksandr Kogan was building an app of his own. It used a personality quiz to collect users' profile information, including their location, gender, name, and Page likes, and then spit out predictions about their personality types. Like Carroll, Kogan knew that when Facebook users took the quizzes, not only would their data be free for the taking, so would the data belonging to millions of their friends. Unlike Carroll, Kogan viewed that not as an invasion of privacy but as an opportunity.

"It didn't even dawn on us that people could react this way," Kogan says.

Beginning in 2014, Kogan paid about 270,000 US Facebook users to take the quiz, which Kogan has said unlocked access to some 30 million people's data. But Kogan wasn't just working on his own. He was collecting this information on behalf of SCL, which had big plans to use it to influence American elections. Kogan sold the data and his predictions to the company, and though he didn't know it then, lit the fuse of a time bomb that would detonate three years down the line.

Carroll knew none of this at the time. But his experience building Glossy made him enough of a self-proclaimed "privacy nerd" that by the time the 2016 election rolled around he was keeping a close eye on the presidential campaigns and their digital strategies. He was watching SCL's spinoff Cambridge Analytica, in particular, because it had taken credit for helping senator Ted Cruz win the Iowa primary, using so-called psychographic targeting techniques. But it wasn't until President Trump's upset victory, in a campaign that had been buoyed by Cambridge Analytica data scientists and consultants, that Carroll, a Democrat, began to worry about what this firm could really do with millions of Americans' information.

He wasn't the only one. Thousands of miles away, in Geneva, Switzerland, a researcher named Paul-Olivier Dehaye, who now runs a digital rights nonprofit called PersonalData.IOt, was deep into a months-long investigation of SCL. At the time, he was trying to answer a fundamental question about the company that was also rumored to have played a hand in promoting the Brexit referendum: Did Cambridge Analytica really know as much as it claimed? Or was it just selling snake oil? One way to answer that question conclusively, Dehaye believed, would be to see what information the company actually held.

The UK's Data Protection Act guarantees the right to access data that's processed within the UK. But in the past, it was mainly British residents who had exercised that right. Few had ever tested whether the law applied to people outside of the country as well. Dehaye believed this would be the perfect opportunity to try, so he began reaching out to American academics, activists, and journalists, urging them to submit what is known as a "subject access request" to the company. It was Americans' data, after all, that Cambridge Analytica seemed most interested in. Carroll was one of Dehaye's targets.

"David was very vocal on Twitter, and he already knew a lot about ad tech," Dehaye says. "That's why I thought I had a chance to convince him."

He was right. Carroll was one of a handful of people who accepted the challenge. He says he viewed the project as an academic experiment at first, and, he says, a good use of his tenure. "I can't get fired for what I do," he said. "My job gives me the freedom to pursue these things. If I don't do it, who's going to?"

In early 2017, Carroll submitted his request, along with a copy of his driver's license, his electric bill, and a £10 fee, which Dehaye paid. Then he waited. Dehaye never really expected Carroll to receive a response. In fact the story may have ended there, had SCL denied that Carroll had the right to his data from the outset. "They could have just said UK law doesn't apply to you because you're an American," Dehaye says.

Instead, one Monday morning about a month later, as Carroll sat alone in his apartment, sipping coffee at the dining room table, an email landed in his inbox from the data compliance team at SCL Group. It included a letter signed by the company's chief operating officer, Julian Wheatland, and an Excel file laying out in neatly arranged rows and columns exactly who Carroll is—where he lives, how he's voted, and, most interestingly to Carroll, how much he cares about issues like the national debt, immigration, and gun rights, on a scale of one to 10. Carroll had no way of knowing what information informed those rankings; the thousands of data points Cambridge Analytica supposedly used to build these predictions were nowhere to be found.

"I felt very invaded personally, but then I also saw it was such a public interest issue," Carroll says.

He promptly tweeted out his findings. To Carroll, his file seemed woefully incomplete. But to Dehaye and other experts of the internet, it seemed like exactly what he needed to prove a case. In answering Carroll at all, Dehaye argued, SCL conceded that even as an American, he was entitled to his data. But in showing him only the smallest slice of that data, Carroll and Dehaye believed, SCL had broken the law.

Dehaye put Carroll in touch with Ravi Naik, a British human rights lawyer, who had worked on data rights cases in the past. "Immediately, he was like, 'This is going to be a massive case. It's going to set precedents,'" Carroll says.

Still, Naik was cautious, knowing that the case law regarding foreigners gaining access to their data was extremely limited, resting on just two cases where death row inmates from Thailand and Kenya had attempted to get their data from the British police. But Naik also viewed Carroll's case as the beginning of a new civil rights movement. "It's really balancing the rights of individuals against those with mass power," Naik says.

In April 2017, Carroll and Naik sent what's known as a "pre-action" letter to SCL, laying out a legal claim. In the UK, these letters are used to determine if litigation can be avoided. In the letter, Naik and Carroll argued that not only had SCL violated the UK's Data Protection Act by failing to give Carroll all of the underlying data, the company hadn't received the proper consent to process data related to his political views to begin with. Under the law, political opinions are considered sensitive data.

Once again, Carroll got no additional data in return. According to Alexander Nix, Cambridge Analytica's then-CEO, the company shared certain data with Carroll as a gesture of "good faith," but received legal advice that foreigners didn't have rights under the Data Protection Act. Asked why the company didn't share more of that data, Nix said, "There was no legal reason to comply with this request, and it might be opening ... a bottomless pit of subject access requests in the United States that we would be unable to fulfill just through the sheer volume of requests in comparison to the size of the company." (After answering *Wired*'s questions, Nix retroactively asked for these answers to be off the record. *Wired* declined.)

Carroll wasn't the only person who had tried and failed to get his data from SCL. Initially, Naik says, about 20 people around the world were on board. But when it came time to bring the case to court, he says, they needed only one complainant, and it was Carroll who was most willing to take the risk. "It says a lot about David that he's willing to stand by not just his own rights but also the rights of everyone affected, to work out what this company was doing," Naik says.

Carroll and Naik spent the bulk of 2017 preparing the case and hedging their bets against worst case scenarios, of which there were many. In the British legal system, whoever loses a legal case winds up paying the winning side's fees. Carroll worried that could amount to hundreds of thousands of dollars, the kind of costs he couldn't bear on his own. So that fall, Carroll launched his own legal defense fund on CrowdJustice and announced his plans to file the complaint in *The Guardian*. Suddenly, he was flooded with support from strangers who'd grown similarly suspicious of Cambridge Analytica. He raised nearly $33,000 in a matter of weeks. Today, he's raised another $10,000 more.

But for all the encouragement Carroll received, almost as soon as he went public with his plans he also got more than a few words of warning. Once, Carroll says, a Cambridge Analytica employee approached him after a film screening at The New School, shook his hand for a few beats too long, and told him to drop the case. Another time, Carroll got a mysterious email about a British journalist who had supposedly been investigating SCL when he died suddenly falling down the stairs. "Please don't forget how powerful these individuals are," the email read.

It was almost certainly a coincidence, and Carroll never followed up with the woman who sent the email. "I didn't want her to talk me out of it," Carroll says. But he still couldn't help but feel spooked. In the fall of 2017, he rightly felt like he had a lot to lose.

The night we met in the coffee shop, I asked Carroll whether all these risks he was taking worried him. He smiled anxiously and said, "It scares the shit out of me."

A few months later, I spotted Carroll across a crowded auditorium at Putin-Con, a gathering of reporters, foreign policy experts, intelligence officials, and professional paranoiacs being held in an undisclosed location in Manhattan. The express purpose of the conference was to discuss "how Russia is crippled by totalitarian rule" and explore how Russian president Vladimir Putin's power "is based in fear, mystery, and propaganda."

But Carroll had other matters on his mind. That day, March 16, 2018, his lawyers in London were finally serving SCL with a formal legal claim, requesting disclosure of his data and laying out their intention to sue for damages. The request had been more than a year in the making, and Carroll spent much of the morning darting out to the hallway, exchanging Signal messages with Naik, even though he was scared that any venue hosting something called PutinCon must have been hacked.

After Naik's colleague served SCL with the paperwork, Carroll stood looking at his phone in satisfied disbelief. "It's finally real," he told me. "It's not just an idea anymore."

There was one other thing. Carroll said he'd heard "rumblings" from British journalist Carole Cadwalladr that some big news regarding Cambridge Analytica was coming from *The Guardian* and the *New York Times*. "It's going to make Facebook look really bad," he said.

Less than 24 hours later, Carroll turned out to be more right than he even knew. The next morning, photos of a pink-haired, self-styled whistleblower and former SCL contractor named Christopher Wylie were splashed across pages of the *New York Times* and *The Guardian*. "Revealed: 50 million Facebook profiles harvested for Cambridge Analytica in major data breach," read the *Guardian* headline. "How Trump Consultants Exploited the Facebook Data of Millions," read the *Times'*. The night before, Facebook had tried to preempt the stories, announcing it was suspending Wylie, Cambridge Analytica, SCL, and Aleksandr Kogan for violating its policies against sharing Facebook data with third parties.

That hardly helped Facebook's case. The news did more than make Facebook look bad. It did what history may judge to be irreparable damage to a company at the peak of its unprecedented power. Facebook's stock price plummeted. Zuckerberg was summoned to Congress. The company gave itself the impossible task of auditing apps that had access to mass amounts of data, and began cutting off other developers from collecting even more. Google searches for "how to delete Facebook" spiked.

In the end, Facebook CEO Mark Zuckerberg acknowledged that as many as 87 million people may have been affected by the data intrusion. Eventually, the Federal Trade Commission launched an investigation into whether Facebook violated a 2011 consent decree regarding its data privacy practices. "I started Facebook, and at the end of the day I'm responsible for what happens on our platform," Zuckerberg wrote on Facebook days after the news broke. "While this specific issue involving Cambridge Analytica should no longer happen with new apps today, that doesn't change what happened in the past."

Earlier this month, the *Washington Post* reported that the FTC is considering "imposing a record-setting fine" against Facebook.

As bad as things were for Facebook, they soon got worse for Cambridge Analytica. Days after Wylie's story first made headlines, Britain's Channel 4 News began airing a series of devastating undercover videos that showed the firm's once sought-after CEO, Alexander Nix, discussing using dirty tricks like bribery and blackmail on behalf of clients. In one case, Nix boasted that using Ukrainian women to entrap politicians "works very well."

Nix has since denied that the company engages in those practices. "That was just a lie to impress the people I was talking to," he told a parliamentary committee last summer. But almost as soon as the videos aired, Nix was replaced as CEO. By May, buried under an avalanche of negative press, SCL Group announced it was shutting down completely and filing for bankruptcy and insolvency in the US and the UK. Today, just one of its many corporate properties—SCL Insights—is still up and running.

As SCL was crumbling, Carroll's case took on a new sense of urgency. He was thrown into the media firestorm, crisscrossing Manhattan as he discussed his claim on an alphabet soup of television networks. Suddenly, this wasn't just a wonky academic endeavor to retrieve data from some company. It was a story about rescuing that data

> **But if he won, Carroll could use that trove of information he received to show the world just how powerless Americans are over their privacy.**

from the one company the public had decided, and Facebook had claimed, was singularly sinister. "Chris Wylie took the story that I knew was a big deal for a long time and made it a worldwide story, a household name," Carroll says.

When the news broke in March, the UK's Information Commissioner's Office was already investigating SCL for its refusal to hand over Carroll's data. Carroll and Naik had filed a complaint with the ICO in 2017. But for months, SCL told the regulator that as an American, Carroll had no more rights to his data "than a member of the Taliban sitting in a cave in the remotest corner of Afghanistan." The ICO disagreed. In May, days after SCL declared bankruptcy, the regulator issued an order, directing the firm to give Carroll his data once and for all. Failure to comply within 30 days, they warned, would result in criminal charges.

SCL never complied. Julian Wheatland, director of SCL Group, told me he thinks the guilty plea the company issued in January is a "shame" and says it merely represented the path of least resistance for SCL's liquidators, who oversee the insolvency proceedings and are duty bound to maximize the company's assets. "There was little option but to plead guilty, as the cost of fighting the case would far outweigh the cost of pleading guilty," Wheatland says. SCL's administrators declined *Wired*'s request for comment.

The ICO fine was ultimately measly. Carroll's slice of it couldn't buy him more than a MetroCard and a bag of groceries. It's also no guarantee he'll get his data. Naik is still waging that battle on Carroll's behalf, as SCL's insolvency proceedings progress. Meanwhile, an ICO spokesperson confirmed that the office now has access to SCL's servers and is "assessing the material on them," which could help to bring Carroll's information to light.

But the ICO's charges were meaningful nonetheless. It clearly underscored the fact that people outside the UK had these rights to begin with. "This prosecution, the first against Cambridge Analytica, is a warning that there are consequences for ignoring the law," the information commissioner, Elizabeth Denham, said in a statement following the hearing. "Wherever you live in the world, if your data is being processed by a UK company, UK data protection laws apply."

By the time I interviewed Carroll in June 2018, about a month after SCL announced it was shutting down and just days after the ICO's deadline had ticked by, the fear Carroll felt that first time we met had almost evaporated. We were in

London to hear Cambridge Analytica's fallen CEO Alexander Nix state his case before a committee of British parliamentarians. It seemed as if the entire cast of characters involved in the story had settled into the hearing room's green upholstered chairs. There was Cadwalladr, *The Guardian* reporter who'd cracked the story open, and Wylie, the pink-haired source who'd helped her do it. Carroll sat to my right, busily tweeting every tense exchange between a defiant and defensive Nix and his inquisitors.

There was also a documentary film crew, stationed toward the back of the room. They'd been trailing Carroll for months.

When husband and wife team Jehane Noujaim and Karim Amer initially set out to make what is now *The Great Hack*, back in 2015, they planned to follow the story of the Sony Pictures breach that had exposed the film studio's secrets in what US intelligence officials said was an attack by North Korea. But as time went on, their attention, like that of the public's, shifted focus from the ways in which private information is straight-up stolen to all of the little ways we give it away to powerful corporations, often without realizing it or knowing what will happen to it—and certainly without any way to claw it back.

That led them to Carroll. "We were initially drawn to David's story because his mission to reclaim his data summarized the complexities of this world into a single question: What do you know about me?" the directors, who were nominated for an Academy Award for their film *The Square*, wrote in an email. "One of the things that has become increasingly clear is that whether David gets his data back or not, his case has brought to light some of the largest questions around data privacy."

This weekend, Carroll will head to Park City, Utah, to see himself on the big screen. For Naik, the fact that a film like this is debuting to mainstream audiences represents an "astonishing step in the data rights movement." "This shows a rapid change in interest in this field and the interest in data rights as a real and enforceable facet of human rights," he says.

Over the past few years, these rights have expanded drastically. Last May, Europe's General Data Protection Regulation went into effect across the European Union, giving Europeans the right to request and delete their data, and requiring businesses to receive informed consent before collecting that data. The law also established stricter reporting protocols around data breaches and created harsh new penalties for those who violate them.

Last summer, the state of California unanimously passed its own privacy law, which lets residents of the state see the information businesses collect on them and request that it be deleted. It also enables people to see which companies have purchased their data and direct businesses to stop selling it at all.

Some of the most influential business leaders in the world have simultaneously rallied around the cause. In Brussels last year, Apple CEO Tim Cook condemned what he called the "data industrial complex" and called for a federal law that would prevent personal information from being "weaponized against us with military efficiency." Even data gobblers like Google, Amazon, and Facebook have finally come out in support of a federal privacy law, partly due to the fact that such legislation could prevent the stricter California bill from taking effect in 2020.

If Congress is ever going to make good on its recent promises to crack down on rampant data mining, this could be the year. So far, senator Ron Wyden (D-Oregon) has floated some draft legislation. Senator Marco Rubio (R-Florida) proposed a bill that would task the FTC with drafting new rules. And in December, senator Brian Schatz (D-Hawaii) introduced a bill of his own, cosponsored by 14 other Democrats, that requires companies to "reasonably secure" personally identifying information and promise not to use it for harm. It would also force businesses and the third parties they work with to notify users of data breaches and gives the FTC new authority to fine violators.

"Just as doctors and lawyers are expected to protect and responsibly use the personal data they hold, online companies should be required to do the same," Schatz said in a statement when the bill was announced. "Our bill will help make sure that when people give online companies their information, it won't be exploited."

Carroll isn't so sure. He says bills like this hardly address the underlying problem. If data is the new oil powering the economy, then what Schatz is proposing is a process for cleaning up the next oil spill. It's not a set of safety procedures to prevent that spill from happening in the first place. That's what Carroll says the United States, whose homegrown tech giants control so much of the world's data, desperately needs. He continues to believe his SCL file would prove how badly it's needed.

Cambridge Analytica may have taken data from Facebook that it didn't have the right to, and Facebook may have made that data too easy to access. But the most overlooked fact in the whole saga is that Cambridge Analytica wasn't alone. From data brokers that track your every purchase to mobile phone carriers that sell your location to social media companies that give far more detail to developers than is necessary, there's an invisible, unregulated marketplace of personal information in the United States. And it's no longer just being used to sell us new boots or connect us with high school classmates. It's being used to influence decisions about who the most powerful people in the world get to be.

"They're not the only ones by any stretch of the imagination," Carroll says of SCL. "It's a dirty business, but sunlight is the best disinfectant."

This is, perhaps, the one issue on which Carroll and Wheatland, SCL's director, see eye to eye. Wheatland predictably disagrees with the broad characterization of his company, whose very name has become a proxy for everything wrong with the data trade. He says Cambridge Analytica was a "lightning rod" for a confluence of feelings about President Trump's election, Facebook, Brexit, and the rising use of data. "We found ourselves at the nexus of all of those and became the whipping boy," he says.

He doesn't find many sympathetic audiences for that message these days. But he, too, says that regulation is imperative, given the "huge power" of data modeling. And he too says there's a risk to casting Cambridge Analytica as somehow unique. "This is an issue that is much bigger than one company," he says. "If we take this villain mentality and think that we've moved on, we haven't. We've lost Cambridge Analytica, but we haven't moved on at all."

Carroll is hardly pouring one out for the loss of Cambridge Analytica. Far from it. As he watched Nix stammer and squirm in his tailored suit that June afternoon in Parliament, Carroll couldn't help but recognize how dramatically their roles had been reversed.

These last two years have been emotionally taxing and at times lonely for Carroll, who's become absorbed by an issue that sometimes even the people closest to him failed to understand. But every new break in the case has provided some validation that it's all been worth it. "I don't feel like I'm up against the wall," he told me the night of Nix's hearing, the documentary crew's cameras trained on his face. "They're up against the wall."

But he stopped short of declaring victory. Not until he gets his data back, and sees some real change come of it. "All I want is everything," he said. "Because I'm entitled to it. And so is everyone."

Print Citations

CMS: Lapowsky, Issie. "One Man's Obsessive Fight to Reclaim His Cambridge Analytica Data." In *The Reference Shelf: Internet Law,* edited by Annette Calzone, 108-118. Amenia, NY: Grey House Publishing, 2020.

MLA: Lapowsky, Issie. "One Man's Obsessive Fight to Reclaim His Cambridge Analytica Data." *The Reference Shelf: Internet Law,* edited by Annette Calzone, Grey House Publishing, 2020, pp. 108-118.

APA: Lapowsky, I. (2020). One man's obsessive fight to reclaim his Cambridge Analytica data. In Annette Calzone (Ed.), *The reference shelf: Internet law* (pp. 108-118). Amenia, NY: Grey House Publishing.

A Dark Web Tycoon Pleads Guilty. But How Was He Caught?

By Patrick Howell O'Neill

MIT Technology Review, February 8, 2020

When the enterprising cybercriminal Eric Eoin Marques pleaded guilty in an American court this week, it was meant to bring closure to a seven-year-long international legal struggle centered on his dark web empire.

In the end, it did anything but.

Marques faces up to 30 years in jail for running Freedom Hosting, which temporarily existed beyond reach of the law and ended up being used to host drug markets, money-laundering operations, hacking groups, and millions of images of child abuse. But there is still one question that police have yet to answer: How exactly were they able to catch him? Investigators were somehow able to break the layers of anonymity that Marques had constructed, leading them to locate a crucial server in France. This discovery eventually led them to Marques himself, who was arrested in Ireland in 2013.

Marques was the first in a line of famous cybercriminals to be caught despite believing that using the privacy-shielding anonymity network Tor would make them safe behind their keyboards. The case demonstrates that government agencies can trace suspects through networks that were designed to be impenetrable.

Marques has blamed the American NSA's world-class hackers, but the FBI has also been building up its efforts since 2002. And, some observers say, they often withhold key details of their investigations from defendants and judges alike—secrecy that could have wide-ranging cybersecurity implications across the internet.

"The overarching question is when are criminal defendants entitled to information about how law enforcement located them?" asks Mark Rumold, a staff attorney at the Electronic Frontier Foundation, an organization that promotes online civil liberties. "It does a disservice to our criminal justice system when the government hides techniques of investigation from public and criminal defendants. Oftentimes the reason they do this kind of obscuring is because the technique they use is questionable legally or might raise questions in the public's mind about why they were doing it. While it's common for them to do this, I don't think it benefits anyone."

Freedom Hosting was an anonymous and illicit cloud computing company running what some estimated to be up to half of all dark web sites in 2013. The operation existed entirely on the anonymity network Tor and was used for a wide range of illegal activity, including the hacking and fraud forum HackBB and money-laundering operations including the Onion Bank. It also maintained servers for the legal email service Tor Mail and the singularly strange encyclopedia Hidden Wiki.

But it was the hosting of sites used for photos and videos of child exploitation that attracted the most hostile government attention. When Marques was arrested in 2013, the FBI called him the "largest facilitator" of such images "on the planet."

Early on August 2 or 3, 2013, some of the users noticed "unknown Javascript" hidden in websites running on Freedom Hosting. Hours later, as panicked chatter about the new code began to spread, the sites all went down simultaneously. The code had attacked a Firefox vulnerability that could target and unmask Tor users—even those using it for legal purposes such as visiting Tor Mail—if they failed to update their software fast enough.

While in control of Freedom Hosting, the agency then used malware that probably touched thousands of computers. The ACLU criticized the FBI for indiscriminately using the code like a "grenade."

The FBI had found a way to break Tor's anonymity protections, but the technical details of how it happened remain a mystery.

"Perhaps the greatest overarching question related to the investigation of this case is how the government was able to pierce Tor's veil of anonymity and locate the IP address of the server in France," Marques's defense lawyers wrote in a recent filing.

In the original indictment, there is little information beyond references to an "investigation in 2013" that found a key IP address linked to Freedom Hosting (referred to in the document as the "AHS," or anonymous hosting service).

Marques's defense lawyers said they received only "vague details" from the government, and that "this disclosure was delayed, in part, because the investigative techniques employed were, until recently, classified."

Peter Carr, a Justice Department spokesperson, said the letter is "not in the public record." The defense attorneys did not respond to questions.

Not-So-Full Disclosure

US government agencies regularly find software vulnerabilities in the course of their security work. Sometimes these are disclosed to technology vendors, while at other times the government decides to keep these exploits for use as weapons or in investigations. There is a formal system for deciding whether an issue should be shared, known as the vulnerabilities equities process. This is meant to default toward disclosure, under the belief that any bug that affects the "bad guys" also has the potential to be used against American interests; an agency that wants to use a major bug in an investigation has to get approval, or else the bug will be publicly disclosed. US officials say the vast majority of such vulnerabilities end up disclosed so that they can be fixed, ideally increasing internet security for everyone.

But if the FBI used a software vulnerability to find Freedom Hosting's hidden servers and didn't disclose the details, it could still potentially use it against others on Tor. This has observers concerned.

"It's not uncommon to play these games where they hide the ball about the source of their information," the EFF's Rumold says.

> **Tor is free software designed to let anyone use the internet anonymously by encrypting traffic and bouncing it through various nodes to obfuscate connections to the original users.**

Tor is free software designed to let anyone use the internet anonymously by encrypting traffic and bouncing it through various nodes to obfuscate connections to the original users. Users could include Americans sick of being tracked by advertising companies, Iranians attempting to circumvent censorship, Chinese dissidents escaping national surveillance, or criminals like Marques attempting to stay ahead of international police. The users are diverse in every way, but software vulnerabilities can affect all of them.

In a 2017 criminal case, the US government put the secrecy of its hacking tools above all else. Prosecutors chose to drop all charges in a case of child exploitation on the dark web rather than reveal the technological means they used to locate the anonymized Tor user.

Freedom Hosting's closure was the first in a series of stunning successes by international law enforcement that shut down some of the most high-profile criminal websites in history.

Two months after Marques was caught, the free-wheeling marketplace Silk Road was shut down in another FBI-led operation. After facilitating at least hundreds of millions of dollars in sales, Silk Road became a symbol of the apparent invulnerability of the criminals inhabiting the dark web. Although it lasted less than three years, it was clear that Silk Road's founder, nicknamed Dread Pirate Roberts, felt invincible. Close to the end, the anonymous figure was giving interviews to magazines like *Forbes* and writing political essays about his cause and the ideology behind it.

Then, in October 2013, Ross Ulbricht—a 29-year-old online bookseller—was arrested in San Francisco and charged with running Silk Road. He was eventually sentenced to life in prison, a punishment that far exceeds whatever Marques might receive at his sentencing date in May.

Freedom Hosting and Silk Road were just the most well-known dark web sites that were brought down by law enforcement despite the anonymity that Tor is meant to provide.

"We can't have a world where a government is allowed to use a black box of technology from which spring these serious criminal prosecutions," Rumold says. "Defendants have to have the ability to test and review and look at the methods that are used in criminal prosecutions."

Print Citations

CMS: O'Neill, Patrick Howell. "A Dark Web Tycoon Pleads Guilty: But How Was He Caught?" In *The Reference Shelf: Internet Law,* edited by Annette Calzone, 119-122. Amenia, NY: Grey House Publishing, 2020.

MLA: O'Neill, Patrick Howell. "A Dark Web Tycoon Pleads Guilty: But How Was He Caught?" *The Reference Shelf: Internet Law,* edited by Annette Calzone, Grey House Publishing, 2020, pp. 119-122.

APA: O'Neill, P.H. (2020). A dark web tycoon pleads guilty: But how was he caught? In Annette Calzone (Ed.), *The reference shelf: Internet law* (pp. 119-122). Amenia, NY: Grey House Publishing.

Hackers Will Be the Weapon of Choice for Governments in 2020

By Patrick Howell O'Neill
MIT Technology Review, January 2, 2020

When Russia was recently banned from the Olympics for another four years in a unanimous decision from the World Anti-Doping Agency (WADA), the instant reaction from Moscow was anger and dismissal. Now the rest of the world is waiting to see how Russia will retaliate this time.

In the history books, 2016 will forever be known for unprecedented Russian interference into an American presidential election, but until that transpired, one of the most aggressive cybercampaigns that year centered on the Olympics. In the run-up to the summer games in Brazil, WADA had uncovered a national Russian doping conspiracy and recommended a ban. In response, Moscow's most notorious hackers targeted an array of international officials and then leaked both real and doctored documents in a propaganda push meant to undermine the recommendation. The International Olympic Committee rejected a blanket ban and allowed each sport to rule individually.

Next, the opening ceremony of the 2018 winter games in South Korea kicked off with all the traditional optimism, bright lights, and pageantry—plus a targeted cyberattack known as Olympic Destroyer that was designed to sabotage the networks and devices at the event. The attack's origins were obfuscated, with breadcrumbs in the malware pointing to North Korea and China—but after investigators untangled the attempts to mislead them, it became apparent that some of the Russian government's most experienced hackers were behind it. In a series of angry blog posts, the hackers charged that "on the pretext of defending clean sport," what they described as "the Anglo-Saxon Illuminati" were fighting for "power and cash in the sports world." It was clear that the Russians viewed the Olympics as one part of a larger world power competition, and looked to hacking as a weapon of choice. Almost nothing has been done to hold anyone responsible.

Indeed, as a new crop of books expertly explain, cybercapabilities are expanding and transforming the old game of statecraft. The Russians are playing right alongside the Americans, Chinese, Iranians, North Koreans, and others in using hackers to shape history and try to bend geopolitics to their will.

"Over two decades, the international arena of digital competition has become ever more aggressive," writes Ben Buchanan, a professor at Georgetown University's

School of Foreign Service, in his upcoming *The Hacker and the State*. "The United States and its allies can no longer dominate the field the way they once did. Devastating cyberattacks and data breaches animate the fierce struggle among states."

> **Whether or not a hack achieves a specific technical goal—malware installed, account taken over, data breached—it can undermine public confidence and democracy.**

With an academic's eye, Buchanan compares and contrasts the emerging tactics with the traditional ways of military conflict, nuclear competition, and espionage to make some sense of the new age. The book dissects how governments use cyberattacks to fundamentally "change the state of play" by "stacking the deck or stealing an opponent's card for one's own use." The Americans have a long history of exploiting their "home field advantage" to this effect, using the country's giant tech and telecom companies as well as its central position in the internet's infrastructure to enable cyberoperations that have helped fight its wars and win rounds of negotiations at the United Nations.

Meanwhile, *Sandworm*, a new book by journalist Andy Greenberg, zeroes in on multiple interrelated Russian hacking groups responsible not only for the sprawling campaign against the Olympics but for an impossibly long list of headline-making hacks. They turned the lights out in Ukraine by breaking into utilities, broke into the Democratic National Committee in America, and brought hospitals, ports, giant corporations, and government agencies to their knees with a piece of malware called NotPetya. This debacle illustrates the big and unanswered questions defining the new era: What are the rules? What are the consequences?

Although it may seem as if cyberattacks target mainly networks and computers, conflict on the internet can affect every human being both directly—when, for example, medical equipment is compromised—and indirectly, by forcefully reshaping the geopolitical reality we're all living in.

"Today, the full scale of the threat Sandworm and its ilk present loom over the future," Greenberg writes. "If cyberwar escalation continues unchecked, the victims of state-sponsored hacking could be on a trajectory for even more virulent and destructive works. The digital attacks first demonstrated in Ukraine hint at a dystopia on the horizon, one where hackers induce blackouts that last days, weeks, or even longer—intentionally inflicted deprivations of electricity that could mirror the American tragedy of Puerto Rico after Hurricane Maria, causing vast economic harm or even loss of life."

As we start a new decade, the most immediate threat in the minds of many Americans is—once again—election interference. The 2020 election threatens to move forward the pattern of escalation that began when Barack Obama's campaign was hacked in 2008, and spiked when Donald Trump became the first to directly benefit from hacking by a foreign power. *Hacker States*, an upcoming book by the British academics Luca Follis and Adam Fish, distinguishes between the different dimensions of destruction. Whether or not a hack achieves a specific technical goal—malware installed, account taken over, data breached—it can undermine public confidence and democracy.

"It is not just about tampering, information warfare, or influence campaigns, but it is also about the very physical infrastructures and complex systems responsible for everything from healthcare to tallying votes," Follis and Fish write.

"In the 2016 US presidential elections, Russian hackers targeted the electronic voting systems of more than one hundred local elections. Even when the tampering is not successful or when damning information is not exfiltrated, the suspicion generated by the discovery of malicious code (or reports of systems penetration) speaks to a new conspiratorial and anxious politics, in which the question of democratic legitimacy is left open and unanswered."

Perhaps the most useful preview of the 2020 election will be, once again, the Olympics. The 2020 summer games will be held in Tokyo, and the Russians have already put a bull's-eye on the event with several successful hacks on relevant organizations. Despite a spotlight on their activities, there have been virtually no consequences for what the Russians did to the Olympics in the past four years, so a repeat performance is a distinct possibility.

The last decade was marked by nations harnessing the power of hacking to win wars, elections, and any other fight they chose. World powers will continue using this distinctly 21st-century weapon to shape politics to their advantage. In both the Olympic Games and elections, even the smallest advantage makes a world of difference.

It's clear that fights on both of those fronts are already well under way.

Print Citations

CMS: O'Neill, Patrick Howell. "Hackers Will Be the Weapon of Choice for Governments in 2020." In *The Reference Shelf: Internet Law,* edited by Annette Calzone, 123-125. Amenia, NY: Grey House Publishing, 2020.

MLA: O'Neill, Patrick Howell. "Hackers Will Be the Weapon of Choice for Governments in 2020." *The Reference Shelf: Internet Law,* edited by Annette Calzone, Grey House Publishing, 2020, pp. 123-125.

APA: O'Neill, P.H. (2020). Hackers will be the weapon of choice for governments in 2020. In Annette Calzone (Ed.), *The reference shelf: Internet law* (pp. 123-125). Amenia, NY: Grey House Publishing.

Proposed US Law Is "Trojan Horse" to Stop Online Encryption, Critics Say

By Jon Brodkin
Ars Technica, March 5, 2020

Two Republicans and two Democrats in the US Senate have proposed a law that aims to combat sexual exploitation of children online, but critics of the bill call it a "Trojan horse" that could harm Americans' security by reducing access to encryption.

The EARN IT (Eliminating Abusive and Rampant Neglect of Interactive Technologies) Act "would create incentives for companies to 'earn' liability protection for violations of laws related to online child sexual abuse material," an announcement by the bill's supporters said today.

Under current law, Section 230 of the Communications Decency Act provides website operators broad legal immunity for hosting third-party content. A 2018 law known as FOSTA-SESTA chipped away at that immunity for content related to prostitution and sex trafficking, and the EARN IT Act would further weaken immunity for website operators who fail to take certain to-be-determined measures to find and remove child sexual-abuse material.

In a related development today, US Attorney General William Barr gave a speech calling for an analysis of how Section 230 affects "incentives for platforms to address [child sexual exploitation] crimes and the availability of civil remedies to the victims."

Bill Lets Trump "Control Online Speech"

The bill doesn't directly prevent websites or online platforms from using encryption. But it would create a commission that would develop "best practices for providers of interactive computer services regarding the prevention of online child exploitation conduct" and require online platforms to certify compliance with those best practices. Not following these practices would make the tech companies more vulnerable to lawsuits. The attorney general would be the chairperson of the commission.

As the Electronic Frontier Foundation notes, the proposed 15-member commission would be "dominated by law enforcement agencies," which have repeatedly urged tech companies to weaken encryption. Critics of the bill worry that the commission's best practices will dissuade tech companies from deploying end-to-end encryption that protects the private communications of Internet users.

"This terrible legislation is a Trojan horse to give Attorney General Barr and [President] Donald Trump the power to control online speech and require government access to every aspect of Americans' lives," Sen. Ron Wyden (D-Ore.) said today. Wyden continued:

> While Section 230 does nothing to stop the federal government from prosecuting crimes, these senators claim that making it easier to sue websites is somehow going to stop pedophiles. This bill is a transparent and deeply cynical effort by a few well-connected corporations and the Trump administration to use child sexual abuse to their political advantage, the impact to free speech and the security and privacy of every single American be damned.

Those "well-connected corporations" include IBM, Marriott, and Disney, as a recent *New York Times* article said. Wyden's statement didn't specifically mention encryption, but his office told *Ars* that "when [Wyden] discusses weakening security and requiring government access to every aspect of Americans' lives, that is referring to encryption."

The EARN IT Act is sponsored by Senate Judiciary Committee Chairman Lindsey Graham (R-S.C.), Judiciary Committee Ranking Member Dianne Feinstein (D-Calif.), Sen. Richard Blumenthal (D-Conn.), and Sen. Josh Hawley (R-Mo.).

The Internet Association, which represents tech companies, said "the EARN IT Act as introduced may impede existing industry efforts to achieve this shared goal" of ending child exploitation online. EARN IT Act sponsors are not receptive to that argument.

"First Big Tech said it needed special immunity from human-trafficking laws," Sen. Hawley said. "Now it says it needs immunity from laws against child pornography. Enough. It's time to stop putting the financial interests of Big Tech above protecting kids from predators. The EARN IT Act is another way to bring today's Internet law into the 21st century."

The Internet Association also said that Section 230 "empowers Internet companies to proactively identify and remove [child sexual abuse material] and other illegal or objectionable material," and that tech companies already coordinate with law enforcement agencies in this area.

Banning Encryption "Without Banning It"

Stanford Law School's Center for Internet and Society (CIS) made a case against the EARN IT Act in late January after draft text of the bill was released. The bill is an attempt to "ban end-to-end encryption without actually banning it," CIS Associate Director of Surveillance and Cybersecurity Riana Pfefferkorn wrote.

Pfefferkorn wrote:

> The bill would, in effect, allow unaccountable commissioners to set best practices making it illegal for online service providers (for chat, email, cloud storage, etc.) to provide

end-to-end encryption—something it is currently 100 percent legal for them to do under existing federal law, specifically CALEA (Communications Assistance for Law Enforcement Act of 1994).

Stewart Baker, who was formerly assistant secretary for policy at the Department of Homeland Security and general counsel at the National Security Agency, wrote in a blog post that "there is nothing radical" about the bill.

"The risk of liability isn't likely to kill encryption or end Internet security," Baker wrote. But Baker acknowledged that the bill will likely make the decision to offer encryption a more difficult one for tech companies:

> To see what this has to do with encryption, just imagine that you are the CEO of a large Internet service thinking of rolling out end-to-end encryption to your users. This feature provides additional security for users, and it makes your product more competitive in the market. But you know it can also be used to hide child-pornography distribution networks. After the change, your company will no longer be able to thwart the use of your service to trade in child pornography, because it will no longer have visibility into the material users share with one another. So if you implement end-to-end encryption, there's a risk that, in future litigation, a jury will find that you deliberately ignored the risk to exploited children—that you acted recklessly about the harm, to use the language of the law.
>
> In other words, EARN IT will require companies that offer end-to-end encryption to weigh the consequences of that decision for the victims of child sexual abuse. And it may require them to pay for the suffering their new feature enables.

Update: The latest version of the bill is now available. The planned commission is now 19 members instead of 15, and the best practices would be submitted to Congress for an additional vote under a fast-tracking process. Pfefferkorn posted an analysis of the updated version, saying "I expect that this process is just a rubber-stamp by Congress, particularly given the fast-tracking provisions that do away with the usual legislative processes. That is: the 'best practices' are still pretty much up to the AG to determine." The current version of the legislation allows the attorney general to approve or deny the commission's recommended best practices; the draft version differed in that it gave the AG power to "modify" the recommendations.

Think of the Children

Similarly to the campaign for the FOSTA-SESTA bill that made websites liable for prostitution-related content, EARN IT supporters try to paint the bill's opponents as being indifferent to child abuse.

"The Internet is infested with stomach-churning images of children who have been brutally assaulted and exploited and who are forced to endure a lifetime of pain after these photographs and videos are circulated online," Sen. Blumenthal said.

Blumenthal argued that tech companies should have to "earn" the "extraordinary special safeguard against legal liability" that they've had under Section 230.

"Companies that fail to comport with basic standards that protect children from exploitation have betrayed the public trust granted them by this special exemption."

> **Critics of the bill worry that the commission's best practices will dissuade tech companies from deploying end-to-end encryption that protects the private communications of Internet users.**

Wyden isn't buying that argument, and he said the government can do more to fight child abuse without jeopardizing online security. The federal government has "spent years ignoring the law and millions of reports of the most heinous crimes against children," Wyden said.

"I'll be offering legislation in the coming days to drastically increase the number of prosecutors and agents hunting down child predators, require a single person in the White House to be personally responsible for these efforts, and direct mandatory funding to the people who can actually make a difference in this fight," Wyden said.

TechFreedom, a libertarian advocacy group, argued that the EARN IT Act might not even accomplish its primary goal of making kids safer. "The EARN IT Act could actually make law enforcement's job significantly harder by ending today's close cooperation between law enforcement and tech companies," TechFreedom President Berin Szóka said.

Print Citations

CMS: Brodkin, Jon. "Proposed US Law is 'Trojan Horse' to Stop Online Encryption, Critics Say." In *The Reference Shelf: Internet Law,* edited by Annette Calzone, 126-129. Amenia, NY: Grey House Publishing, 2020.

MLA: Brodkin, Jon. "Proposed US Law is 'Trojan Horse' to Stop Online Encryption, Critics Say." *The Reference Shelf: Internet Law,* edited by Annette Calzone, Grey House Publishing, 2020, pp. 126-129.

APA: Brodkin, J. (2020). Proposed US law is "Trojan horse" to stop online encryption, critics say. In Annette Calzone (Ed.), *The reference shelf: Internet law* (pp. 126-129). Amenia, NY: Grey House Publishing.

Does the CFAA Apply to Voting Machine Hacks?

By Derek B. Johnson
FCW, August 30, 2018

For decades, the Computer Fraud and Abuse Act served as the U.S. government's most powerful tool to prosecute hackers. Over the years, virtually every high-profile cybercrime case in which federal prosecutors brought forth charges—from Aaron Swartz and Marcus Hutchins to Russian and Iranian-backed hacking groups – has used the CFAA as its cornerstone statute.

As the U.S. heads into the 2018 mid-term elections, the government is facing intense political pressure to harden the security around election systems, while the Trump administration has also come under fire for not doing enough to draw bright lines around election infrastructure and signal to foreign nations that interference will come with great consequences.

Recent documents and comments from the Department of Justice indicate that when it comes to prosecuting the most high-profile form of interference – hacking and compromising voting machines – the government may end up going to war without its most potent weapon.

In July, the DOJ cyber digital task force released a report assessing the department's work in the cyber arena. While it calls CFAA the "principal tool" for prosecuting computer-related crimes, buried within the report are several passages expressing skepticism over whether the law would apply to individuals who hack into electronic voting machines.

The CFAA "currently does not prohibit the act of hacking a voting machine in many common situations," the report reads. "In general, the CFAA only prohibits hacking computers that are connected to the Internet (or that meet other narrow criteria for protection). In many conceivable situations, electronic voting machines will not meet those criteria, as they are typically kept off the Internet."

The heart of the CFAA allows the government to prosecute anyone who has "knowingly accessed a computer without authorization or exceeding authorized access." It has been used over the years to prosecute and convict a wide range of digital activities, from hacking into an organization's systems and networks, stealing or altering sensitive data or designing and spreading malware. Controversially, it has also been interpreted and used to criminally charge far less nefarious activities that have opened the law up to criticisms of overreach.

In congressional testimony August 21, Associate Deputy Attorney General Sujit Raman expanded on the department's position, saying that the CFAA draws a substantial portion of its authority from the Commerce Clause, an enumerated power in the U.S. Constitution that gives Congress and the federal government broad jurisdiction over activities that affect intra- and interstate commerce. However, DOJ officials worry that because voting machines are (in theory though not always in practice) disconnected from the Internet, their ability to affect interstate commerce is limited.

"We are concerned that courts might conclude that the Commerce Clause power, alone, does not reach voting machine computers that are not used in a commercial setting, are not used in interstate communication, and are typically never connected to the Internet or to any other network," Raman stated in his written testimony.

The CFAA has come under fire in the past by white hat hackers and digital rights groups for criminalizing activities, such as software vulnerability research, that are considered widely legitimate activities today. The DOJ's position has puzzled some legal experts, particularly those who have in the past criticized the government for relying on overly broad interpretations of the 1986 law's applicability.

> **Congress could conceivably rely on other authorities, such as its constitutional power to regulate federal elections, to criminally prosecute hackers who compromise voting machines.**

Law professor Orin Kerr wrote on Twitter that "it doesn't seem hard to argue that computers, in the aggregate, have an effect on interstate commerce."

Kerr also questioned whether the DOJ's legal interpretation was being influenced by politics. By setting a lower bar for its current legal authorities, it could provide cover for lawmakers to give the appearance of taking action on a hot-button issue.

"It's also possible that this is a fake problem that enables a fake solution: By suggesting the CFAA doesn't apply to voting machines, Congress can 'do something' about election hacking by passing a law that explicitly covers voting machines — even though the law covers this now," Kerr continued.

Both the DOJ report and Raman note that Congress could conceivably rely on other authorities, such as its constitutional power to regulate federal elections, to criminally prosecute hackers who compromise voting machines, but do not cite any specific laws. Raman pressed lawmakers to update the CFAA, unamended since 2008, in a number of ways, including specifying that electronic voting machines would quality as protected computers.

Sen. Richard Blumenthal (D-Conn.), who recently referred to alleged Russian interference and influence operations during the 2016 presidential election as "an act of war," introduced legislation in July that would include voting machines and other election information systems under the CFAA.

Print Citations

CMS: Johnson, Derek B. "Does the CFAA Apply to Voting Machine Hacks?" In *The Reference Shelf: Internet Law,* edited by Annette Calzone, 130-132. Amenia, NY: Grey House Publishing, 2020.

MLA: Johnson, Derek B. "Does the CFAA Apply to Voting Machine Hacks?" *The Reference Shelf: Internet Law,* edited by Annette Calzone, Grey House Publishing, 2020, pp. 130-132.

APA: Johnson, D.B. (2020). Does the CFAA apply to voting machine hacks? In Annette Calzone (Ed.), *The reference shelf: Internet law* (pp. 130-132). Amenia, NY: Grey House Publishing.

Helicopter Government? How the Internet of Things Enables Pushbutton Regulation from a Distance

By Clyde Wayne Crews Jr.
Forbes, **November 11, 2019**

Artificial intelligence can be curiously stupid. My Android phone still thinks I'm "wing Cruz" and doesn't know my kids. Pandora overplays The Church and Deadmau5 (no offense).

As hackable as Alexa, Jeep Cherokees and credit card services are over a public Internet not designed for security, the networked gadgetries enabled by the Internet of Things (IoT) continue to dazzle. An overwhelming number of them will be on display again in January at the 2020 Consumer Electronics Show (#CES2020).

The primary vulnerability of the IoT is not hackers, though, but IoT *policy*.

Technology that overcomes "market failure" in the provision of goods and services should enable the reduction and streamlining of regulatory burdens. Instead it sometimes threatens to foster the expansion of government power.

That is, the same IoT that animates objects can also mean instantaneous nanny-state regulation from a distance—of drones, vehicles, buildings, social media use, schooling and more.

You've heard of free-range kids vs. helicopter parenting?

Well, the society fancying itself on the verge of flying cars may face helicopter government instead; assorted bureaucrats clicking and swiping from afar, using the IoT to control the IoT.

It's one thing for Tesla to send its own software updates to its customers' cars. We definitely want such things to happen—a lot.

But as Jason Dorrier noted in *Singularity Hub*, "regulations. . . written into software" could be highly appealing to regulators. A "No drones within 100 feet of federal buildings," rule, for example, could be enforced by requiring the uploading to networked objects of software patches altering GPS coordinates, and disabling them in event of non-compliance.

Dorrier named other examples: software patches imposing speed restrictions and no-drive zones on vehicles, preventing cars from starting without seatbelt attachment, and mandating thermostate settings and water use restrictions in buildings.

Entrepreneur Marc Andreessen long ago described software eating the world.

Titans in sectors from "movies to agriculture to national defense" are now software companies, run on software and delivered as online services.

Unfortunately, while software has eaten business models, it is not eating traditional top-down central regulatory regimes in the sense of displacing them.

Those systems are preparing to eat the IoT instead.

The next step in this "evolution" could go beyond rules mandating the updating or patching of software, to unelected bureaucrats simply doing it themselves remotely by clicking and swiping rather than enacting a law or rule, Constitution notwithstanding. The use of guidance documents, informal directives and other "offers you can't refuse" are already a prominent regulatory concern highlighted by the Administrative Conference of the United States. The IoT could magnify such abuse.

In Long Beach, California, water authorities used smart meters to nab alleged water-wasting villains. The "logical" next step is government remotely overriding commercial building water and energy usage, perhaps even drafting the utility to countermand people's own smart home preferences. This is particularly galling since it ignores governments' culpability in the prevalence of shortages.

For policymakers infected with Green New Deal (GND) fever and taking steps like installing rooftop-mounted carbon-footprint monitors, one need not speculate on how authoritarian they are prepared to be when it comes to tweaking office buildings and regional tailpipes. Google's Street View cars fitted with chemical sensors now map air quality in several cities and provide that information to governments. The Environmental Protection Agency (EPA) has already invested in technology tracking office workers' energy and water usage, complete with visual alerts.

The EPA has protested exemptions to the Digital Millennium Copyright Act that might permit owners and researchers to access and modify vehicle software on the grounds that emissions might increase. But one suspects a future GND-lubricated EPA would itself love to remotely modify emission control software in vehicles – but punish you harshly if you do the same.

Politicians like Sen. Josh Hawley (R-Missouri) take addiction psychology seriously, and Hawley has introduced legislation to require Big Tech to eliminate "infinite scrolling" and set timers on gaming and social media. Future rules would be written and enforced by the Federal Trade Commission under

> **Indeed, technology helps expose regulatory malpractice and expands the case for separation of tech and state.**

this (so far, unpopular) scheme. Since these services are cloud based too, helicopter government may elect to ensure future compliance should such a regime emerge. For the children, of course.

In a progressive society bent on turning professors and administrators into government employees via "free" college, major textbook publishers are going digital. So do not be surprised if students are required to use the government's preferred "constantly updated texts, tethering students schools exclusively to the publisher's digital platform."

And so on.

The "Smart Cities" movement potentially may present the most significant incarnation of Regulation from A Distance, though. Versions I've noticed seem to involve heavy governmental control, "partnered" with large corporations or government-preferred players.

Despite inherent operational difficulties like procurement challenges, public-private partnerships indeed can play important roles in society (the more open to transition to fully market operations they are, the better, in my view). But "PPPS" present problems if they trend toward the "public" piece running the show and locking in a permanent regulated public infrastructure and utility mindset rather than ever envisioning any path to voluntarism and privatization. Here especially, the very IoT technology capable of overcoming ancient market failure justifications for government regulations and steering can be misused to expand the administrative state instead. As in any field, the political entrepreneurs among Big Tech's ranks will be happy to oblige and offer the licensed/approved technologies, such as traffic routing, vehicle to infrastructure V2I communications, securing a monopoly on emergent local or regional drone deliveries, or scoring coveted e-scooter contract (while I can't park my motorcycle on the sidewalk).

It may be perfectly reasonable for Uber and other ride-sharing outfits to collect and share vast amounts of anonymized locational and traffic data with public authorities. But for reasons apart from the emissions tweaking noted, authorities in "smart" cities are also attracted to remote override capabilities over automated vehicles for clearing lanes for emergency vehicles, routing around police and fire activity, or shutting down the vehicle of a fleeing suspect. On an already insecure-by-design Internet on which targeted hacking could cause monumental stranding and gridlock (or even weaponize vehicles) this global "LoJack" is concerning and feeds into a suspicion that smart cities will be primarily surveillance cities that ignore requirements for court orders, echoing abuses of red light traffic cameras and boimetrics. In China, many vehicle manufacturers have been sending locational information to the government without the vehicle owner's awareness, and facial recognition there enables jaywalkers to be outed on giant public screens.

Ironically, local city planners themselves sometimes game the useful traffic routing apps commuters rely upon to thwart them, and even create gridlock to drive distressed people into biking or public transport. Smart city planners can be similarly suspect.

The most significant issues in the IoT, properly, entail hazards or injury to third parties. But government can aggravate those. The federal government pursued a V2V (vehicle to vehicle) mandate that would have locked in obsolete technology and increased an array of risks across networked infrastructure. Furthermore, governments are prone to inappropriately indemnifying favored industries from the harms they cause, such as homeland security legislation that indemnified manufacturers of security technologies (like weapon alarms and bomb detectors) for losses above insured levels in the event of failure. Similarly, in the nascent space commercialization sector, the Spurring Private Aerospace Competitiveness and Entrepreneurship

(SPACE) Act of 2015 (in Sec. 103's extension of "Indemnification for Space Flight Participants") absolves launch providers from catastrophic losses or for injury to third parties (through September 2025). In this vein, it is likewise interesting that the orbital space debris that has become a concern has happened primarily without a large private sector presence in space.

So in spite of the default to government that is now apparent in IoT, continuous safety and due care advances are not a challenge for industry, they are the normal goal and operational mode. Big Tech has lives and assets to protect.

Indeed, technology helps expose regulatory malpractice and expands the case for separation of tech and state. But it will be difficult to unspool opportunistic government entrenchment like that sought in the IoT if the bureaucratic impulse is allowed to prevail. Instead of worrying about autonomous vehicles, we'd best thwart *autonomous regulation* and ensure ample opportunities for opt-out, evasive entrepreneurish, and alternative business models.

And for goodness sake *stop trying to do everything in the city*. In colonial America, settlers sailed up the James and other rivers and built cities once they hit the rocks. Now the cities *are the rocks*. Rather than jump the gun with VTOL (vertical take-off and landing) air taxis, for example, practice in the county and the peripheries on networks of private land and construct altogether new property rights/corridor/route and infrastructure regimes. Then, sit back and enjoy the emergence of "new" cities *out there*. Afterward take the lessons learned and improve the old-school cities. Above all, do not use the IoT to "solve" a "city problem" and inflict it on the nation. Offer it as one option, sure, but not the only.

Foundational issues like these need to be worked out experimentally, not imposed push-button style. Scientists debate whether the best approach to AI is to program everything in, or to let it learn like a baby, or some mix. Routing by AI algorithm can save lives in airspace and highways by eliminating the human-error hazard, but it doesn't have to be and ought not be government dominating this. I've joked that technology and tracking could eventually make it possible to pack the sky like a neutron star with commercial and personal drones, with defined corridors respecting rights. Data sharing by entities like the Space Data Association's satellite operators plays a large already prevalent role in risk management and situational awareness in space with insights that could potentially cross fertilize what happens on the ground with cars, and in-between with drones. Instead, drones are being absorbed into decades old commercial airspace models, not to mention already required to be registered with the federal government.

Contractual devices, insurance and liability innovations that mitigate risk become easier, not harder in the normal course of events. Will those smart cities consist of hive-mind "roadway management systems" and networked cars rather than *actually* independent autonomous vehicles that detect on their, not imposed, terms? Not so far. Instead, fusion of the (regulated) vehicle and the (hyper-regulated) infrastructure is the path we are on now, and it may or may not be the right one, depending on the setting (cities vs. country, for example). Amazon has patented a networking technology to allow self-driving vehicles en bloc to navigate reversible lanes. Amazon, not the automakers, would own and operate such a network and presumably let any makers vehicles participate, and it seems a better, intermediate, approach than governmental management.

But bottom-up and top-down approaches need to remain viable, because what governments seem to want is not localized, independent control from inside smart, autonomous vehicles (and intermediate-scale networking innovations atop that), but external control over everything. It's noteworthy that plain old ice-skating rinks thrive without somebody with a megaphone telling everybody where to go, and the same can be true over tomorrow's networked world if allowed. Maybe it's best for city planners to control roadway signals, rather than potentially individual vehicles or fleets of them.

Rather than top-down push button rules for the most complicated cases of cities, the rocks-in-the-river experimental stance also preserves the ability to explore trespass, peeping tom and vicious animal-style rules against misuse of drones and other IoT-enabled vehicles. as entrepreneur John Chisholm described in defense of "organic" rather than imposed regulation in *Unleash Your Inner Company*. Heck, given the pace of miniaturization, maybe there won't be smart cars at all, but husks or "sleds" that we snap our mobile devices into. But that can't be the case if smart cities amount to the major automakers teaming up with planners for a lock on the market.

By this point it should be clear that another major problem with remote regulation at a distance is that it steamrolls over synergies with sibling and cousin network infrastructures that should be evolving in parallel. The planners' approaches so far preserve the siloed regulation of infrastructure that prevails today (power, water, sewer, transportation). The expansion of 5G and air and land corridors invites huge possibilities for simultaneous infrastructure development like privately managed drone docking/recharge stations (such as on lampposts and church property) and other heavy-duty networking assets. But such symbiosis isn't happening that I can see.

The gaps and sub-optimality imposed by the threat of top-down, siloed IoT regulation are symptomatic of the myth that federal agencies offer expertise, let alone the myth of impartiality. Expertise in the modern IoT context necessarily consists of extending institutions of complex property rights and contract on land and in air and space. Bureaucrats, as well as the entire smart city concept, ignore that pretty much entirely in favor of the default public utility model as the backdrop and framework.

The concerns preoccupying IoT policy seem not to be the actual complex property rights problems needing resolution, but rather seem self-reinforcing of regulatory bureaucracy, even cronyism. The Internet of Things also needs to be the Internet of Thinks; that means not entrenching dumb, permanent market-socialist policy via misuse of remote regulation and pushbutton bureaucracy.

A main point of Jason Dorrier was that, while software updates typically add functionality, they can also take functionality away. While I might fantasize about pushing a button to ground Leonardo Decaprio's next high-carbon-footprint jet flight to a global warming confab, I'd better not.

But the same goes for bureaucrats when it comes to All Things IoT; they'd best not. We've a long way to go to get even the easy stuff right; take it from wing Cruz.

Print Citations

CMS: Crews, Clyde Wayne, Jr. "Helicopter Government? How the Internet of Things Enables Pushbutton Regulation from a Distance." In *The Reference Shelf: Internet Law,* edited by Annette Calzone, 133-138. Amenia, NY: Grey House Publishing, 2020.

MLA: Crews, Clyde Wayne, Jr. "Helicopter Government? How the Internet of Things Enables Pushbutton Regulation from a Distance." *The Reference Shelf: Internet Law,* edited by Annette Calzone, Grey House Publishing, 2020, pp. 133-138.

APA: Crews, C.W., Jr. (2020). Helicopter government? How the internet of things enables pushbutton regulation from a distance. In Annette Calzone (Ed.), *The reference shelf: Internet law* (pp. 133-138). Amenia, NY: Grey House Publishing.

Doublecheck That Ballot: Controversial Voting Machines Make Their Primary Debut in South Carolina

By Eric Geller
Politico, **February 28, 2020**

South Carolina's Democratic primary on Saturday won't just be a high-stakes contest to decide whether Joe Biden can hold the line against a surging Bernie Sanders. It will also be a huge, highly scrutinized test for a new breed of voting machines intended to offer safeguards against hacking and other digital threats.

But the machines have drawn a lot of doubts about whether they're up to the task.

The state is among 14 that have scrambled to replace their insecure, paperless voting equipment since the 2016 election, according to a *Politico* survey. Nationwide, 47 states and the District of Columbia rely at least partially on the kinds of devices South Carolina has adopted: touchscreen machines that produce paper ballots for every vote. But Saturday's primary in South Carolina, which spent $51 million last year to install roughly 13,500 voting machines, is the first statewide presidential election primary being run on these devices.

While the paper-based machines are supposed to make the vote more resistant to digital tampering, they also introduce new uncertainty into an election already marked by widespread warnings that Russia is determined to interfere in yet another U.S. presidential race. Many South Carolina voters and precinct workers will be encountering the new machines for the first time — less than four weeks after the Democrats' bungled Iowa caucus showed the pitfalls of introducing new technology into a high-stakes election.

The technology behind the ballot-printing touchscreen machines has also raised hackles among cyberresearchers, election security advocates and the National Academies of Sciences, Engineering and Medicine. They say the machines may be more secure than the totally paperless systems still used in 11 states—but they're not as safe as paper ballots that voters mark by hand.

Bothered by the Barcode

South Carolina lawmakers decided in June to buy a model called ExpressVote from the country's largest election technology company, Election Systems &

> **They say the machines may be more secure than the totally paperless systems still used in 11 states—but they're not as safe as paper ballots that voters mark by hand.**

Software. Counties in at least seven states—Florida, Indiana, Kansas, New Jersey, Pennsylvania, Tennessee and Texas—have also replaced their paperless machines with the ExpressVote since 2018, according to a *Politico* survey. Delaware bought another model from ES&S, called the ExpressVote XL, and Georgia has purchased similar machines from another manufacturer.

The ExpressVote is a so-called ballot-marking device, and its most prominent feature is a large touchscreen for voters to make selections. But unlike older electronic machines, this one produces a paper record at the end of the process showing which candidates the voter selected.

That slip of paper, which serves as the official ballot, also embeds those votes in a barcode that the state's tabulators will scan to tally the results on Saturday.

The problem, according to the security experts: The voting machines are still vulnerable to tampering that could cause them to print barcodes that don't match the voter's choices—for example, changing "Sanders" to "Biden" or vice versa. Voters, who can't read barcodes, would be unable to tell that such a change had occurred.

In a close election, a recount could uncover any tampering by verifying the official results against the text on the ballots. But a hacked machine could also change that text as well—and research shows that most voters do not doublecheck printouts from electronic voting machines. One University of Michigan study published in January found that participants missed more than 93 percent of errors on their printed ballots, although verification improved when poll workers prompted the voters to check the ballots' accuracy.

"Until [ballot-marking devices] are shown to be effectively verifiable during real-world use," the researchers wrote, "the safest course for security is to prefer hand-marked paper ballots."

"Everyone should be concerned about voters not verifying their BMD printouts," said Eddie Perez, the global director of technology development at the OSET Institute, which advocates for open-source election systems.

South Carolina election commission spokesperson Chris Whitmire disagreed that any danger exists, saying the state "works to educate voters on how to use the system." That training specifically emphasizes the importance of verification, he said.

"South Carolina's voting system is tested, certified and proven," Whitmire said.

Ballot-printing voting machines have also provoked controversy in states like Georgia—where the state pushed ahead with spending $150 million on the devices despite voluminous criticism from security experts—and Pennsylvania, where Philadelphia city election commissioners overrode objections from the state auditor general.

Overstated Worries?

Other experts expressed less concern about these relatively new machines, saying the ballot-printing touchscreens are probably not the most promising avenue for hackers looking to disrupt an election.

In terms of possible cyberattacks from nations like Russia, "malware implants on BMDs are much lower on the bang-for-the-buck list" than attacks on other links in the election security chain, said Dan Wallach, a computer science professor at Rice University. Those include the tabulating machines that count the votes, the websites that report them, states' voter registration databases and the laptops or tablets that precinct workers use to check-in voters at polling places.

"That said," he added, "the risk that malware somehow finds its way into these machines is a legitimate security threat."

But Whitmire noted that ExpressVote machines have already had trial runs in South Carolina, where some jurisdictions have used the devices in smaller elections, including an Oct. 1 special election for a state House district and roughly 200 mostly municipal elections on Nov. 5.

"We have not experienced any issues with the operation of the system, and we expect it to continue to perform as designed in all future elections," he said.

But voting security experts said those tiny test-runs don't prove much.

"That doesn't mean that [the machines] work perfectly," said Jeremy Epstein, vice chairman of the Association for Computing Machinery's U.S. Technology Policy Committee. "I disagree with those who insist on hand-marked paper, but it would be good to have additional testing to ensure that [BMDs] work correctly under a variety of circumstances."

Another Weak Spot: The Check-in Process

South Carolina's unusual system for checking in voters poses another potential problem.

While many states buy tablet computers preloaded with check-in software from the same vendor, South Carolina lets counties buy their own off-the-shelf laptops and provides them with its check-in software. (Counties also have backup paper voter lists in case the machines malfunction, something that occurred in some North Carolina polling places during the November 2016 election.)

A now-defunct South Carolina firm called TiBA Solutions created the software around 2006, Whitmire said, and a tech company called NWN Corp. later updated it. Both that company and the state government tested the program before deploying it, Whitmire said. He called it "a tested, tried and proven system."

To guard against hacking, the state requires counties to disable WiFi, Bluetooth and other network connections on the check-in laptops. Asked if the state oversees whether they comply, Whitmire said, "The laptops are owned and maintained by county election officials."

That arrangement worried some security experts.

"I cannot say I am happy with the idea that we are trusting the pollbooks to be disabled from connections," said Duncan Buell, a computer science professor and voting security expert at the University of South Carolina.

Security protocols will be "largely left to chance" without uniform enforcement, said Perez, who added that letting counties buy whatever laptops they wanted created the risk of "inconsistencies in configuration and performance."

The Results Are In—But Are They Right?

Another risk comes from the platform that South Carolina will use to report the results on election night, which is developed and managed by the Spanish technology company Scytl.

Tampering with this system wouldn't change the results themselves but could delay them and cause confusion—something 2020 already saw when the Democrats' process for reporting results collapsed in Iowa.

Scytl is also controversial in the election security community because of its advocacy for internet voting, which nearly all experts consider extremely unsafe and unwise. Researchers have identified multiple weaknessses in the online voting platform that Scytl developed for the Swiss government.

"Scytl has exhibited a pattern of overstating the capabilities of its security architecture," Perez said. "The fact that the company has attempted to position questionable online voting experiments as 'secure' ... leaves [me] skeptical of Scytl's security-centric engineering practices."

But South Carolina has used Scytl's results-reporting platform since 2008 and has experienced no problems, said Whitmire, who added that "hundreds of jurisdictions" in the U.S. and other countries use it.

Only two people at the state election commission can gain access to the system's administrative functions, while county employees must log in with two-factor authentication—which provides more security than mere passwords—before they can upload results data to it. The state trains county officials to use the platform before every statewide election.

Fortunately, disruptions in this late stage of the primary wouldn't be catastrophic, because counties preserve all their paper ballots until the results are certified.

"The good news is that reporting discrepancies can be corrected," said Wallach. "The bad news is that corrections might take a while and, if it's a tight race, we could always have more of the same confusion that we saw with the Iowa caucus results."

Print Citations

CMS: Geller, Eric. "Doublecheck That Ballot: Controversial Voting Machines Make Their Primary Debut in South Carolina." In *The Reference Shelf: Internet Law,* edited by Annette Calzone, 139-142. Amenia, NY: Grey House Publishing, 2020.

MLA: Geller, Eric. "Doublecheck That Ballot: Controversial Voting Machines Make Their Primary Debut in South Carolina." *The Reference Shelf: Internet Law,* edited by Annette Calzone, Grey House Publishing, 2020, pp. 139-142.

APA: Geller, E. (2020). Doublecheck that ballot: Controversial voting machines make their primary debut in South Carolina. In Annette Calzone (Ed.), *The reference shelf: Internet law* (pp. 139-142). Amenia, NY: Grey House Publishing.

Zoombombing and the Law

By Eugene Volokh
The Volokh Conspiracy, **April 7, 2020**

Friday, the top federal prosecutor in Detroit wrote, "You think Zoom bombing is funny? Let's see how funny it is after you get arrested. If you interfere with a teleconference or public meeting in Michigan, you could have federal, state, or local law enforcement knocking at your door." Is that so? Or, perhaps more usefully, when is that so?

Well, as with so many buzzwords, such as "trolling," "doxxing," "bullying," and the like, "Zoombombing" can cover many different things (as the vague word "interfere" suggests). Let's start by looking at what behavior might be covered by the term, and consider (as the law often does) the physical-world analogs of such behavior.

[1.] Hacking into closed, password-protected Zoom meetings. This is indeed likely a crime under the federal Computer Fraud and Abuse Act, which bars accessing computers "without authorization." Think of this as **cyber-breaking-and-entering**.

[2.] Accessing non-password-protected Zoom meetings to which the public wasn't invited. This could be a conversation among friends or coworkers, or a meeting between a business and its clients (or students and their professor). It may feel like a sort of **cyber-trespass**, but it's not clear when it would be a crime: Much depends on the particular state trespass laws involved, but I doubt that a court would be willing to read a typical state criminal trespass statute, written with the physical world in mind, as applying to unauthorized access to virtual spaces.

Computer crime laws are, of course, made with computer access in mind; but there too things aren't clear. Accessing publicly accessible computer-based *meetings* that are publicly accessible on the Internet, but that the operator doesn't want the public to access, is in some ways similar to accessing publicly accessible computer-based *web pages*. Federal courts have split on whether such access to web pages violates the CFAA (either in general or when the site operator announces that the scraping is forbidden). For more, see this post by our own Orin Kerr, likely the nation's leading CFAA expert.

It's also possible that some state computer crimes laws might apply here, at least if the Zoombomber has reason to know which state the meeting organizer is located in. (For a sense of how courts deal with claims that state laws can't apply to the

Internet, see this Mary-
land upholding a state
anti-spam law, which also
discusses other cases that
have struck down state
anti-pornography laws;
and see also this more
recent case.) But a lot de-

> **Content-neutral laws that bar people from accessing others' property are thus generally constitutional, even when someone wants to violate them in order to speak.**

pends on the text of the particular state computer crime law, and any precedents
interpreting it; so while Zoombombing of this sort could be outlawed, it's not clear
whether it is.

[3.] **Accessing Zoom meetings to which the public was invited, and display-
ing offensive materials,** for instance in the video feed that's coming from your
computer. This is like showing up at a publicly accessible talk wearing offensive
messages on your T-shirt, or carrying offensive signs. I doubt that this would generally be a crime, though you could get kicked out of the meeting for that. Likewise, if
the meeting opens up its chat function, I think that posting offensive content in the
chat isn't likely a crime. (Same if it opens up its share screen function, though wise
meeting organizers generally won't do that.)

[4.] **Accessing Zoom meetings to which the public was invited, and saying
offensive things using your audio,** thus making it harder for the speakers' audio
to be heard. That's the equivalent of **cyber-heckling**, and might in principle be
punishable by state laws banning disrupting a lawful assembly (see, e.g., here and
here). I think such laws might be applicable to online speech, though the boundaries of the law themselves are complicated and not entirely clear. But note that
these laws, to the extent they are constitutional, are constitutional because they are
content-neutral—because they target conduct based on its disruptive noise, and
don't target messages based on their offensive content.

[5.] **Accessing Zoom meetings of any sort, and posting true threats of
violence or other crime.** Such threats are punishable whatever the medium—
phone, fax, text message, Zoom, or whatever else. The same is true for speech that is
criminalized via some of the narrow First Amendment exceptions, such as obscenity
(hard-core pornography) or child pornography.

It's also conceivable that the threshold for finding pornography to be obscene
and thus constitutionally unprotected would be lower if it's communicated to unwilling viewers. But to fit within the obscenity exception, the material would still
have to be pornographic and not merely violent, racist, or otherwise offensive to
some people.

What about the First Amendment? Generally speaking, you don't have a First
Amendment right to speak on others' property, if they want to exclude you—and
you certainly don't have a First Amendment right to speak in ways that physically

interrupts others' speech, or changes the tenor of a conversation that others are choreographing. Content-neutral laws that bar people from accessing others' property are thus generally constitutional, even when someone wants to violate them in order to speak.

But:

[1.] The laws involved must indeed be content-neutral, and applied in a content-neutral way (again, except to the extent they involve unprotected speech, such as true threats). Thus, if people hack into a meeting to say racist things, they can be punished for the hacking, but not for the content of their message.

Hate crimes laws can ban violence or vandalism that targets victims because of the victims' race, religion, and the like: They are constitutional precisely because they ban such nonspeech conduct, rather than mere speech. Hate crimes law thus can't punish, say, showing up to a publicly accessible Zoom meeting wearing a T-shirt with a racist message. And while hate crimes laws could in principle ban trespass or hacking motivated by the target's race, religion, and such, federal hate crimes laws don't extend to that (and, to my knowledge, most state hate crimes laws don't, either).

[2.] If the Zoom meeting is organized by the government, the government may not exclude listeners based on the viewpoint expressed on their video feeds, or even the viewpoint of their heckling. Say, for instance, a public university organizes an event, and invites the public (or even just students). It can't then exclude attendees because of the offensive political messages on their T-shirts; likewise, it can't exclude them because of the offensive political messages on their video feeds.

And while the university could have a policy of imposing discipline on all students who heckle speakers (or even having such students prosecuted), it can't discipline hecklers who shout racist messages but not hecklers who shout, say, anti-Trump messages. The same, I think, would be true of Zoom-heckling.

Note, though, that this involves decisions by the public university itself, or a public university department, or other government bodies. A public university professor who organizes his own Zoom meeting can pick and choose what attendees to invite and which ones to exclude, since he's not using his government powers (cf. *Naffe v. Frey* (9th Cir. 2015) for more on the state action requirement generally).

This, by the way, highlights the value of public universities and other public government entities have clear policies forbidding heckling, whether on Zoom or in person: If the university allows people to heckle expressing some viewpoints, it can't then punish them or have them prosecuted for heckling expressing other viewpoints.

But let's get real: I've offered a quick, high-level glance at the law in theory. But in practice, you're usually going to have a hard time getting a prosecutor to do anything about most of these problems, except perhaps some kinds of hacking. Federal prosecutors tend to focus on big-ticket items; even many criminal frauds are seen as too small potatoes for them.

State prosecutors may have lower prosecution thresholds, but they may be reluctant to get involved in cases where the offender may be in another state or otherwise hard to get at: Even if they technically have jurisdiction over the offense (because the defendant knew or should have known that he was, say, interrupting a meeting that was organized by someone in that state), the investigation could be a huge hassle, especially if it requires extradition and extensive cooperation with prosecutors in other jurisdictions. And imagine if the defendant is in a foreign country; it would take a lot to get prosecutors willing to deal with that.

The solution, it seems to me, is generally **technologically enabled self-protection**—features such as muting, passwords, and waiting rooms provided by the videoconferencing systems. These features make it possible to block outsiders altogether, or at least to eject someone who is misbehaving and then keep them from rejoining.

As with much on the Internet, Zoombombing may cause more problems than, say, in-person heckling, because it's **easier, cheaper, and in some ways less risky for the bad guys**. (Compare, for instance, the relationship between spamming and traditional junk mail.) But it's also **easier, cheaper, and less risky for the good guys** to fight it: Ejecting a Zoom-heckler is annoying, but much less annoying than trying to deal with a real person (or a mob) who might physically resist such ejection.

These technological self-protection features aren't a perfect solution; like all security features, they create something of a hassle, and at times a bit of an arms race (for instance, if you eject a Zoom-heckler from a deliberately publicly accessible meeting, and he then tries to get back on, perhaps using a different user id). But relying on prosecutors is an even less perfect solution. And the technological self-protection features are likely to quickly get better over time, especially given competition between software providers. Prosecutor responsiveness isn't likely to quickly get better.

Print Citations

CMS: Volokh, Eugene. "Zoombombing and the Law." In *The Reference Shelf: Internet Law,* edited by Annette Calzone, 144-147. Amenia, NY: Grey House Publishing, 2020.

MLA: Volokh, Eugene. "Zoombombing and the Law." *The Reference Shelf: Internet Law,* edited by Annette Calzone, Grey House Publishing, 2020, pp. 144-147.

APA: Volokh, E. (2020). Zoombombing and the law. In Annette Calzone (Ed.), *The reference shelf: Internet law* (pp. 144-147). Amenia, NY: Grey House Publishing.

5
Digital Nationalism and the Splinternet

By Hamed Saber, via Wikimedia.

The anti-aircraft missiles guarding the Natanz nuclear facility in Iran were unable to defend Iran's nuclear program from Stuxnet, a malicious worm jointly created by U.S. and Israeli intelligence agencies that extended beyond digital damage and caused centrifuges to malfunction.

From Unity to Division

Despite the visionary optimism that characterized much of its early days, the Internet has not proven to be a free, unregulated, globally unifying "space" of its own. State-sponsored cyberwarfare and ever-increasing censorship and surveillance have divided citizens from their own governments and nation-states from one another. Will one country or a bloc of countries largely control the existing Internet? Or will it ultimately divide into three or more separate networks? Will the division be based on political philosophy? Where does 5G fit into all this? The influence that the Internet now has in the realm of daily and political life give it the potential to drastically alter our lives, for better or for worse.

Digital Warfare

Although longstanding fears of nation-states attacking entire infrastructures and bringing whole countries to a standstill have not materialized, smaller-scale attacks have still had devastating consequences. Intellectual property theft by China, covert influence campaigns like Russian interference in the 2016 presidential election, and hacking into banks, have eroded trust in the Internet. Former U.S. Under Secretary of Defense for Policy Michèle Flournoy and former Belfer Center cyber project director Michael Sulmeyer warn of U.S. vulnerability in a recent *Foreign Affairs* article: "For the U.S. military, this represents a particularly acute risk. It is so reliant on the Internet that an attack on its command-and-control, supply, or communications networks could undermine its ability to project power overseas and leave forces disconnected and vulnerable."[1] They go on to recommend the formation of a cabinet-level agency subject to congressional oversight, similar to the United Kingdom's National Cyber Security Centre. This agency would be tasked with not only protecting the government from cyberattacks but also U.S. citizens. It would partner with private tech firms and work with state and local authorities to improve security.

They are not alone in this recommendation. National Security Administration (NSA) advisory board member Ted Schlein argues that such an agency would provide organization, authority to act, and capability. Schlein notes in a *Wall Street Journal* article: "This is not an area where being second best will suffice, where being good but not great will win, and where turf wars can be allowed to rule the day. To be safe, the U.S. must be the greatest superpower on Earth in cyberspace, and to do that we need to gather our cyber assets into one cabinet-level agency." In the same article, former U.S. Department of Homeland Security Under Secretary Suzanne Spaulding counters that a new agency would do more harm than good by disrupting cybersecurity in existing departments or replicating existing activities and expertise, significantly increasing costs and private-sector confusion. Spaulding notes that the only way to improve security is "to continue the hard work of clarifying roles, harmonizing guidance and regulations, and coordinating activity among various agencies. We need strong White House leadership in that coordination and in the development of a national strategy that deters adversaries, builds resilience in the wake of cyberattacks, and includes the expertise of the private sector."[2]

The Electronic Frontier Foundation (EFF), in an open letter to the Obama administration, weighed in by stressing transparency and public accountability in whatever manner the U.S. government chooses to pursue enhanced cybersecurity: "The task of improving security will require sustained and detailed commitment across many entities and over many years. This task cannot be done well—and with proper attention to the government's duty to secure privacy and civil liberties while it secures the information infrastructure—if it is driven by events and a crisis mentality. The rhetoric of crisis and urgency can lead to intemperate, overreaching actions. Thus, we emphasize institutional processes over any specific technical actions. And these institutional processes must be transparent and accountable."[3]

In the opinion of Ben & Jerry's Ice Cream cofounder Ben Cohen, "It's not enough for the United States to spend more than half of our country's discretionary budget each year on endless war. Now we're told that we must spend trillions more, sacrifice our privacy and essentially nationalize Google. All in the name of national security. . . . It is a tragic waste of money. But more than that, it is a fool's errand. It's an arms race in which the whole world loses. Including us. . . . We cannot buy our way to security with weapons and counter-weapons and counter-counter-weapons. The only way we will achieve security is through cooperation and mutual aid. Deride me as a hippie peace and love child."[4]

The Effect of 5G

Countries are beginning to invest seriously in 5G, a technology that will transform the Internet. Though it may seem like not being tethered to a wire would result in more freedom, in fact for any device—phones, self-driving cars, pacemakers—to work, they must be within a certain range of the rest of the system, making the Internet in fact more grounded by its infrastructure than it ever was. The surveillance and security implications are significant, and it remains to be seen whether governments or corporations will exert the most control over 5G technology. Large multinational tech firms like Amazon's AWS, Google Cloud, Microsoft Azure, and Alibaba currently own the most data centers, and are aiming to continue building networks that are scalable across borders. But in 2019 France and Germany announced plans to build a "European cloud" that would give preference to local companies over the multinationals, although this network would not have the same computing capability. Another issue is that the cloud does not currently operate seamlessly among the major multinationals, in effect requiring "corporate visas" to cross "corporate borders." As journalist Scott Malcolmson points out in a recent *Foreign Affairs* article, "This amounts to a redistribution of sovereignty from state to corporation so far-reaching that states will push back—as indeed they already are. The techlash is not a blip. What the Trump administration is doing to Huawei, and

China once did to Google, is what the EU might do to AWS. Silicon Valley's 'tomorrow belongs to us' period is ending."[5]

The End of the World as We Know It

A 2018 article by the editorial board of the *New York Times* raises the possibility of three internets—China, the United States, and Europe. All three are creating differing sets of rules and norms, in addition to the problem of data being confined to national data centers. The monopoly of larger tech firms, particularly in regard to infrastructure, also plays a role. If a company with a large market share chooses to comply with a law, smaller companies often have no choice but to do the same. The article notes:

> The power of a handful of platforms and services combined with the dismal state of international cooperation across the world pushes us closer and closer to a splintered internet. . . . Yet even the best possible version of the disaggregated web has serious—though still uncertain—implications for a global future: What sorts of ideas and speech will become bounded by borders? What will an increasingly disconnected world do to the spread of innovation and to scientific progress? What will consumer protections around privacy and security look like as the internets diverge? And would the partitioning of the internet precipitate a slowing, or even a reversal, of globalization?[6]

China's Great Firewall—which restricts its citizens' access to content not approved by the state—served as an early example of what it called "digital sovereignty." Its relative success has led to Iran's "halal net," North Korea's Kwangmyong network, and possibly a future Russian Runet. Many totalitarian states have a "kill switch" which allows them to shut down the global network, a trend that has been increasing. A less intrusive form of digital sovereignty are data localization requirements, which stipulate that data from a country's citizens must be physically stored within that country. Though motivated by legitimate privacy concerns, this can also be used to repress dissidents. Content is already restricted by certain countries, and recent regulations in Europe mandating fines for hate speech have had the effect, at least initially, of some companies deciding to withhold content. Brazil once thought of building an undersea cable link to the EU in response to Edward Snowden's revelations of U.S. surveillance under the Patriot Act, effectively nationalizing infrastructure. The inherent risk of these measures is the possible breakup of the Internet—often referred to as the "splinternet." As New York University GovLab senior fellow Akash Kapur explains in the *Wall Street Journal*, "In the old vision [of the internet], nation-states were the enemy of innovation and freedom. Those were the Wild West days, and it is understandable that internet purists—and many average users—are nostalgic for them. But things have changed a lot. . . . Amid the creeping nationalism and illiberalism of today, we may no longer have the luxury of rejecting governance and governments. Fifty years after the birth of the internet, it may well be that national governments, wielding enlightened regulation, are the last best hope for maintaining a network that is—at least relatively—open and free."[7]

Works Used

Cohen, Ben, and Ray Rothrock. "On Cybersecurity: Two Scoops of Perspective." *The New York Times*. Sept. 29, 2019. https://www.nytimes.com/2019/09/29/opinion/letters/cybersecurity.html.

"Does the U.S. Need a Cabinet-Level Department of Cybersecurity?" *The Wall Street Journal*. June 3, 2019. https://www.wsj.com/articles/does-the-u-s-need-a-cabinet-level-department-of-cybersecurity-11559586996.

Flournoy, Michèle, and Michael Sulmeyer. "Battlefield Internet: A Plan for Securing Cyberspace." *Foreign Affairs*. September/October 2018. https://www.foreignaffairs.com/articles/world/2018-08-14/battlefield-internet.

Kapur, Akash. "The Rising Threat of Digital Nationalism." *The Wall Street Journal*. Nov. 1, 2019. https://www.wsj.com/articles/the-rising-threat-of-digital-nationalism-11572620577.

Malcolmson, Scott. "The Real Fight for the Future of 5G." *Foreign Affairs*. Nov. 14, 2019. https://www.foreignaffairs.com/articles/2019-11-14/real-fight-future-5g.

Tien, Lee, and Peter Eckersley. "Open Letter to the Whitehouse Cyber Security Review Team." *Electronic Frontier Foundation*. https://obamawhitehouse.archives.gov/files/documents/cyber/Electronic%20Frontier%20Foundation%20-%20To%20the%20White%20House%20Cyber%20Security%20Review%20Team.pdf.

"There May Soon Be Three Internets: America's Won't Necessarily Be the Bets." Editorial Board. *The New York Times*. Oct. 15, 2018. https://www.nytimes.com/2018/10/15/opinion/internet-google-china-balkanization.html.

Notes

1. Flournoy and Sulmeyer, "Battlefield Internet: A Plan for Securing Cyberspace."
2. "Does the U.S. Need a Cabinet-Level Department of Cybersecurity? *The Wall Street Journal*.
3. Tien and Eckersley, "Open Letter to the White House Cyber Security Review Team."
4. Cohen and Rothrock, "On Cybersecurity: Two Scoops of Perspective."
5. Malcolmson, "The Real Fight for the Future of 5G."
6. "There May Soon Be Three Internets: America's Won't Necessarily Be the Best," The *New York Times*.
7. Kapur, "The Rising Threat of Digital Nationalism."

Society's Dependence on the Internet: 5 Cyber Issues the Coronavirus Lays Bare

By Laura DeNardis and Jennifer Daskal
The Conversation, March, 27, 2020

As more and more U.S. schools and businesses shutter their doors, the rapidly evolving coronavirus pandemic is helping to expose society's dependence—good and bad—on the digital world.

Entire swaths of society, including classes we teach at American University, have moved online until the coast is clear. As vast segments of society are temporarily forced into isolation to achieve social distancing, the internet is their window into the world. Online social events like virtual happy hours foster a sense of connectedness amid social distancing. While the online world is often portrayed as a societal ill, this pandemic is a reminder of how much the digital world has to offer.

The pandemic also lays bare the many vulnerabilities created by society's dependence on the internet. These include the dangerous consequences of censorship, the constantly morphing spread of disinformation, supply chain vulnerabilities and the risks of weak cybersecurity.

1. China's censorship affects us all.

The global pandemic reminds us that even local censorship can have global ramifications. China's early suppression of coronavirus information likely contributed to what is now a worldwide pandemic. Had the doctor in Wuhan who spotted the outbreak been able to speak freely, public health authorities might have been able to do more to contain it early.

China is not alone. Much of the world lives in countries that impose controls on what can and cannot be said about their governments online. Such censorship is not just a free speech issue, but a public health issue as well. Technologies that circumvent censorship are increasingly a matter of life and death.

2. Disinformation online isn't just speech—it's also a matter of health and safety.

During a public health emergency, sharing accurate information rapidly is critical. Social media can be an effective tool for doing just that. But it's also a source of disinformation and manipulation in ways that can threaten global health and personal safety—something tech companies are desperately, yet imperfectly, trying to combat.

Facebook, for example, has banned ads selling face masks or promising false preventions or cures, while giving the World Health Organization unlimited ad space. Twitter is placing links to the Centers for Disease Control and Prevention and other reliable information sources atop search returns. Meanwhile, Russia and others reportedly are

> **Others are using the coronavirus to spread racist vitriol, in ways that put individuals at risk.**

spreading rumors about the coronavirus's origins. Others are using the coronavirus to spread racist vitriol, in ways that put individuals at risk.

Not only does COVID-19 warn us of the costs—and geopolitics—of disinformation, it highlights the roles and responsibilities of the private sector in confronting these risks. Figuring out how to do so effectively, without suppressing legitimate critics, is one of the greatest challenges for the next decade.

3. Cyber resiliency and security matter more than ever.

Our university has moved our work online. We are holding meetings by video chat and conducting virtual courses. While many don't have this luxury, including those on the front lines of health and public safety or newly unemployed, thousands of other universities, businesses and other institutions also moved online—a testament to the benefits of technological innovation.

At the same time, these moves remind us of the importance of strong encryption, reliable networks and effective cyber defenses. Today network outages are not just about losing access to Netflix but about losing livelihoods. Cyber insecurity is also a threat to public health, such as when ransomware attacks disrupt entire medical facilities.

4. Smart technologies as a lifeline.

The virus also exposes the promise and risks of the "internet of things," the globe-spanning web of always-on, always-connected cameras, thermostats, alarm systems and other physical objects. Smart thermometers, blood pressure monitors and other medical devices are increasingly connected to the web. This makes it easier for people with pre-existing conditions to manage their health at home, rather than having to seek treatment in a medical facility where they are at much greater risk of exposure to the disease.

Yet this reliance on the internet of things carries risks. Insecure smart devices can be co-opted to disrupt democracy and society, such as when the Mirai botnet hijacked home appliances to disrupt critical news and information sites in the fall of 2016. When digitally interconnected devices are attacked, their benefits suddenly disappear—adding to the sense of crisis and sending those dependent on connected home diagnostic tools into already overcrowded hospitals.

5. Tech supply chain is a point of vulnerability.

The shutdown of Chinese factories in the wake of the pandemic interrupted the supply of critical parts to many industries, including the U.S. tech sector. Even Apple had to temporarily halt production of the iPhone. Had China not begun to recover, the toll on the global economy could have been even greater than it is now.

This interdependence of our supply chain is neither new nor tech-specific. Manufacturing—medical and otherwise—has long depended on parts from all over the world. The crisis serves as a reminder of the global, complex interactions of the many companies that produce gadgets, phones, computers and many other products on which the economy and society as a whole depend. Even if the virus had never traveled outside of China, the effects would have reverberated—highlighting ways in which even local crises have global ramifications.

Cyber Policy in Everything

As the next phase of the pandemic response unfolds, society will be grappling with more and more difficult questions. Among the many challenges are complex choices about how to curb the spread of the disease while preserving core freedoms. How much tracking and surveillance are people willing to accept as a means of protecting public health?

As Laura explains in *The Internet in Everything* cyber policy is now entangled with everything, including health, the environment and consumer safety. Choices that we make now, about cybersecurity, speech online, encryption policies and product design will have dramatic ramifications for health, security and basic human flourishing.

Print Citations

CMS: DeNardis, Laura, and Jennifer Daskal. "Society's Dependence on the Internet: 5 Cyber Issues the Coronavirus Lays Bare." In *The Reference Shelf: Internet Law,* edited by Annette Calzone, 155-157. Amenia, NY: Grey House Publishing, 2020.

MLA: DeNardis, Laura, and Jennifer Daskal. "Society's Dependence on the Internet: 5 Cyber Issues the Coronavirus Lays Bare." *The Reference Shelf: Internet Law,* edited by Annette Calzone, Grey House Publishing, 2020, pp. 155-157.

APA: DeNardis, L., & Daskal, J. (2020). Society's dependence on the internet: 5 cyber issues the coronavirus lays bare. In Annette Calzone (Ed.), *The reference shelf: Internet law* (pp. 155-157). Amenia, NY: Grey House Publishing.

Battlefield Internet: A Plan for Securing Cyberspace

By Michèle Flournoy and Michael Sulmeyer
Foreign Affairs, September/October 2018

Cyberspace has been recognized as a new arena for competition among states ever since it came into existence. In the United States, there have long been warnings of a "cyber–Pearl Harbor"—a massive digital attack that could cripple the country's critical infrastructure without a single shot being fired. Presidential commissions, military task force reports, and congressional investigations have been calling attention to such a risk for decades. In 1984, the Reagan administration warned of the "significant security challenges" of the coming information age. And just this year, Dan Coats, the director of national intelligence, said of such threats, "the lights are blinking red."

Yet the Internet has always been much more than a venue for conflict and competition; it is the backbone of global commerce and communication. That said, cyberspace is not, as is often thought, simply part of the global commons in the way that the air or the sea is. States assert jurisdiction over, and companies claim ownership of, the physical infrastructure that composes the Internet and the data that traverses it. States and companies built the Internet, and both are responsible for maintaining it. Actions taken in the public sector affect the private sector, and vice versa. In this way, the Internet has always been hybrid in nature.

So, accordingly, is the real cyberwar threat. It turns out that for all the increasingly vehement warnings about a cyber–Pearl Harbor, states have shown little appetite for using cyberattacks for large-scale destruction. The immediate threat is more corrosive than explosive. States are using the tools of cyberwarfare to undermine the very foundation of the Internet: trust. They are hacking into banks, meddling in elections, stealing intellectual property, and bringing private companies to a standstill. The result is that an arena that the world relies on for economic and informational exchange has turned into an active battlefield.

To reverse this development, the United States and its allies will have to recognize what China, Iran, North Korea, and Russia already have: that state sovereignty is alive and well on the Internet. Washington must accept that the only way to restore trust is to hold those who abuse it accountable, both at home and abroad. It is time, then, for the United States to reassert leadership on the global stage and take greater responsibility for protecting the country's communities, businesses, and government from digital threats. Leaving the market alone, as some have called for, will not do. What's required is an inclusive, government-led approach that protects the public in an increasingly dangerous era.

The New, New Threat

Cyber-operations are emblematic of a new style of competition in a world where less power is concentrated in the hands of a single superpower. They are deniable and scalable, and suitable for war, peace, and much in between. In operation after operation, many of them hardly registered by the wider world, states are weaponizing the Internet.

As Russia's attempts to meddle in the 2016 U.S. presidential election showed, it is now possible to undertake cyber-operations in support of a sophisticated campaign of covert influence. In a textbook information-warfare operation, Moscow hacked into e-mail accounts belonging to the Democratic National Committee and one of Hillary Clinton's top aides, not only to collect intelligence but also to find embarrassing information to publicize. The hackers shared their trove of stolen e-mails with WikiLeaks, which released them to the public, driving negative media coverage of the Democratic candidate in the run-up to voting day. In the months before the election, Russian companies linked to the Kremlin also went on an ad-buying spree on Facebook and created an army of Twitter accounts backing Donald Trump, the Republican nominee. The Internet gave Russia's security services the unprecedented ability to reach millions of American voters with propaganda.

Nations have also taken advantage of the Internet to launch asymmetric attacks when more traditional strategies were unavailable or unwise. Perhaps the best example of this type of operation occurred in 2014, when North Korea hacked into Sony Pictures' network, destroyed its servers, and leaked confidential information in retaliation for the release of The Interview, a comedy depicting the assassination of North Korea's leader, Kim Jong Un. For months, Sony Pictures had to operate by pen and paper as it rebuilt a functioning IT system. In a 2016 heist linked to North Korea, hackers managed to withdraw tens of millions of dollars from Bangladesh's central bank, thus undermining the international campaign to isolate North Korea from the global economy.

In a similar vein, China is also engaging in Internet-enabled theft for economic advantage. For at least a decade, the country has stolen the intellectual property of countless foreign firms to gain the upper hand in economic negotiations and compensate for its lack of homegrown innovation. According to a 2017 report by the Commission on the Theft of American Intellectual Property, U.S. losses from intellectual property theft range from $225 billion to $600 billion per year, much of which can be blamed on China.

All these incidents occurred in a gray zone of conflict—below the threshold of outright war but above that of purely peacetime behavior. But states are increasingly drawing on cyber-capabilities during traditional military operations, too. During the 1999 NATO bombing of Yugoslavia, as the journalist Fred Kaplan has reported, a Pentagon unit hacked into Serbia's air defense systems to make it appear as if U.S.

planes were coming from a different direction than they really were. Many of the details remain classified, but U.S. officials have admitted that the Pentagon has also used cyberattacks in the fight against the Islamic State (or ISIS). In 2016, Robert Work,

> **The United States and its allies will have to recognize what China, Iran, North Korea, and Russia already have: that state sovereignty is alive and well on the Internet.**

then the U.S. deputy secretary of defense, admitted that the United States was dropping "cyberbombs" on ISIS (although he did not elaborate on what that entailed). In at least one instance, such attacks forced ISIS fighters to abandon a primary command post and flee toward other outposts, thereby revealing their location.

Of course, it's not just the United States that is using such tactics. During its invasion of Georgia in 2008, Russia employed denial-of-service attacks to silence Georgian television stations ahead of tank incursions to create panic. Almost certainly, Russia was also behind the 2015 hack of Ukraine's electrical grid, which interrupted the power supply for some 225,000 customers. Now, dozens of militaries have established or are establishing cyber commands and are incorporating cyber-operations into official doctrine.

Tomorrow's Attack

Military strategists have focused much of their attention on how online operations could affect combat outside cyberspace. In theory, at least—with no track record in a major war, it is too soon to tell for sure—cybertools give a military the ability to overcome physical distance, generate disruptive effects that can be turned off at a moment's notice, and reduce collateral damage relative to even the most sophisticated conventional ordnance.

For the U.S. military, this represents a particularly acute risk. It is so reliant on the Internet that an attack on its command-and-control, supply, or communications networks could undermine its ability to project power overseas and leave forces disconnected and vulnerable. As William Lynn, then the U.S. deputy secretary of defense, revealed in this magazine, the Pentagon fell victim to a hacking attack undertaken by a foreign intelligence agency in 2008. The malware was eventually quarantined, but not before it made its way into classified military networks. A 2014 congressional investigation of the Pentagon's Transportation Command revealed something else that many had long feared: U.S. adversaries were exploring how to threaten not just its important military networks but also its ability to move forces and materiel.

But given the unique nature of the online battlefield, the relevance of this trend extends beyond military operations, since civilians will likely suffer major collateral damage from attacks directed at governments. Imagine, for instance, that a cyber-attack were launched against parts of the U.S. electrical grid in an attempt to cut off power to military bases. The malware used could spread beyond the intended targets to interrupt the power supply to the surrounding civilian population, making hospitals go dark, shutting down heating or cooling systems, and disrupting the supply chains for basic goods. This scenario is not so remote: in 2017, malware that was spread through a Ukrainian tax preparation software program (an attack presumably launched by Russia and intended to compromise Ukrainian companies) ended up catching Western firms in the crossfire. The Danish shipping conglomerate Maersk estimated its costs from the attack at between $200 million and $300 million.

In that case, many of the private companies affected were inadvertent victims, but in the future, states may increasingly threaten nonmilitary targets deliberately. Despite international law's prohibition against targeting civilians on the battlefield, states are already doing so online. The bulk of Estonian society was knocked offline in a 2007 attack carried out by patriotic hackers tied to Russia, and South Korean banks and their customers were the target of a cyberattack in 2013, no doubt launched by North Korea.

The first task is to go beyond merely naming and shaming hackers and their government backers and to set forth clear consequences for cyberattacks.

To date, no one has produced evidence that anyone has ever died from a cyberattack, but that may change as more and more infrastructure that was once isolated, such as electrical grids and hospitals, goes online. Cars are connecting to WiFi and Bluetooth, and the Internet of Things is already penetrating the most private spaces of people's homes. Some technologists are even promoting an "Internet of Bodies," which envisions networked implants. All these devices are, or will soon be, targets.

These threats to the stable operation of the Internet mean that the trust that everyone places in it will erode even further, and people and governments may seek to wall themselves off. Many have tried "air-gapping" important systems—that is, physically isolating secure networks from the Internet—but the method is not foolproof. Air-gapped systems still need to receive outside software updates, and computer scientists have even shown that it is possible to "jump" the gap by way of acoustic resonance or radio frequencies. Some states have acted on the same impulse at the national level, trying to create their own separate internets, with mixed results. China's Great Firewall is designed to limit what people can read online, but clever citizens can evade it. The same is true in Iran, where authorities have set up a restrictive "halal net."

Flawed Fixes

The many gaping vulnerabilities in cyberspace have long been obvious to governments and companies, but they have consistently failed to patch the holes. For decades, information sharing has been the clarion call, the idea being that the sooner potential victims are tipped off about impending threats and the sooner actual victims reveal how they have been compromised, the better defended the entire system will be. In practice, however, information sharing has taken hold only in certain sectors—in the United States, mostly among financial institutions and between defense contractors and the military. And these are exceptions: government and corporate cultures still disincentivize acknowledging a breach, which makes it more likely that others will remain vulnerable to attack.

In addition, companies have often resisted investing fully in cybersecurity, believing it cheaper to clean up a mess than to prevent it in the first place. But this hack-by-hack approach has resulted in devastating losses in the aggregate. Beyond the billions of dollars in intellectual property stolen from companies every year, there is also damage inflicted by the pilfering of defense secrets from military contractors and by the deep reconnaissance that adversaries have undertaken to understand critical infrastructure such as water and power systems—intrusions that have dealt the United States a strategic blow.

At the international level, Washington and over a dozen other governments have sought to fashion "rules of the road," norms for conduct in cyberspace during peacetime. Both the G-7 and the G-20, for example, have issued joint statements committing their members to good behavior online. But despite the little consensus these efforts have reached, malicious conduct has continued unabated. These endeavors fall far short of what is really needed: a concerted diplomatic push to build a substantial coalition of like-minded states willing not just to sign on to these norms but also to impose serious economic and political costs on those who violate them.

Another effort has centered on public-private partnerships, through which government and industry can work together to secure the Internet and promote better behavior online. Building such partnerships is essential, but it is also difficult, as the two sides often have competing interests. For example, the U.S. government has pressed Facebook, Twitter, and YouTube to remove terrorist-related content and "fake news" from their sites, yet in complying, these companies have found themselves uncomfortable with acting as arbiters of good and bad content. What's more, the technology sector is not a monolith: Apple, Facebook, Google, and Twitter have very different business models and approaches to such issues as data privacy and data sharing. Despite this complexity, the U.S. government cannot meaningfully enhance the nation's cybersecurity by itself; it must work with the private sector.

What Now?

What is needed most is leadership from the United States, which should work with governments that share its commitment to privacy, freedom, and stability in cyberspace. The first task is to go beyond merely naming and shaming hackers and their government backers and to set forth clear consequences for cyberattacks. For starters, the United States could assert that as a matter of policy, any cyberattacks that result in civilian harm will be treated as equivalent to comparable physical attacks and will be met with equally serious consequences. The perils of such redlines are no secret: too specific, and the adversary will press right up against the line; too vague, and the opponent will be left unsure about what conduct will trigger a response. Multiple administrations, both Democratic and Republican, have struggled with this challenge, and the specific message will undoubtedly evolve, but it is long past time for the United States to lead its allies in responding to online aggression more seriously. An obvious and long-overdue first step would be for the Trump administration to warn Russia against meddling in future U.S. elections and to spell out in no uncertain terms the consequences it could expect if it does so.

Since public declarations alone are unlikely to deter all nations from conducting cyberattacks, the United States must back up its threats by imposing real costs on perpetrators. That means not only developing offensive options, such as retaliatory cyberattacks, but also drawing on a broad array of national tools. For too long, officials have been unwilling to upset areas of policy that do not directly involve the Internet when responding to cyberattacks, but there is no reason the United States cannot punish an aggressor through, say, increased economic sanctions, tariffs, diplomatic isolation, or military pressure. Deterrence will not be established overnight, but demonstrating credibility through consequences will bolster it over time.

In the meantime, the United States needs to break through the conceptual block of looking at its own cyber-capabilities primarily as instruments of foreign surveillance. It can also use them judiciously to degrade its adversaries' ability to perpetrate cyberattacks by hacking foreign hackers before they hack U.S. targets. The U.S. military and the FBI should proactively thwart imminent attacks, and Washington should work more aggressively with its partners abroad to form mutual cyberdefense pacts, in which countries pledge to come to one another's aid in the event of a serious attack.

At home, the U.S. government needs to fundamentally rethink its approach to cyberdefense. Historically, the government has seen itself as responsible for protecting only government systems and has left everyone else to fend for themselves. That must change. Just as the federal government takes responsibility for protecting Americans from physical attacks, so must it protect them from digital ones. The United States can look to its close ally for inspiration: in 2016, the United Kingdom set up the National Cyber Security Centre, which is designed to protect both government and society from cyberattacks. The United States should set up something similar: a new cyberdefense agency whose purpose would be not to share information or build criminal cases but to help agencies, companies, and communities prevent attacks. One of its top priorities would have to be bolstering the resilience of the United States' most critical systems—its electrical grid and emergency services chief among them. It could also work with state and local authorities to help them improve election security.

To be successful, this new organization would have to be an independent, cabinet-level agency, insulated from politics while subject to congressional oversight. Creating such an agency would require some painful reorganization within the executive branch and Congress, but continuing to rely on an outdated structure to achieve an ever-expanding set of cybersecurity objectives all but guarantees failure. It is not enough to merely raise the profile of cybersecurity within the Department of Homeland Security, as some have proposed, given how many competing priorities there are within that department. Creating a stand-alone agency would also enable that agency to change the culture of cybersecurity within the government, blending the spirit of innovation from the private sector with the responsibility of security from the government.

For the government to be an effective player in this space, it will have to do far more than reorganize: it will have to invest more in the appropriate human capital. To that end, it should create a program modeled on the Reserve Officer Training Corps, or ROTC, but for civilians interested in cyberdefense. Participating students would have their college or graduate school tuition paid for in exchange for a set number of years of government service. Washington should also create more opportunities for midcareer experts from technology hubs such as Silicon Valley to do a tour of service in the federal government. Not every computer engineer will want to contribute to national cyberdefense, of course, but the success of the U.S. Digital Service, a program created after the failure of HealthCare.gov that brings private-sector talent into the government, shows how much is possible.

The final challenge is to promote greater accountability in the technology sector for the products and services its companies put into the market. Just as the federal government regulates prescription drugs, mutual funds, electronics, and more, so should it ensure that when companies sell flawed services and products in the digital marketplace, those harmed can seek redress.

A Call to Action

Cyberspace has already become a domain of intense economic competition and information warfare, and states have begun testing the waters in preparation for weaponizing it during actual wars. The United States and its allies have responded to these rapidly changing realities far too slowly. For many in the U.S. government, cybersecurity has been seen as a matter for the IT help desk to address. But as new vulnerabilities crop up in nearly every corner of Americans' lives and American infrastructure, it is more important than ever to safeguard the country against cyberattacks.

In 1998, L0pht, a security-minded hacking collective from Boston, testified before Congress about just how vulnerable the online world was. One of the group's members warned that it would take any one of them just 30 minutes to bring down the entire Internet. Had such an attack come to fruition then, it would have been an annoyance. Today, it would be a catastrophe. Cyberattacks are not merely a problem for Americans, for businesses, or for governments. Everyone who values trust and stability online loses out if the threat grows. But with U.S. leadership, there is much that can be done to make these attacks happen less frequently and inflict less damage.

Print Citations

CMS: Flournoy, Michèle, and Michael Sulmeyer. "Battlefield Internet: A Plan for Securing Cyberspace." In *The Reference Shelf: Internet Law,* edited by Annette Calzone, 158-165. Amenia, NY: Grey House Publishing, 2020.

MLA: Flournoy, Michèle, and Michael Sulmeyer. "Battlefield Internet: A Plan for Securing Cyberspace." *The Reference Shelf: Internet Law,* edited by Annette Calzone, Grey House Publishing, 2020, pp. 158-165.

APA: Flournoy, M., & Sulmeyer, M. (2020). Battlefield internet: A plan for securing cyberspace. In Annette Calzone (Ed.), *The reference shelf: Internet law* (pp. 158-165). Amenia, NY: Grey House Publishing.

The Rising Threat of Digital Nationalism

By Akash Kapur

The Wall Street Journal, November 1, 2019

Fifty years ago this week, at 10:30 on a warm night at the University of California, Los Angeles, the first email was sent. It was a decidedly local affair. A man sat in front of a teleprinter connected to an early precursor of the internet known as AR-PANET and transmitted the message "login" to a colleague in Palo Alto. The system crashed; all that arrived at the Stanford Research Institute, some 350 miles away, was a truncated "lo."

The network has moved on dramatically from those parochial—and stuttering—origins. Now more than 200 billion emails flow around the world every day. The internet has come to represent the very embodiment of globalization—a postnational public sphere, a virtual world impervious and even hostile to the control of sovereign governments (those "weary giants of flesh and steel," as the cyberlibertarian activist John Perry Barlow famously put it in his *Declaration of the Independence of Cyberspace* in 1996).

But things have been changing recently. Nicholas Negroponte, a co-founder of the MIT Media Lab, once said that national law had no place in cyberlaw. That view seems increasingly anachronistic. Across the world, nation-states have been responding to a series of crises on the internet (some real, some overstated) by asserting their authority and claiming various forms of digital sovereignty. A network that once seemed to effortlessly defy regulation is being relentlessly, and often ruthlessly, domesticated.

From firewalls to shutdowns to new data-localization laws, a specter of digital nationalism now hangs over the network. This "territorialization of the internet," as Scott Malcomson, a technology consultant and author, calls it, is fundamentally changing its character—and perhaps even threatening its continued existence as a unified global infrastructure.

The phenomenon of digital nationalism isn't entirely new, of course. Authoritarian governments have long sought to rein in the internet. China has been the pioneer. Its Great Firewall, which restricts what people can read and do online, has served as a model for promoting what the country calls "digital sovereignty." China's efforts have had a powerful demonstration effect, showing other autocrats that the internet can be effectively controlled. China has also proved that powerful tech multinationals will exchange their stated principles for market access and that limiting online globalization can spur the growth of a vibrant domestic tech industry.

Several countries have built—or are contemplating—domestic networks modeled on the Chinese example. To control contact with the outside world and suppress dissident content, Iran has set up a so-called "halal net," North Korea has its Kwangmyong network, and earlier this year, Vladimir Putin signed a "sovereign internet bill" that would likewise set up a self-sufficient Runet. The bill also includes a "kill switch" to shut off the global network to Russian users. This is an increasingly common practice. According to the *New York Times*, at least a quarter of the world's countries have temporarily shut down the internet over the past four years.

Most assertions of government authority aren't quite so heavy-handed. Recent years have seen the emergence of a softer form of digital nationalism, evident in the proliferation of so-called data localization (or data protectionism) laws in countries as varied as Vietnam, India, Argentina, Venezuela and Nigeria. Broadly, these laws take two approaches. Some countries require that data on their citizens (or certain types of data, such as medical or financial information) must be physically stored on servers within their countries. Others allow the data to leave their borders but insist on a copy remaining domestically.

Many of the justifications cited for such laws are valid, ranging from privacy concerns to national security. But sometimes the very real failings of the internet, such as hate speech and disinformation, are co-opted to justify laws that give repressive governments a way to monitor online activity and speech. For all of the undeniable faults of the multinational tech companies, a Vietnamese or Cambodian dissident might still prefer their information to be under the control of Google or Facebook rather than their own governments.

> **The great risk is that digital nationalism will Balkanize the internet, breaking it up into a patchwork of incompatible and irreconcilable fiefs. This scenario, referred to as Splinternet, is already happening at the level of content and services.**

According to a recent study by a Brussels think tank, at least 45 countries now have some version of data localization requirements in place. The trend is no longer restricted to authoritarian states. Australia, Canada, New Zealand, South Korea and Switzerland are among the countries that now restrict cross-border flows of data. The European Union's influential General Data Protection Regulation (GDPR), while not specifically about localization, imposes such stringent obligations that it makes it hard for companies to move data across borders, thus effectively serving as a similar requirement.

The cumulative effect of all these laws is starting to be felt throughout the network. Companies that work with data in multiple jurisdictions are among the hardest hit. Peter Yared, the founder of InCountry, a San Francisco startup that helps businesses comply with international data regulations, says that companies are struggling to understand local requirements, purchase or rent servers, hire staff and deploy new software to comply with a panoply of emerging (and often fluctuating) laws. "People in compliance, information security and technical operations departments are starting to sweat a little bit right now," he says. "It hasn't quite hit business leaders yet that they could face large fines or be ejected out of large markets like India."

Many of these laws are ostensibly designed to rein in Western multinationals, but bigger companies are generally better able to accommodate the resulting uncertainty than smaller ones, which lack the necessary resources. Likewise, developing countries, often at the forefront of digital nationalism, could end up being among its chief victims. Countries such as India and the Philippines have important outsourcing sectors that rely on a unified global information network. Their moves to set up roadblocks on that network could come back to haunt them.

The great risk is that digital nationalism will Balkanize the internet, breaking it up into a patchwork of incompatible and irreconcilable fiefs. To an extent, this scenario, sometimes referred to as Splinternet, is already happening at the level of content and services. China's population (around a fifth of humanity) does not have access to Wikipedia, Facebook and most of Google. When the EU's GDPR first came into effect, many American media companies decided that the safest course of action, at least temporarily, was simply to stop offering their content to European consumers.

This Balkanization also could play out in the internet's underlying core technical infrastructure. Over the last decade, several countries, citing cultural sensitivities, have considered banning or otherwise restricting the .xxx top-level domain name (generally used for pornography), raising the prospect that the internet's naming system could eventually fracture. Responding to Edward Snowden's revelations about U.S. spying, Brazil mooted the idea of building a separate undersea cable link to the EU to bypass existing internet infrastructure. And recent debates at the Engineering Task Force, a key internet standards committee, have sometimes been tense. In the lead-up to the introduction last year of a new security standard, representatives who wanted to maintain a backdoor for government agencies clashed with those advocating more robust encryption.

None of these debates has so far managed to shake the underlying foundations of the network, but the prospect of a technical Splinternet is no longer as inconceivable as it once was. In the decades ahead, we may look back wistfully to a time when data could move freely across the globe, without virtual customs or immigration checkpoints.

The internet was never just a technology or an engine of globalization. It was, at its core, an idea. Stefaan Verhulst, a co-founder of the GovLab at New York University (a think tank where I am a senior fellow), argues that, in its early days, the internet was very much a project of classical liberalism, embedded with "ideals like human rights, freedom of expression and free trade. If you care about those notions, then internet fragmentation is a problem."

Like classical liberalism, the internet may also be a good idea in urgent need of updating. Much as the individualism and freedom of classical liberalism have been distorted into the inequalities and ethical transgressions of modern capitalism, so the internet's culture of "permissionless innovation" has been abused, transformed into the centralized, controlled network of today. The original dream of an unfettered global public sphere is probably over. Understanding why that happened is the first step to reclaiming at least part of the original vision and to mitigating the most damaging effects of digital nationalism.

It's no coincidence that the rise of digital nationalism corresponds with a similar resurgence of its offline variety. A technology community that has long prided itself on its radical difference, its apartness, turns out to be susceptible to many of the trends that influence the world at large. Over the last decade or so, the internet has suffered the same distortions of wealth and power—and the same resulting resentments—that have spurred the rise of illiberal nationalism and populism. Google today accounts for around 90% of online searches around the world; Facebook and Google together draw an estimated 84% of global advertising dollars (excluding China). Amazon accounts for 49% of online spending in the U.S., and Alibaba claims 60% in China. This was not the original dream.

Many of the anxieties to which this consolidation of power has given rise are legitimate; some are spurious and are used to advance ulterior motives. It has all been fertile ground for digital nationalism. When governments call for regulation to combat fake news, they tap into real concerns over the unaccountable power of social media; they also open up avenues for censorship. When developing countries insist on keeping their citizens' data to combat "data colonization," they raise genuine issues about the Western, especially American, bias of the internet; they also create backdoors to eavesdrop on citizens and erect barriers to protect local commercial interests. Modern nationalism, as the Harvard sociologist Bart Bonikowski has noted, depends on the widespread "mobilization of resentment"; this is true of both its digital and offline variants.

It turns out that the way to deal with offline and online nationalism may be quite similar: Restore a sense of inclusiveness and fair play, flatten some of the sharpest inequalities and rediscover and stress the principles that made the network so inspiring (and radically creative) in the first place. As it happens, there is a tool kit, both existing and emerging, to do some of this.

Mr. Verhulst, from the GovLab at NYU, argues that laws and principles from a previous era should be updated for the 21st century, by applying telecom universal service obligations to broadband, for example, and diversity and equal-time rules (sometimes applied to radio and television) to large news and social-media networks. "It's not like we don't know how to go about this," he says. "We just have to be more creative and think of what we can learn from models that were used in the past." Competition law is another area that has received a lot of attention, specifically the need to update its provisions to take account of the (nominally) free business models practiced by many digital companies.

Another idea is to develop "club"- or "zone"-based approaches to running the internet—discrete, interconnecting blocs whose nation-members would make commitments to liberal principles like free trade, privacy and freedom of expression. Such blocs would be a far cry from the original vision of a single global network. But adherents, like Geoff Mulgan, the former head of Nesta, a British innovation foundation, argue that such "coalitions of the willing" are the best way to arrest the continuing fragmentation of the network. "I don't see what the alternative is," Mr. Mulgan says. "The old global vision is breaking up."

The question is no longer whether national governments should have a say but what form their authority will take and how it will ultimately shape the network. In the old vision, nation-states were the enemy of innovation and freedom. Those were the Wild West days, and it is understandable that internet purists—and many average users—are nostalgic for them.

But things have changed a lot since that first email was sent in California. Amid the creeping nationalism and illiberalism of today, we may no longer have the luxury of rejecting governance and governments. Fifty years after the birth of the internet, it may well be that national governments, wielding enlightened regulation, are the last best hope for maintaining a network that is—at least relatively—open and free.

Print Citations

CMS: Kapur, Akash. "The Rising Threat of Digital Nationalism." In *The Reference Shelf: Internet Law,* edited by Annette Calzone, 166-170. Amenia, NY: Grey House Publishing, 2020.

MLA: Kapur, Akash. "The Rising Threat of Digital Nationalism." *The Reference Shelf: Internet Law,* edited by Annette Calzone, Grey House Publishing, 2020, pp. 166-170.

APA: Kapur, A. (2020). The rising threat of digital nationalism. In Annette Calzone (Ed.), *The reference shelf: Internet law* (pp. 166-170). Amenia, NY: Grey House Publishing.

Make the Internet American Again?

By John Hendel
Politico, January 23, 2018

President Donald Trump's pick for a top Commerce Department post privately assured Republican senators that he would look at reversing the Obama administration's decision to give up U.S. oversight of the internet, according to documents newly obtained by *Politico*.

David Redl, now the head of Commerce's National Telecommunications and Information Administration, made the pledge last summer to Sens. Ted Cruz (R-Texas) and Mike Lee (R-Utah), who had condemned the move to international control as a giveaway that could empower authoritarian governments. Trump has also attacked former President Barack Obama's handover, describing it as a "stupid" decision that would turn over "the internet to foreigners."

Redl promised the senators that he would recommend convening a "panel of experts to investigate options for unwinding the transition," according to a letter that *Politico* obtained through a Freedom of Information Act request.

It's unclear whether Redl, who took office two months ago, has followed through on the pledge, or whether the Commerce Department even has the ability to reverse the handover at this point. But his words appear to contradict public statements from both Redl and Commerce Secretary Wilbur Ross—while offering signs that Trump's "America First" mantra may be intruding into the administration's approach to the internet.

The Senate confirmed Redl in November after he overcame objections from Cruz, who has long railed against Obama's move to relinquish U.S. government authority over ICANN, the global nonprofit that manages the internet's domain name system. The change took effect in October 2016, meaning that ICANN has now been an independent entity for more than a year.

Cruz has repeatedly warned that giving up that control would lead to an online power grab by countries like China and Russia and threaten freedom of speech around the world. He told Redl's predecessor, Larry Strickling, that he could go to jail over the internet transition plan.

During the latter stages of the 2016 campaign, Trump sided with Cruz, his one-time bitter rival for the Republican presidential nomination, calling the handover "just one more way Obama-Clinton have sold out the citizens of this country."

Spokespeople for NTIA, the Commerce Department and Cruz didn't immediately respond to requests for comment.

ICANN handled domains like ".com" and ".org" under a U.S. government contract for years, but the Obama administration said it was always envisioned that U.S. oversight would be temporary and that the global "multistakeholder" model would eventually operate on its own. In practice, that meant untethering ICANN from its U.S. contract. Despite vocal criticism from a number of congressional Republicans, efforts to block the transition through legislation fell short.

Redl's private assurances to Cruz are striking given that both he and Ross appeared to take the opposite view in public, casting doubt on the possibility of reversing Obama's decision. During his June confirmation hearing, Redl said it would be "very difficult to put the genie back in the bottle," while Ross said in January 2017 that he was "not aware that there's a realistic way to do anything about it."

> **The idea of undoing the internet transition "may be an interesting political topic" but is ultimately a "fantasy."**

But that stance appeared to change during Redl's protracted confirmation process. Cruz took issue with Redl's statements about the internet transition and put a hold on the nominee, sparking months of closed-door negotiations.

"I am not aware of any specific proposals to reverse the ... transition, but I am interested in exploring ways to achieve this goal," Redl told Cruz and Lee in his written responses, before suggesting the "panel of experts" be convened to look at reversing the handover.

He also said he would continue to monitor ICANN, which is based in Los Angeles.

"ICANN remains a California corporation, subject to the laws of the United States," Redl wrote. "I will work with all parts of the U.S. government to ensure that ICANN operates with a level hand and respects the laws of the United States."

Ross, in his own Aug. 1 letters to Cruz and Lee, said Redl "understands my position regarding ICANN" and "is eager to learn of any possible [mechanism] for reversing it."

Cruz never disclosed his reasons for lifting his hold on Redl, a mystery that alarmed Democrats at the time.

Sen. Brian Schatz (D-Hawaii) briefly blocked Redl himself over concerns that he'd cut some deal with Cruz, but he ultimately lifted his hold after about two weeks.

In an interview, Schatz said the idea of undoing the internet transition "may be an interesting political topic" but is ultimately a "fantasy."

"We feel confident that there's no going back," he said, adding that Redl understands it's "simply not practicable to go back to the old way even if we wanted to."

Print Citations

CMS: Hendel, John. "Make the Internet American Again?" In *The Reference Shelf: Internet Law,* edited by Annette Calzone, 171-173. Amenia, NY: Grey House Publishing, 2020.

MLA: Hendel, John. "Make the Internet American Again?" *The Reference Shelf: Internet Law,* edited by Annette Calzone, Grey House Publishing, 2020, pp. 171-173.

APA: Hendel, J. (2020). Make the internet American again? In Annette Calzone (Ed.), *The reference shelf: Internet law* (pp. 171-173). Amenia, NY: Grey House Publishing.

Should the U.S. Reclaim Control of the Internet? Evaluating ICANN's Administrative Oversight since the 2016 Handover

By Mark Grabowski

Nebraska Law Review, August 6, 2018

I. INTRODUCTION

About two years ago, the United States of America surrendered oversight of the Internet Corporation for Assigned Names and Numbers (ICANN), an obscure, private company that oversees the Internet's backbone: the domain-name system, IP address allocation, and network protocol number assignments. The hope was this power transfer would usher in an era of international cooperation on Internet governance. But, after taking one step forward, it appears the Internet has taken two steps back. The transition has arguably exacerbated existing Internet governance problems, according to experts. Now, the U.S. government is mulling snatching back control. This paper argues that government officials should pressure ICANN to fix its problems, but stop short of a power reversal.

II. BACKGROUND

Global cooperation on Internet governance has always been a challenge. No one country owns the Internet, and each nation regulates how its citizens use the Internet within the framework of its political, legal, moral and cultural values. Because online activities often involve actors and intermediaries in multiple physical locations, diverse sets of potentially incompatible laws and rules overlap and frequently are in conflict.[1]

But, with a few exceptions—such as North Korea, which has its own intranet that is isolated from the rest of the world—the vast majority of nations have at least agreed to participate in the global Internet that is administered by ICANN.[2] ICANN acts as the phonebook of the Internet by assigning and matching domain names with IP addresses. To reach a website or person on the Internet, a user gives his or her computer a destination—usually entered as a name or number.[3] That destination has to be unique so computers know where to find each other. Humans prefer to find web and email addresses by name, such as google.com.[4] But computers know each other by numbers, or Internet Protocol address-es. ICANN coordinates these

---

ICANN's struggles threaten to put the security, interoperability, and openness of the entire Internet at risk.

---

matches. Without their coordination, we would not have one global Internet.

Although this non-profit, Los Angeles-based organization has typically made its own decisions on how to best manage these behind-the-scenes technical op-erations, it ultimately answered to the U.S. government.[5] That is because America essentially invented the Internet and thus decided who manages it. U.S. officials always kept an eye on ICANN and let it know when its policies had gone astray. But this all changed in September 2016. Then-President Barack Obama decided ICANN was better off without any government intervention. As a result, ICANN has had absolute control of key Internet infrastructure and has answered to no one since September 30, 2016.

Proponents insisted this power shift was necessary for various reasons.[6] They argued that the Internet had become too American–centric. Since countries such as China and India have many more Internet users than the U.S., proponents rea-soned it was no longer fair for one nation to control the world's communication tool. Moreover, the world no longer trusted the U.S. to oversee the Internet after the Ed-ward Snowden spying scandal.[7] There was a risk that other countries could form an alternate Internet rather than participate in our existing global and interconnected cyberspace.[8]

The power transfer, while controversial, was widely lauded. The Internet is "best protected by . . . geeks, rather than any government or agency," journalists argued.[9] The U.S. surrendering control is not a big deal, academics said.[10] This will "not affect Internet users and their use of the Internet," assured ICANN, which also promised to govern using a global multistakeholder model based on consen-sus.[11] "The U.S. government's willingness to allow the Internet to be a more truly global asset will improve the[ir] stature . . . as a global citizen," predicted Greg Shatan, a partner at New York City law firm McCarter & English, who assisted ICANN with its transition.[12]

However, the handover was not without notable detractors.[13] For example, Sena-tor Ted Cruz and then-presidential candidate Donald Trump preferred that the U.S. government maintained oversight of ICANN and took an "if it ain't broke, don't fix it" viewpoint. Some lawmakers even attempted, albeit unsuccessfully, to block the transfer through a lawsuit. Others supported ICANN's independence, but were concerned the transition plan was hasty and needed more fine-tuning.

Now, as the two-year anniversary of ICANN's independence approaches, Pres-ident Trump's administration is reevaluating the decision. On June 5, 2018, the National Telecommunications and Information Administration (NTIA) published a formal notice of inquiry in the *Federal Register* asking, "Should the [ICANN] Transi-tion be unwound? If yes, why and how? If not, why not?"[14] Those questions were among twenty-three posed by U.S. government officials who are seeking public comment on the handover. Other questions included, "What are the challenges to the free flow of information online?"; "Are the existing accountability structures within multistakeholder internet governance sufficient?"; and "Does the multistakeholder approach continue to support an environment for the internet to grow and thrive?"[15] NTIA stated that they would use the public's input to shape their policy agenda going forward.[16]

III. ANALYSIS

The Register, an online tech publication that has closely followed the transition, called the inquiry "extraordinary given how controversial such a reversal would be," stating "nobody expected the question to be [so] blunt . . . which risks exploding what most feel is a settled matter."[17] But it is understandable why the U.S. government may want to backtrack. Since the handover, many experts argue that ICANN has fallen short of meeting its goals. Moreover, they argue that ICANN's struggles threaten to put the security, interoperability and openness of the entire Internet at risk. Consider some of ICANN's post-transition problems related to free speech, accountability, governance and the Internet's future.

A. Controversial Policy Changes

First, ICANN has implemented controversial policy changes since assuming total control of the Internet. After the handover occurred, the Internet continued to function as usual and the average user likely did not notice any differences in his or her online experience. But, as time has passed, ICANN has made decisions that could potentially harm Internet users worldwide.

Some observers contend that ICANN's core values have been compromised since it is no longer subject to U.S. jurisdiction and the First Amendment, a federal constitutional right that provides freedom of speech and transparency.[18] For example, Whois—ICANN's worldwide database containing who owns which website and how to contact these owners—will no longer be publicly available despite strong objections from U.S. officials.[19] Businesses and law enforcement rely on these open records to track down scammers, copyright pirates, child pornographers and other bad actors online.[20]

Mission creep could worsen at ICANN, experts warn, due to a changing company culture that endangers ICANN's mission of managing Internet traffic in a neutral way. "The company started hiring the wrong type of people," explained *Domain Name Wire*'s editor Andrew Allemann.[21]

It started hiring people that don't want to do boring work. People who want to make a name for themselves. It hired people who want to be at the helm of a growing organization that takes on an important role in the world. . . . Hiring people that want to make a difference is usually a good thing, but not for an organization that should be boring.[22]

ICANN has long tried to play the role of Switzerland in virtual world conflicts, maintaining that it "is not the Internet [c]ontent [p]olice." But digital rights group Electronic Frontier Foundation cautioned that censorship is a "real concern."[24] In the past year, several American tech companies have been criticized for censoring online speech—one highlighted instance being a Twitter employee temporarily deactivating President Trump's account.[25] Likewise, ICANN is facing increasing pressure to engage in censorship of offensive online speech. An ICANN employee could conceivably punish Russia for election meddling or "resist" a democratic nation that elects a contentious leader by disabling their Internet domain. Individual employees have the power to bring the entire Internet to its knees, *Business Insider* revealed.[26] Had ICANN remained an arm of the U.S. government, it would have been prohibited from engaging in such censorship due to the U.S. Constitution's free speech protections.[27] However, the First Amendment prohibits only U.S. government censorship, and not censorship from private companies inside America.

B. Financial Mismanagement

A more pressing concern is ICANN's financial woes. ICANN is struggling with what watchdogs call a "budget crisis." Revenues have not kept up with ballooning expenses, highlighted by an ever-expanding bureaucracy that is handsomely compensated with high salaries, generous benefits and essentially "free vacations."[28] As a result, ICANN needs to find a way to cut several millions of dollars from its proposed $138 million budget for the 2019 fiscal year.

Some watchdogs worry that these financial problems could corrupt ICANN officials' handling of important issues, such as whether the disputed dot-amazon domain be given to Brazil's rain forest or to Amazon's Jeff Bezos.[29] ICANN executives have a history of engaging in conflict-of-interest domain sales that have drawn criticism from watchdog groups. In 2011, for example, ICANN's chairman approved selling new domains to a company he left to join less than a month later.[30] There may be insufficient checks and balances to prevent this from happening again. ICANN boasts of its multistakeholder governance model, which solicits input from government representatives, tech experts and others. But ICANN's board can decide to take their advice or not. Sometimes the board disregards even its own bylaws, one independent review found.[31]

C. Power Struggles

In addition to all of its internal issues, ICANN is now struggling to maintain its authority over the Internet. The European Union has "started rejecting the organization's authority," *The Register* reported.[32] Brazil officials told ICANN that only governments control the Internet.[33] It seems that with the U.S. no longer backing ICANN, the organization is being easily bullied by other nations to bend to their will. "ICANN lost 99% of its spine when the U[.]S[.] relinquished control over it. It now lost the remaining 1%," observed industry analyst Theo Develegas of *Acroplex*.[34] *The Register* agreed: "Since that handover on September 30, 2016, two things have become clear: 1. ICANN continues to make terrible decisions, and 2. European governments have decided that they will use their collective power as the EU to force changes on how the Internet functions."[35] Due to its perceived weakness, many critics now mockingly refer to ICANN as "ICANN'T."[36]

ICANN could soon face a much greater existential threat. Russia announced it is developing its own Internet that will operate separate from ICANN's.[37] Brazil,

India, China, Turkey and South Africa could join them in this "splInternet," leaving Americans and Europeans cut off from half of the world's Internet users.[38] Smaller nations, such as Taiwan, could face a dilemma: join China's Internet, which will be in its native Mandarin language but highly censored, or participate in the West's Internet, which enjoys great freedom of expression, but its content is primarily in English and caters to users located thousands of miles away.

IV. CONCLUSION

Given all of ICANN's woes, the United States is justifiably concerned about its ability to manage the Internet. However, more upheaval may not be the remedy to this instability. *The Register* warned that if the U.S. attempts to reclaim power, "such a move would risk fragmenting the internet's global addressing systems."[39] But they speculate, "More likely is that the NTIA is using its notice of inquiry to put pressure on ICANN."[40] Indeed, it is uncertain whether U.S. officials can reverse the handover even if they want to. David Redl, President Trump's top Internet policy advisor, stated at a 2017 U.S. Senate hearing that "it would be very difficult to put the genie back in the bottle on ICANN."[41] One thing seems clear, however. As the two-year anniversary of the ICANN stewardship transition approaches, things have not gone as envisioned. In fact, the power shift may have caused more problems than it solved. Unless these issues get resolved quickly, the future of a connected world may be in peril. The U.S. is not wrong to second-guess whether the handover was the right decision.

1. *See generally* Joel R. Reidenberg, *Technology and Internet Jurisdiction*, 153 U. Pa. L. Rev. 1951 (2005), https://papers.ssrn.com/sol3/papers.cfm?abstract_id=691501.

2. Meghan Keneally, *Here's What the Internet Looks Like in North Korea*, ABC News (Dec. 23, 2014, 11:25 AM), https://abcnews.go.com/International/internet-north-korea/story?id=27789459.

3. Elizabeth Weise, *U.S. Set to Hand Over Internet Address Book*, USA Today (Sept. 29, 2016, 8:52 PM), https://www.usatoday.com/story/tech/news/2016/09/29/icann-iana-internet-address-book-autonomous-department-of-commerce-ip-address-transition-internet-corporation-for-assigned-names-and-numbers/91281960.

4. Mark Grabowski, *Obama's Risky Internet Giveaway*, Wash. Exam'r (Sept. 26, 2016, 12:03 AM), http://www.washingtonexaminer.com/obamas-risky-internet-giveaway/article/2602802.

5. *Id.*

6. *Id.*

7. *See* Edward Wyatt, *U.S. to Cede its Oversight of Addresses on the Internet*. N.Y. Times (March 14, 2014), https://www.nytimes.com/2014/03/15/technology/us-to-give-up-role-in-internet-domain-names.html.

8. Claire Ricke, *Texas AG Files Lawsuit Against Obama Over 'Internet Control'*, KXAN (Sept. 29, 2016, 3:56 AM), http://www.kxan.com/news/texas-ag-files-lawsuit-against-obama-over-Internet-control/995016013.

9. David Ignatius, *Let the Geeks Rule Over the Internet*, Wash. Post (Aug. 2, 2016), https://www.washingtonpost.com/opinions/let-the-geeks-rule-over-the-Internet/2016/08/02/7121eb68-58f6-11e6-9767-f6c947fd0cb8_story.html.

10. Jonathan Zittrain, *No, Barack Obama Isn't Handing Control of the Internet Over to China: The Misguided Freakout Over ICANN*, New Republic (Mar. 24, 2014), https://newrepublic.com/article/117093/us-withdraws-icann-why-its-no-big-deal.

11. *Frequently Asked Questions About the Transition*, ICANN (March 14, 2014), https://www.icann.org/en/system/files/files/functions-transfer-faqs-14mar14-en.pdf.

12. Grabowski, *supra* note 4.

13. *Id.*

14. National Telecommunications and Information Administration; International Internet Policy Priorities, 83 Fed. Reg. 26,036, 26,038 (June 5, 2018), https://regmedia.co.uk/2018/06/05/ntia-internet-policy-noi-jun18.pdf.

15. *Id.*

16. *Id.*

17. Kieren McCarthy, *US Govt Mulls Snatching Back Full Control of the Internet's Domain Name and IP Address Admin*, Register (June 5, 2018, 9:30 PM), https://www.theregister.co.uk/2018/06/05/us_government_icann_iana.

18. U.S. Const. amend. I.

19. Kieren McCarthy, *Uncle Sam Slams Plans to Give Govts Final Say Over Domain Privacy*, Register (Mar. 13, 2018, 10:29 PM), https://www.theregister.co.uk/2018/03/13/us_government_icann_domain_privacy.

20. John D. McKinnon, *U.S., Tech Firms Warn Against Internet Monitor's Privacy Tightening*, Wall St. J. (Mar. 15, 2018, 8:22 AM), https://www.wsj.com/articles/u-s-tech-firms-warn-against-internet-monitors-privacy-tightening-1521115200.

21. Andrew Allemann, *My Thoughts on ICANN's Budget Crisis*, Domain Name Wire (Apr. 10, 2018), https://domain-namewire.com/2018/04/10/my-thoughts-on-icanns-budget-crisis (last visited Aug. 5, 2018).

22. *Id.*

23. Allen R. Grogan, *ICANN is Not the Internet Content Police*, ICANN (June 12, 2015), https://www.icann.org/news/blog/icann-is-not-the-Internet-content-police (last visited Aug. 5, 2018).

24. Jeremy Malcolm, *Oversight Transition Isn't Giving Away the Internet, But Won't Fix ICANN's Problems*, Elec. Frontier Found. (Oct. 3, 2016), https://www.eff.org/deeplinks/2016/09/oversight-transition-isnt-giving-away-Internet-wont-fix-icanns-problems (last visited Aug. 5, 2018).

25. Haley Tsukayama, Rachel Siegel & J. Freedom du Lac, *Rogue Twitter Employee Deactivated Trump's Personal Account on Last Day on the Job, Company Says*, Wash. Post (Nov. 3, 2017), https://www.washingtonpost.com/news/the-switch/wp/2017/11/02/trumps-twitter-account-was-temporarily-deactivated-due-to-human-error.

26. Julie Bort, *The Internet is Still Actually Controlled by 14 People Who Hold 7 Secret Keys*, Bus. Insider (Oct. 21, 2016, 1:56 PM), http://www.businessinsider.com/the-internet-is-controlled-by-secret-keys-2016-10.

27. *See* U.S. Const. amend. I.

28. Kevin Murphy, *ICANN Slashes Millions from its Budget*, Domain Incite (Jan. 22, 2018, 11:50 PM), http://domainincite.com/22559-icann-slashes-millions-from-its-budget.

29. Kevin Murphy, *"We Own Your Name" Government Tells Amazon in Explosive Slapdown*, Domain Incite (Oct. 29, 2017, 9:43 PM), http://domainincite.com/22231-we-own-your-name-government-tells-amazon-in-explosive-slapdown.

30. Eric Engleman, *ICANN Departures Draw Criticism*, Wash. Post (Aug. 20, 2011), https://www.washingtonpost.com/business/icann-departures-draw-criticism/2011/08/19/gIQAzpeDTJ_story.html.

31. Kieren McCarthy, *Months After it Ordered a Review into Allegations of Mismanagement, How's That ICANN Accountability Drive?*, Register (May 9, 2017, 7:02 AM), https://www.theregister.co.uk/2017/05/09/icann_latest_screw_up.

32. Kieren McCarthy, *As GDPR Draws Close, ICANN Suggests 12 Conflicting Ways to Cure Domain Privacy Pains*, Register (Feb. 9, 2018, 7:28 AM), https://www.theregister.co.uk/2018/02/09/icann_whois_gdpr.

33. Kieren McCarthy, *Dot-Amazon Spat Latest: Brazil Tells ICANN to Go Fsck Itself, Only 'Govts control the Internet,'* Register (Sept. 27, 2017, 9:04 PM), https://www.theregister.co.uk/2017/09/27/brazil_dot_amazon_gtld.

34. Theo Develegas, Comment to Andrew Allemann, *I Just Fixed Whois and GDPR*, Domain Name Wire (April 13, 2018, 2:03 PM), https://domainnamewire.com/2018/04/13/i-just-fixed-whois-and-gdpr/#comment-2249232.

35. *https://www.theregister.co.uk/2018/06/01/whats_next_for_whois_and_icann/?page=3.*

36. *See, e.g.,* Kieren McCarthy, *ICANN't Get No Respect: Europe Throws Whois Privacy Plan in the Trash*, Register (July 6, 2018, 6:30 AM), https://www.theregister.co.uk/2018/07/06/europe_no_to_icann_whois.

37. Tracy Staedter, *Why Russia is Building its Own Internet*, IEEE Spectrum (Jan. 17, 2018, 9:30 PM), https://spectrum.ieee.org/tech-talk/telecom/internet/could-russia-really-build-its-own-alternate-internet.

38. Katja Bego, *The 'Splinternet' is Coming: Why Countries Will Break Away from Today's Internet*, Qrius (Mar. 17, 2018), https://qrius.com/the-splInternet-is-coming-why-countries-will-break-away-from-todays-Internet (last visited Aug. 5, 2018).

39. McCarthy, *US Govt Mulls Snatching Back Full Control of the Internet's Domain Name and IP Address Admin, supra* note 17.

40. *Id.*

41. *Id.*

Print Citations

CMS: Grabowski, Mark. "Should the U.S. Reclaim Control of the Internet? Evaluating ICANN's Administrative Oversight since the 2016 Handover." In *The Reference Shelf: Internet Law,* edited by Annette Calzone, 174-179. Amenia, NY: Grey House Publishing, 2020.

MLA: Grabowski, Mark. "Should the U.S. Reclaim Control of the Internet? Evaluating ICANN's Administrative Oversight since the 2016 Handover." *The Reference Shelf: Internet Law,* edited by Annette Calzone, Grey House Publishing, 2020, pp. 174-179.

APA: Grabowski, M. (2020). Should the U.S. reclaim control of the internet? Evaluating ICANN's administrative oversight since the 2016 handover. In Annette Calzone (Ed.), *The reference shelf: Internet law* (pp. 174-179). Amenia, NY: Grey House Publishing.

Bibliography

Ahasker, Abhijit. "How Cyberattacks Are Being Used by States against Each Other." *Livemint*. June 21, 2019. https://www.livemint.com/technology/tech-news/how-cyberattacks-are-being-used-by-states-against-each-other-1561100711834.html.

Band, Jonathan. "The Copyright Paradox: Fighting Content Piracy in the Digital Era." *Brookings*. Dec. 1, 2001. https://www.brookings.edu/articles/the-copyright-paradox-fighting-content-piracy-in-the-digital-era/.

Band, Jonathan. "The Digital Millennium Copyright Act." *ALA Washington Office*. Nov. 25, 1998. http://www.ala.org/advocacy/sites/ala.org.advocacy/files/content/copyright/dmca/pdfs/dmcaanalysis.pdf.

Bettilyon, Tyler Elliot. "Network Neutrality: A History of Common Carrier Laws 1884–2018." *Medium*. Dec. 12, 2017. https://medium.com/@TebbaVonMathenstien/network-neutrality-a-history-of-common-carrier-laws-1884-2018.

Bowles, Nellie. "Thermostats, Locks, and Lights: Digital Tools of Domestic Abuse." *The New York Times*. June 23, 2018. https://www.nytimes.com/2018/06/23/technology/smart-home-devices-domestic-abuse.html.

Brodsky, Rachel. "The Music Modernization Act, One Year Later." *Advocacy*. Oct. 11, 2019. https://www.grammy.com/advocacy/news/music-modernization-act-one-year-later.

Cohen, Ben, and Ray Rothrock. "On Cybersecurity: Two Scoops of Perspective." *The New York Times*. Sept. 29, 2019. https://www.nytimes.com/2019/09/29/opinion/letters/cybersecurity.html.

"Complicit in Censorship? Amazon and the Suppression of Online Expression in Ecuador." George Washington University Law School. International Human Rights Clinic. Apr. 2017. https://www.law.gwu.edu/sites/g/files/zaxdzs2351/f/downloads/GWU-Amazon-Ecuador-Report-Final.pdf.

Cope, Sophia. "EFF Supports Senate Email and Location Privacy Bill." *Electronic Frontier Foundation*. July 27, 2017. https://www.eff.org/deeplinks/2017/07/eff-applauds-senate-email-and-location-privacy-bill#:~:text=ECPA%20was%20first%20passed%20in,and%20the%20habits%20of%20users.

Cox, Kate. "Biden Wants Sec. 230 Gone, Calls Tech 'Totally Irresponsible,' 'Little Creeps'." *Ars Technica*. Jan. 17, 2020. https://arstechnica.com/tech-policy/2020/01/joe-biden-is-so-mad-at-facebook-he-wants-to-revoke-sec-230-for-everyone/.

Crews, Clyde Wayne, Jr. "Helicopter Government? How the Internet of Things Enables Pushbutton Regulation from a Distance." *Forbes*. Nov. 11, 2019.

Darlington, Shasta. "Battle for .amazon Domain Pits Retailer Against South

American Nations." *The New York Times*. Apr. 18, 2019. https://www.nytimes.com/2019/04/18/world/americas/amazon-domain-name.html.

Davis, Wendy. "Covid-19 Crisis Shows Need for Net Neutrality Rules, Advocates Say." *Digital News Daily*. Apr. 20, 2020. https://www.mediapost.com/publications/article/350285/covid-19-crisis-shows-need-for-net-neutrality-rule.html

"The Digital Arts: Web, Internet, and Software." Copyright website. https://www.benedict.com/.

"Does the U.S. Need a Cabinet-Level Department of Cybersecurity?" *The Wall Street Journal*. June 3, 2019. https://www.wsj.com/articles/does-the-u-s-need-a-cabinet-level-department-of-cybersecurity-11559586996.

Dyson, Lauren. "Code Is Law, Law Is Code: Law.gov & the Local Challenge for Legal Transparency." *Code for America*. Feb. 22, 2011. https://www.codeforamerica.org/blog/2011/02/22/code-is-law.

Ehrlich, Ev. "A Brief History of Internet Regulation." Progressive Policy Institute. 2014. https://www.progressivepolicy.org/wp-content/uploads/2014/03/2014.03-Ehrlich_A-Brief-History-of-Internet-Regulation.pdf.

"Electronic Communications Privacy Act." *ScienceDirect*. https://www.sciencedirect.com/topics/computer-science/electronic-communications-privacy-act.

Flournoy, Michèle, and Michael Sulmeyer. "Battlefield Internet: A Plan for Securing Cyberspace." *Foreign Affairs*. September/October 2018. https://www.foreignaffairs.com/articles/world/2018-08-14/battlefield-internet.

Ghoshal, Abhimanyu. "A Nostalgic Look Back at Digital Music Piracy in the 2000s." *TNW*. Dec. 28, 2018. https://thenextweb.com/insights/2018/12/28/a-nostalgic-look-back-at-digital-music-piracy-in-the-2000s/.

Gilbertson, Scott. "In 2019, Multiple Open Source Companies Changed Course—Is It the Right Move?" *Ars Technica*. Oct. 16, 2019. https://arstechnica.com/information-technology/2019/10/is-the-software-world-taking-too-much-from-the-open-source-community/.

Giles, Martin. "Five Reasons 'Hacking Back' Is a Recipe for Cybersecurity Chaos." *MIT Technology Review*. June 21, 2019. https://www.technologyreview.com/2019/06/21/134840/cybersecurity-hackers-hacking-back-us-congress/.

Goldman, Eric, and Jess Miers. "Why Can't Internet Companies Stop Awful Content?" *Ars Technica*. Jan. 27, 2019. https://arstechnica.com/tech-policy/2019/11/why-cant-internet-companies-stop-awful-content/.

Grabowski, Mark. "Should the U.S. Reclaim Control of the Internet? Evaluating ICANN's Administrative Oversight Since the 2016 Handover." *Nebraska Law Review*. Aug. 6, 2018. https://lawreview.unl.edu/Should-the-U.S.-Reclaim-Control-of-the-Internet%3F.

Greenberg, Andy. "It's Been 20 Years Since This Man Declared Cyberspace Independence." *Wired*. Feb. 8, 2016, https://www.wired.com/2016/02/its-been-20-years-since-this-man-declared-cyberspace-independence.

"Hacker Hat Colors: An Inside Look at the Hacking Ecosystem." *Alpine Security*. https://alpinesecurity.com/blog/hacker-hat-colors-an-inside-look-at-the-hacking-ecosystem/.

Harmon, Elliot, and Ernesto Falcon. "EFF Defends Section 230 in Congress." *Electronic Frontier Foundation*. Oct. 16, 2019. https://www.eff.org/deep-links/2019/10/eff-defends-section-230-congress.

Herrera, Sebastian. "Activist Behind California's New Privacy Law Already Wants to Improve It." *The Wall Street Journal*. Dec. 29, 2019. https://www.wsj.com/articles/activist-behind-californias-new-privacy-law-already-wants-to-improve-it-11577615401.

Hersko, Tyler. "AT&T Ignores Net Neutrality: HBO Max Won't Hit Data Caps but Competing Streamers Will." *IndieWire*. June 4, 2020. https://www.indiewire.com/2020/06/att-net-neutrality-hbo-max-no-data-caps-1202235538/.

Hurley, Lawrence. "U.S. Supreme Court Ends Fight over Obama-Era Net Neutrality Rules." *Reuters*. Nov. 5, 2018. https://www.reuters.com/article/us-usa-court-netneutrality/u-s-supreme-court-ends-fight-over-obama-era-net-neutrality-rules-idUSKCN1NA1UW.

"Internet Regulation." *Encyclopedia.com*. June 12, 2020. https://www.encyclopedia.com/law/encyclopedias-almanacs-transcripts-and-maps/internet-regulation.

Johnson, Derek B. "Does the CFAA Apply to Voting Machine Hacks?" *FCW*. Aug. 30, 2018. https://fcw.com/articles/2018/08/30/cfaa-voting-hacks-johnson.aspx.

Kapur, Akash. "The Rising Threat of Digital Nationalism." *The Wall Street Journal*. Nov. 1, 2019. https://www.wsj.com/articles/the-rising-threat-of-digital-nationalism-11572620577.

Kearns, Abby. "How the New York Times Got Open Source Wrong." *Medium*. Dec. 19, 2019. https://medium.com/@ab415/how-the-new-york-times-got-open-source-wrong-e67bf1283988.

Khana, Derek. "White House Petition on Cellphone Unlocking Receives over 100,000 Signatures." *Forbes*. Feb. 25, 2013. https://www.forbes.com/sites/derekkhanna/2013/02/25/white-house-petition-on-cellphone-unlocking-receives-over-100000-signatures/#1dda62c536bd.

Lee, Timothy B. "Court: Violating a Site's Terms of Service Isn't Criminal Hacking." *Ars Technica*. Mar. 30, 2020. https://arstechnica.com/tech-policy/2020/03/court-violating-a-sites-terms-of-service-isnt-criminal-hacking/.

LoMonte, Frank. "The Law That Made Facebook What It Is Today." *The Conversation*. Apr. 11, 2018. https://theconversation.com/the-law-that-made-facebook-what-it-is-today-93931.

Madigan, Kevin. "Senators and Creators Say Notice and Takedown System Is Broken, While Platforms Blame the Systems' Failures on Creators." *Copyright Alliance*. June 4, 2020. https://copyrightalliance.org/ca_post/senators-and-creators-say-notice-and-takedown-system-is-broken-while-platforms-blame-creators/.

Makena, Kelly. "Self-Isolation Has Stressed Networks, and No One Knows if the FCC Can Step In." *The Verge*. Mar. 31, 2020. https://www.theverge.com/2020/3/31/21200992/fcc-coronavirus-net-neutrality-networks-att-comcast-carriers.

Malcolmson, Scott. "The Real Fight for the Future of 5G." *Foreign Affairs*. Nov. 14, 2019. https://www.foreignaffairs.com/articles/2019-11-14/real-fight-future-5g.

Marks, Joseph. "The Cybersecurity 202: There's Finally a Supreme Court Battle over the Nation's Main Hacking Law." *The Washington Post*. Apr. 24, 2020. https://www.washingtonpost.com/news/powerpost/paloma/the-cybersecurity-202/2020/04/24/the-cybersecurity-202-there-s-finally-a-supreme-court-battle-coming-over-the-nation-s-main-hacking-law/5ea1ade6602ff140c1cc5f51/.

May, Timothy C. "The Crypto Anarchist Manifesto." Nov. 22, 1992. https://www.activism.net/cypherpunk/crypto-anarchy.html/

Milner, Greg. "The Wild, Baffling, and Sometimes Terrifying History of Crypto-Anarchy." *BreakerMag*. Sept. 14, 2018. https://breakermag.com/the-wild-baffling-and-sometimes-terrifying-history-of-crypto-anarchy/.

Mohney, Gillian. "Murder on Facebook Spotlights Rise of 'Performance Crime' Phenomenon on Social Media." *ABC News*. Apr. 18, 2017. https://abcnews.go.com/US/murder-facebook-spotlights-rise-performance-crime-phenomenon-social/story?id=46862306.

Moules, Danny. "A History of Hacking and Hackers." *Computer Weekly*. Oct. 25, 2017. https://www.computerweekly.com/opinion/A-history-of-hacking-and-hackers.

O'Neill, Patrick Howell. "A Dark Web Tycoon Pleads Guilty: But How Was He Caught?" *MIT Technology Review*. Feb. 8, 2020. https://www.technologyreview.com/2020/02/08/349016/a-dark-web-tycoon-pleads-guilty-but-how-was-he-caught/.

O'Neill, Patrick Howell. "Hackers Will Be the Weapon of Choice for Governments in 2020." *MIT Technology Review*. Jan. 2, 2020. https://www.technologyreview.com/2020/01/02/23/hackers-will-be-the-weapon-of-choice-for-governments-in-2020/.

Overly, Steven, and Nancy Scola. "The Trump-Twitter Fight Ropes in the Rest of Silicon Valley." *Politico*. May 30, 2020. https://www.politico.com/news/2020/05/30/trump-twitter-fight-silicon-valley-290759.

"Overview of the GNU System." *GNU Operating System*. https://www.gnu.org/gnu/gnu-history.en.html#:~:text=Overview%20of%20the%20GNU%20System,GNU%20Project%20in%20September%201983.

Pinsker, Joe. "Where Were Netflix and Google in the Net-Neutrality Fight?" *The Atlantic*. Dec. 20, 2017. https://www.theatlantic.com/business/archive/2017/12/netflix-google-net-neutrality/548768/.

Power, Katrina. "The Evolution of Hacking." *Tripwire*. Aug. 17, 2016. https://www.tripwire.com/state-of-security/security-data-protection/cyber-security/the-evolution-of-hacking/.

Reardon, Marguerite. "What You Need to Know about the FCC's 2015 Net Neutrality Regulation." *CNET*. Mar. 14, 2015. https://www.cnet.com/news/13-things-you-need-to-know-about-the-fccs-net-neutrality-regulation/.

Roberts, Jeff John. "The Splinternet Is Growing." *Forbes*. May 29, 2019. https://fortune.com/2019/05/29/splinternet-online-censorship/.

Robertson, Adi. "Copyright Could Be the Next Way for Congress to Take on Big Tech."

The Verge. Feb. 13, 2020. https://www.theverge.com/2020/2/13/21133754/congress-dmca-copyright-reform-hearing-tillis-coons-big-tech.

Ruiz, Rebecca R. "F.C.C. Sets Net Neutrality Rules." *The New York Times.* Mar. 12, 2015. https://www.nytimes.com/2015/03/13/technology/fcc-releases-net-neutrality-rules.html.

"Section 1201 Study." Copyright.gov. June 22, 2017. https://www.copyright.gov/policy/1201/#:~:text=Enacted%20in%201998%20as%20part,in%20technology%20or%20services%20that.

"Senator Hawley Introduces Legislation to Amend Section 230 Immunity for Big Tech Companies." June 19, 2019. https://www.hawley.senate.gov/senator-hawley-introduces-legislation-amend-section-230-immunity-big-tech-companies.

Soderberg-Rivkin, Daisy. "The Lessons of FOSTA-SESTA from a Former Content Moderator." *RStreet.* Apr. 8, 2020. https://www.rstreet.org/2020/04/08/the-lessons-of-fosta-sesta-from-a-former-content-moderator/.

Stroud, Matt. "These Six Lawsuits Shaped the Internet." *The Verge.* Aug. 14, 2019. https://www.theverge.com/2014/8/19/6044679/the-six-lawsuits-that-shaped-the-internet.

Szoldra, Paul. "This Is Everything Edward Snowden Revealed in One Year of Unprecedented Top-Secret Leaks." *Business Insider.* Sept. 16, 2016. https://www.businessinsider.com/snowden-leaks-timeline-2016-9.

"There May Soon Be Three Internets: America's Won't Necessarily Be the Best." Editorial Board. *The New York Times.* Oct. 15, 2018. https://www.nytimes.com/2018/10/15/opinion/internet-google-china-balkanization.html.

Thompson, Ben. "A Framework for Regulating the Internet." *Stratechery.* Apr. 9, 2019. https://stratechery.com/2019/a-regulatory-framework-for-the-internet/.

Tien, Lee, and Peter Eckersley, "Open Letter to the Whitehouse Cyber Security Review Team." *Electronic Frontier Foundation.* https://obamawhitehouse.archives.gov/files/documents/cyber/Electronic%20Frontier%20Foundation%20-%20To%20the%20White%20House%20Cyber%20Security%20Review%20Team.pdf.

Trendacosta, Katherine. "Reevaluating the DMCA 22 Years Later: Let's Think of the Users." *Electronic Frontier Foundation.* Feb. 12, 2020. https://www.eff.org/deeplinks/2020/02/reevaluating-dmca-22-years-later-lets-think-users.

Wakayaba, Daisuke. "Prime Leverage: How Amazon Wields Power in the Technology World." *The New York Times.* Dec. 15, 2019. https://www.nytimes.com/2019/12/15/technology/amazon-aws-cloud-competition.html.

Webb, Maureen. *Coding Democracy: How Hackers Are Disrupting Power, Surveillance, and Authoritarianism.* Cambridge, MA: MIT Press, 2020.

"What Is Hacking?" *Malwarebytes.* https://www.malwarebytes.com/hacker/.

"What Is ICANN and Why Does It Matter?" *Data Foundry.* July 11, 2016. https://www.datafoundry.com/blog/what-is-icann.

"What Is the Computer Fraud and Abuse Act?" *Cybersecurity Masters Degree.org.* n.d. https://www.cybersecuritymastersdegree.org/what-is-the-computer-fraud-and-abuse-act/.

"Will 'Right to Repair' Be a Thing of the Past for Motorcyclists?" *Ultimate Motorcycling*. Mar. 10, 2020. https://ultimatemotorcycling.com/2020/03/10/will-right-to-repair-be-a-thing-of-the-past-for-motorcyclists/.

Wong, Julia Carrie. "Overreacting to Failure: Facebook's New Strategy Baffles Local Activists." *The Guardian*. Feb. 7, 2019. https://www.theguardian.com/technology/2019/feb/07/facebook-myanmar-genocide-violence-hate-speech.

"The Worst and Weirdest IoT Hacks of All Time." *Finance Monthly*. Sept. 2019. https://www.finance-monthly.com/2019/09/the-worst-and-weirdest-iot-hacks-of-all-times/.

Wu, Tim. "How the FCC's Net Neutrality Plan Breaks with 50 Years of History." *Wired*. Dec. 6, 2017. https://www.wired.com/story/how-the-fccs-net-neutrality-plan-breaks-with-50-years-of-history/.

Zhang, Wendy. "Comprehensive Federal Privacy Law Still Pending." *JD Supra*. Jan. 10, 2020. https://www.jdsupra.com/legalnews/comprehensive-federal-privacy-law-still-66167/#:~:text=Online%20Privacy%20Act%3A%20This%20act,enforce%20the%20rights%20and%20requirements.

Websites

Berkeley Center for Law & Technology (BCLT)
https://www.law.berkeley.edu/research/bclt/

Established in 1995, the BCLT is an award-winning multidisciplinary research center at the University of California, Berkeley, School of Law. The first of its kind, the center focuses on intellectual property, cybercrime and cybersecurity, privacy, biotech, telecommunications regulation, patents, healthcare law, and digital entertainment. Recent and ongoing projects include software intellectual property protections, cloud computing and transborder government, video game artist rights, machine testimony in the courtroom, and governance of artificial intelligence. Affiliates include the Samuelson Law, Technology, and Public Policy Clinic and the Miller Institute for Global Challenges and the Law. BCLT faculty file amicus briefs in Supreme Court cases, testify at legal hearings, and serve on governmental advisory boards.

Berkman Klein Center for Internet & Society at Harvard University
https://cyber.harvard.edu/

The Berkman Klein Center is a research center at Harvard University. Founded in 1996 as the Center on Law and Technology, it traditionally focused on Internet-legal issues. Lawrence Lessing joined as the first Berkman professor in 1997. Now a major interdisciplinary center at Harvard, the center explores how social context inspires the development of Internet-related technologies. It sponsors events and conferences, hosts visiting lecturers and research fellows, and puts out *The Buzz* newsletter. The center has conducted public policy reviews of major issues, such as a 2010 accountability study on the International Corporation for Assigned Names and Numbers (ICANN). Major research topics include teens and media, monitoring, privacy, digital art, internet governance, cloud computing, and censorship. The Digital Media Law Project —which offers legal assistance to online media and works to protect online freedom of speech—is hosted by the Berkman Klein Center. Other projects include the Digital Public Library of America, StopBadware, Internet and Democracy Project, and Ethics and Governance of Artificial Intelligence.

Center for Democracy and Technology (CDT)

https://cdt.org/

The Center for Democracy and Technology is a nonprofit organization founded in 1994 by former Electronic Frontier Foundation executive and policy director Jerry Berman. CDT works to preserve online freedom of expression, protect privacy rights, and place stronger controls on government surveillance. The center has opposed wiretapping laws, the Communications Decency Act, and certain copyright protection acts and has been involved in crafting the Children's Online Privacy Protection Act. CDT was one of the few civil organizations involved in the founding of the International Corporation for Assigned Names and Numbers (ICANN). CDT project teams include privacy and data, free expression, security and surveillance, Internet architecture, and European Union. The center is partially funded by grants (including the MacArthur Foundation) and industry organizations.

Electronic Frontier Foundation (EFF)

www.eff.org

The EFF is an international nonprofit digital rights group founded in 1990 by John Gilmore, John Perry Barlow, and Mitch Kapor. The EFF works to defend civil liberties and consumer rights, providing funds for legal defense, presenting amicus curiae briefs, and exposes government overreach. The EFF regularly brings lawsuits at all levels of the legal system and has been involved in many significant technology law cases, including *MGM Studios, Inc., v. Grokster, Ltd.*, and *Apple v. Does*. Initiatives include the Patent Busting Project and advocating for paper audit trails for voting machines. In partnership with the Open Technology Institute, the Center for Democracy and Technology, and the American Civil Liberties Union (ACLU), the EFF has worked on content moderation reform. The EFF has published books, developed software, and maintains the *DeepLinks* blog.

Free Software Foundation (FSF)

www.fsf.org

The FSF is a nonprofit organization founded in 1985 by Richard Stallman to promote free and open-source software, as well as distributing software on a copyleft (share alike) basis., such as its own GNU General Public License. Funding has been used to employ software developers to write free software for the GNU project and has shifted to include legal and structural issues for the free software movement. The FSF updates GNU licenses, operates the GNU Press for affordable computer science publications, maintains the Free Software Directory and h-node list hardware compatible with free software, and hosts software development on its Savannah website. The FSF campaigns against software patents and digital rights management.

Internet Society

www.internetsociety.org

The Internet Society is an American nonprofit organization that promotes open development and access to the Internet. It supports research and education initiatives as well as Internet-related standards. Founded in 1992 by Vint Cerf, Bob Kahn, and Lyman Chapin, it incorporated the Internet Architecture Board, the Internet Engineering Task Force, and the Internet Research Task Force. The center works on building community networks, fostering infrastructure, and encryption. The society hosts international conferences and workshops.

Stanford Center for Internet and Society

cyberlaw.stanford.edu

The Stanford Center for Internet and Society was founded by Lawrence Lessig in 2000 as a public interest law and policy program at Stanford Law School. The center provides educational resources for law students and the public at large. Bringing together academic scholars, legislators, students, programmers, security researchers, and scientists, the center explores how the meeting of technology and the law can promote freedom of speech, innovation, privacy, diversity and scientific inquiry. The Fair Use Project also provides legal representation to clients in cases that raise important civil rights issues. The center also sponsors a range of speaker series, conferences, and workshops.

Index